The Technology of Video and Audio Streaming

The Technology of Video and Audio Streaming

David Austerberry

OXFORD   AMSTERDAM   BOSTON   LONDON   NEW YORK   PARIS
SAN DIEGO   SAN FRANCISCO   SINGAPORE   SYDNEY   TOKYO

Focal Press
An imprint of Elsevier Science
Linacre House, Jordan Hill, Oxford OX2 8DP
225 Wildwood Avenue, Woburn, MA 01801-2041

First published 2002

British Library Cataloguing in Publication Data
A catalogue record for this book is available from the British Library

Library of Congress Cataloguing in Publication Data
A catalogue record for this book is available from the Library of Congress

ISBN 0 240 51694 X

For information on all Focal Press publications visit our website at:
www.focalpress.com

TRADEMARKS/REGISTERED TRADEMARKS
Computer hardware and software brand names mentioned in this book
are protected by their respective trademarks and are acknowledged.

Composition by Genesis Typesetting, Rochester, Kent
Printed and bound in Great Britain by MPG Books Ltd, Bodmin, Cornwall

Contents

Foreword

The evolution of Internet-based communication, from e-mail to the Web, and more recently to streaming media, has developed exceptionally quickly. In a fraction of the time it took television to reach mainstream adoption, both TV and radio stations from all over the globe now broadcast online ('webcast').

The Internet is still evolving, and the Web and broadcasting are now converging to create new services that span PCs, interactive TV and mobile devices. This is leading to equally rapid development of new methods of communication in business, government and consumer sectors.

The Internet, however, differs very significantly from existing broadcast media. It has global reach and open access: anyone may now webcast from anywhere to anywhere, at any time.

The potential impact of this is as great as the impact we have already experienced with e-mail, and the social impact of combining existing web resources with webcasting may be greater than traditional television itself.

Streaming media, a key technique for the delivery of webcasts, combines a surprisingly broad range of concepts, technology and skills. Traditional broadcasting, software development, global network infrastructure, graphic design and information architecture skills are all required in the development of these new services.

Everyone in this new production world should have a thorough understanding of the concepts and processes behind them. This work provides a much-needed introduction to the breadth and depth of streaming media and will assist in this process.

Gavin Starks B.Sc., M.Mus.
CEO, Tornado Productions Ltd (http://www.tornadoproductions.com)
Chairman, International Webcasting Association (Europe)
(http://www.webcasters.org)

Acknowledgements

The original idea for a book stemmed from a meeting with Jennifer Welham of Focal Press at a papers session during an annual conference of the National Association of Broadcasters. I would like to thank Philip O'Ferrall for suggesting streaming media as a good subject for a book; we were building an ASP to provide streaming facilities. I received great assistance from Colin Birch at Tyrell Corporation, and would like to thank Joe Apted at ClipStream (a VTR company) for the views of an encoding shop manager. I am especially grateful to Gavin Starks for his assistance and for reading through my draft copy.

The web sites of RealNetworks, Microsoft and Apple have provided much background reading on the three main architectures.

While I was undertaking the research for this book I found so many dead links on the Web – many startups in the streaming business have closed down or have been acquired by other companies. I wanted to keep the links and references up to date in this fast-changing business, so rather than printing links in the text, all the references for this book are to be found on the associated web site at

www.davidausterberry.com/streaming.html

Section 1

Basics

1 Introduction

Streaming media is an exciting addition to the rich media producers' toolbox. Just as the cinema and radio were ousted by television as the primary mass communication medium, streaming is set to transform the WorldWide Web. The original text-based standards of the Web have been stretched far beyond the original functionality of the core protocols to incorporate images and animation, yet video and audio are accepted as the most natural way to communicate. Through the experience of television, we have now come to expect video to be the primary vehicle for the dissemination of knowledge and entertainment. This has driven the continuing developments that now allow video to be delivered over the Internet as a live stream.

Streaming has been heralded by many as an alternative delivery channel to conventional radio and television – video over IP. But that is a narrow view; streaming can be at its most compelling when its special strengths are exploited. As part of an interactive rich media presentation it becomes a whole new communication channel that can compete in its own right with print, radio, television and the text-based Web.

500 years of print development

It has taken 500 years since Gutenberg introduced the printing press to reach the electronic book of today. In the short period of 10 years, we have developed on from the textual web page to rich media. Some of the main components of the illuminated manuscript still exist in the web page. The illustrated drop-capital (called a historiated initial) and the floral borders or marginalia have been replaced by the GIF image. The illustrations, engravings and half-tones of the print medium are now JPEG images. But the elements of the web page are not that different from the books of 1500.

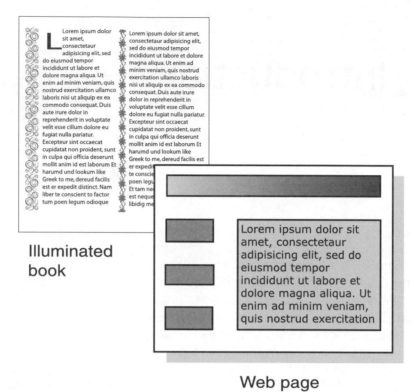

Illuminated book

Web page

Figure 1.1 The evolution of text on a page.

We can thank Tim Berners-Lee for the development of the hypertext markup language that has exploded into a whole new way of communicating. There can be few businesses today that do not place great reliance on a company web site to provide information on their products and services, along with a host of corporate information and possibly file downloads. Soon after its inception the Web was exploited as a medium that could be used to sell the products and services. But all the time if the sales department wanted to give a presentation to a customer, the only ways open to them were either face-to-face or through the medium of television.

100 years of the moving image

The moving image, by contrast, has only been around for 100 years. Since the development of cinematography in the 1890s by the Lumière brothers and Edison, the movie has become part of our general culture and entertainment. Fifty years later the television was introduced to the public, bringing moving images

Jo Coleman
Information Update Service
Butterworth-Heinemann
FREEPOST SCE 5435
Oxford
Oxon
OX2 8BR
UK

always been simple, limited
low vertical resolution of
of small character heights.
g a more web-like design.
tional content is displayed
what is lacking is interactivity with the viewer.
Television can support a limited interactivity: voting responding to a short list of
different choices, and on-screen navigation.

The Web meets television

Rich media combines the Web, interactive multimedia and television in an
exciting new medium in its own right. The multimedia CD-ROM has been with us
for some time. It is very popular for training applications with interactive
navigation around a seamless combination of graphics, video and audio. The
programs were always physically distributed on CD-ROM, and now on DVD.
Unfortunately the MPEG-1 files were much too large for streaming. Advances in
audio and video compression now make it possible for such files to be
distributed in real-time over the Web.

Flash vector graphics were a stepping-stone on the evolution from hypertext
to rich media. The web designers and developers used a great deal of creativity

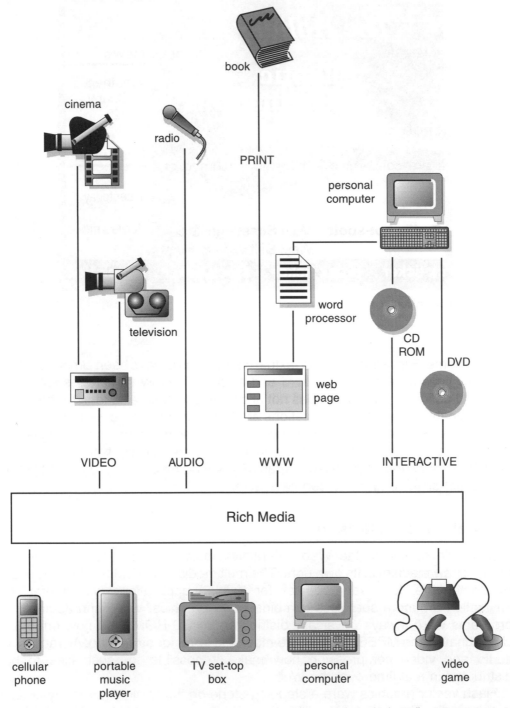

book

cinema

radio

PRINT

personal
computer

television

word
processor

CD
ROM

DVD

web
page

VIDEO   AUDIO   WWW   INTERACTIVE

Rich Media

cellular
phone

portable
music
player

TV set-top
box

personal
computer

video
game

Figure 1.3 Evolution from diverse media to a new generation of integrated media.

and innovative scripting to make some very dynamic, interactive web sites using Flash, but they still lacked the ability to deliver live video and audio.

So by combining the production methods of the multimedia disk, with the skills of the web developer, a whole new way to communicate ideas has been formulated.

Convergence

The media are converging – there is a blurring of the edges between the traditional divides of mass communication. Print now has e-books, and the newspapers have their own web sites carrying background to the stories and access to the archives. The television set-top box can be used to surf the Web, send e-mail, or to interact with the program and commercials. Now a web site may have embedded video and audio.

New technologies have emerged, notably MPEG-4 and third-generation wireless. MPEG-4 has taken a leap forward as a platform for rich media. You can now synchronize three-dimensional and synthetic content with regular video and images. For the creative artist it is a whole new toolbox.

The new wireless devices can display pictures and video as well as text and graphics. The screens can be as large as 320×240 pixels, and in full color. These mobile devices can display pictures and video as well as text and graphics. The bandwidth may be much lower than the hundreds of kilobits downloaded through a cable modem, but much is possible for the innovative content creator.

This convergence has raised many challenges. How to contain production costs? How to manage content? How to integrate different creative disciplines? Can content be repurposed for other media by cost-effective processes? The technologies themselves present issues. How do you create content for the tiny screen on a wireless device and for high-definition television?

What is streaming?

Streaming media and webcasting are often used synonymously. In this book I refer to webcasting as the equivalent of television broadcasting, but delivered over the Web. Live or pre-recorded content is streamed to a schedule and pushed out to the viewer. The alternative is on-demand delivery, where the user pulls down the content, often interactively.

Webcasting embraces both streaming and file download. Streamed media is delivered direct from the source to the player in real-time. This is a continuous process, with no intermediate storage of the media clip. In many ways this is much like conventional television. Similarly, if the content has been stored for on-demand delivery, it is delivered at a controlled rate to the display in real-time as if it were live. Contrast this with much of the MP3 music delivery, where the file is downloaded in its entirety to the local disk drive before playback, a process called download-and-play.

So true streaming could be considered a subset of webcasting. But streaming does not have to use the Web, streams can be delivered through wireless networks or over private intranets. So the boundaries between streaming and webcasting are indistinct.

Streaming media has been around for 70 years. The conventional television, that is familiar to all, would be called streaming media if it were invented today. The original television systems delivered live pictures from the camera, via the distribution network, to the home receiver. In the 1950s, Ampex developed a means of storing the picture streams – the videotape recorder. This gave broadcasters the option of live broadcast (streaming), or to play pre-recorded programs from tape. The television receiver has no storage or buffering, the picture is displayed synchronized to the emissions from the transmitter. Television is normally transmitted over a fixed bandwidth connection with a high quality of service (QoS).

Today, streaming media is taken to mean digitally encoded files delivered over the WorldWide Web to PCs, or 'IP broadcasting'. Whereas television has a one-way channel to the viewer, Internet Protocol (IP) delivery has a bidirectional connection between the media source and the viewer. This allows a more interactive connection enabling additional facilities not possible with conventional television.

The first facility is that content can be provided on demand. This has often been promised for conventional television, but has not yet proved to be financially viable. The second is that the media source (the server) can adapt to cope with varying availability of bandwidth. The goal is to deliver the best picture possible in the prevailing network conditions.

A normal unicast stream over IP uses a one-to-one connection between the server and the client (the media player). Scheduled streaming can also be multicast, where a single IP stream is served to the network. The routers deliver the stream to all the viewers that have requested the content. This allows great savings in the utilization of corporate networks for applications like live briefings or training sessions (but cannot be used for on-demand delivery).

Like subscription television, streaming media can offer conditional access to content using digital rights management. This can be used wherever the owner of the content wants to retain control over who is viewing. This could be for reasons of corporate confidentiality, or if entertainment content is to be sold through an e-commerce site.

What is real-time?

Steaming is often referred to as real-time; this is a somewhat vague term. It implies viewing an event as it happens. Typical television systems have latency; it may be milliseconds, but with highly compressed codecs the latency can be some seconds. The primary factor that makes a stream real-time is that there is no intermediate storage of the data packets. There may be some short buffers, like frame stores in the decoder, but the signal essentially streams all the way from the camera to the player. Streamed media is not stored on the local disk in the client machine, unless a download is specifically requested (and allowed).

Just because streaming is real-time does not mean it has to be live. Pre-recorded files can also be delivered in real-time. The server delivers the packets to the network at a rate that matches the correct video playback speed.

Applications

Wherever electronic communication is used, the applications for streaming are endless. Streaming can be delivered as a complete video package of linear programming, as a subscription service, or as pay-per-view (PPV). It can form part of an interactive web site or it can be a tool in its own right – for video preview and film dailies.

- Internet broadcasting (corporate communications)
- Education (viewing lectures and distance learning)
- Web-based channels (IP-TV, Internet radio)
- Video on-demand (VOD)
- Music distribution (music on-demand)
- Internet and intranet browsing of content (asset management)

The big advantage of streaming over television is the exploitation of IP connectivity – a ubiquitous medium. How many office workers have a television on their desk and a hookup to the cable television system?

Europe and the US

Over the years different standards have been adopted by the US and Europe that impact upon this book. The first is the television standards, with the US adopting a 525-line/30-frame format versus the European standard of 625 lines/ 25 frames per second. The other is the different telecommunications standards, with the Bell hierarchy in the US giving a base broadband rate of 1.5 Mbit/s

(T-1), and the 2 Mbit/s (E-1) of the Europe Telecommunications Standards Institute (ETSI). It is relatively easy to convert from one to another, so the differing standards are not an obstacle to international media delivery.

The production team

Much like web design, streaming media production requires a multi-disciplinary team. A web site requires content authors, graphic designers and web developers. The site also needs IT staff to run the servers and security systems.

To utilize streaming you will have to add the video production team to this group of people. This is the same as a television production team, but the videographer should understand the limitations of the medium. Streaming media players are not hi-def television.

If you are producing rich media, many of the skills should already be present in your web team. These include the design skills plus the ability to write the SMIL and TIME scripts used to synchronize the many elements of an interactive production. So, with luck, you may not need to add to your web production team to incorporate streaming.

How this book is organized

This book is divided into three sections. The first is a background to telecommunications and audio/video compression. The second section is the core chapters on streaming. The final section covers associated technologies and some applications for streaming media.

The book is not intended to replace the operation and installation manuals provided by the vendors of streaming architectures. Those will give much more detail on the specifics of setting up their products.

Summary

Streaming media presents the professional communicator with a whole new way to deliver information, messages and entertainment. By leveraging the Internet, distribution costs can be much lower than the traditional media.

The successful webcaster will need to assemble a multi-skilled and creative team to produce high-quality streaming media content. The Web audience is unforgiving, so content has to be compelling to receive worthwhile viewing figures that will give a return on the investment in streaming.

The development of streaming has benefited from a very wide range of disciplines. We can thank the neurophysiologists for the research in understanding the psychoacoustics of human hearing that has been so vital to the

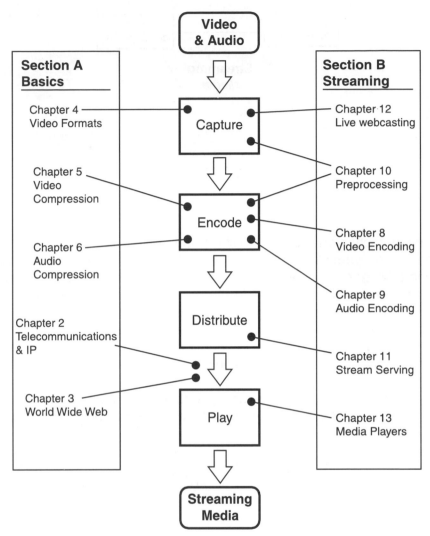

Figure 1.4 The chapter content.

design of audio compression algorithms. Similar work has led to advances in video compression. The information technology engineers are constantly improving content delivery within the framework of the existing web infrastructure. We must not forget the creativity of the multimedia developer in exploiting the technologies to produce visually stimulating content. And a final word for Napster; peer-to-peer distribution has driven the need to deploy digital rights management systems to protect the intellectual property of the content creators and owners.

Figure 1.5 The production team.

Streaming technology is very fast-moving. New versions of codecs are released every year. New technologies obsolete the incumbent, so any streaming content creation and management system should be designed to be flexible and extensible. Some of the newer applications like the mobile and wireless are likely to be more stable. The phone manufacturers prefer fixed standards to ensure reliable operation and low manufacturing cost.

Perhaps the greatest advances to benefit the content creator are the recent emergence of tools to aid the production processes. Just as the word processor brought basic DTP to every desktop, these tools will allow the small business and corporate user to deploy streaming without the need to outsource. The streaming production shop will be freed to concentrate on the more creative content creation.

2 IP networks and telecommunications

Introduction

Why is a network drawn as a cloud? In all but the smallest of enterprises, the IT department maintains the computer network infrastructure. How many of us are concerned what happens beyond the RJ-45 jack on the wall? It says a lot for computer networks that we often forget the network is there. We haul files across the world at the click of a mouse, and they arrive seconds later.

With video media, things are different, we place much more demands on the network. So it helps to understand a little more about the IP network, and the telecommunications infrastructure that underpins it.

The first thing that is different about the delivery of multimedia streams is that usually they do not use the universal TCP. Second, the media files are very large compared with the average web page. Third, delivery in real-time is a prerequisite for smooth playback of video and audio.

A new set of network protocols has been developed to support multimedia streaming. Advances in Internet protocols (IPs) now support multicasting where one stream serves hundreds or thousands of players. This is a handy facility for optimizing network resources if you want to webcast live to large audiences.

The media files are streamed over the general telecommunications network. Again this is something we rarely think about, unless we want a new telephone switch. Communications channels become an issue as soon as you start to encode. The codec configuration menu will offer a number of compression choices: dial-up modem, dual-ISDN, DSL, T-1. So it helps to understand the pipes through which the media is delivered. Streaming is not like a web page. The content arrives after a short delay, but how it reached the browser is of little concern to the user.

Most streaming files are delivered over a data network. For internal corporate communications it may be the local network or, for an enterprise with widely dispersed sites, a wide-area network. For business-to-business and consumer streaming, the Internet is a likely carrier. The Internet has become ubiquitous for data communications, from simple e-mail through to complex electronic commerce applications. The Internet needs a physical layer, the fiber and copper that carry the data. For this we turn to the telcos. It may be your incumbent telephony supplier, or one of the new wideband fiber networks. In all probability an end-to-end Internet connection will use a combination of many carriers and networks.

This chapter gives an overview of the connections that carries the stream. The first section is about data networks. The second is about telecommunications, with the focus on the last mile to your browser. This final link includes the two popular broadband consumer products: DSL and the cable modem.

Network layers

The concept of interconnected networking, or the Internet, has its origins in the quest by the US military to connect research institutions over a packet-switched network. In the 1970s the US Department of Defense DARPA project developed the multi-layer model of network protocols that evolved into the Internet that we know today. The International Standards Organization later augmented the communication protocols. These evolved into the Open Systems Interface

Figure 2.1 Multi-layer network model.

model (the ISO OSI). The Internet does not wholly adhere to the open systems interface; Figure 2.1 shows the relationship, but note that the principles are similar. Later protocols do adhere more closely to the ISO seven-layer model.

The DARPA model defined four layers:

● Network access layer
● Internet layer
● Host-to-host layer
● Process layer

The network access layer includes a number of protocols that deliver the data over the physical network, the copper and fiber. The one chosen depends upon the type of physical network. The Internet layer delivers the data packets from the source to the destination address. It masks the network technology in use from other layers.

The host-to-host layer handles the connection rendezvous and manages the data flow. The process layer is for the implementation of the user application, like e-mail and file transfer.

Internet Protocol

Internet Protocol is the main network (layer 3) communication protocol. The other protocols at layer 3 are used for control of the network routers to set up the connections. IP has a drawback; it is an unreliable delivery system.

● There is variable network latency
● The packets can arrive in a different order from transmission
● Packets can be lost

These potential problems are corrected by the higher layer protocols and applications. The most well known is at the transport layer, Transport Control Protocol (TCP). This is used together with Internet Protocol – the ubiquitous TCP/IP. One of the great strengths of TCP is its reliability. The built-in error protection of TCP makes it an excellent protocol for the delivery of general-purpose data, but the way this is implemented proves to be a disadvantage for streaming applications.

TCP sequences the data bytes with a forwarding acknowledgement number that indicates to the destination the next byte the source expects to receive. If bytes are not acknowledged within a specified time period they are retransmitted. This feature of TCP allows devices to detect lost packets and request a retransmission. The repeated transmission will add to the communication latency, but that is not normally an issue with data exchange. TCP also provides flow control of the data.

With audio and video, the viewer requires a continuous stream to view the source in real-time. Retransmission of data is going to add delays; retransmission also uses up bandwidth in the data channel. Ultimately, high levels of network transmission errors will empty the receive buffer in the media player. The interruption to the stream will ultimately lead to interruptions to the video playback.

The alternative is to ignore lost packets. This may cause loss or distortion of a single video frame, but that is a transient event that will be ignored by the viewer. So for real-time applications, timely delivery is more important than error-free transmission.

User Datagram Protocol – UDP

Streaming needs a transmission protocol that can ignore data errors. Such a protocol is the User Datagram Protocol (UDP). It is used as a transport protocol for several application-layer protocols, notably the Network File System (NFS), Simple Network Management Protocol (SNMP) and the Domain Name System (DNS). UDP has neither the error correction, nor the flow control of TCP, so this

Table 2.1 TCP versus UDP

TCP	UDP
Connection oriented	Connectionless
Reliable	Unreliable
Controls data flow	No flow control

Table 2.2 Popular Internet applications and their underlying transport protocols

Application	Application-layer Protocol	Typical Transport Protocol
E-mail	SMTP	TCP
Remote terminal access	Telnet	TCP
Web	HTTP	TCP
File transfer	FTP	TCP
Remote file server	NFS	UDP
Streaming media	RTSP or proprietary	UDP
Voice-over IP	Proprietary	UDP
Network management	SNMP	UDP
Routing protocol	RIP	UDP
Name translation	DNS	UDP

task has to be handled by an application at a higher layer in the stack. It does, however, carry a checksum of the payload data. The media players can often mask video data errors.

IP version 6

Most of the Internet uses IP version 4. This protocol has been around since 1981, but is showing its age as use of the Internet has spiraled. It now has many shortcomings, so IP version 6 is offering to solve many of the problem issues.

The first is lack of addresses. As more and more users log on version 4 addresses are going to run out. The use of always-on broadband connections means that the dynamic sharing of IP addresses can no longer be used to advantage. The class D multicast addresses are particularly limited. If multicasting is to be fully used to save network congestion, many more addresses are required.

IP version 6 solves the address space by increasing from 32-bit address space to 128 bits. This gives 6×10^{23} IP addresses per square meter of the earth's surface. This may seem to be a ridiculous overkill, but it allows far more freedom for multi-level hierarchies of address allocation. This is the same as telephone numbers, with the hierarchy of area codes. The big advantage of this hierarchy is that the tables in the network routers can be simplified, so the fine-grain routing need only be done at the destination router.

Many other improvements have been incorporated into the version 6 protocol, including a simplified packet header, again to improve router throughput.

The advantages specific to streaming will be two-fold. The increased address space and the opportunity to manage quality of service (QoS). One header field is the traffic flow identification. This will allow routers to distinguish real-time data from mail and file transfer (FTP).

MPEG-4 could potentially take advantage of this packet priority. The scalable coding option provides a baseline low-resolution image, with helper packets to add detail to an image for higher resolution, albeit requiring a higher bandwidth. The low-resolution image could be allocated a higher priority than the high-resolution helper signals. So if the network becomes congested the resolution degrades gracefully as packets are dropped, rather than the stalling that we see with conventional codecs.

Routers compliant with IP version 6 support multicasting as a standard facility.

Real-time protocols

A number of different protocols have been developed to facilitate real-time streaming of multimedia content. Streaming means that the mean frame rate of

Table 2.3 Summary of protocols used for multimedia sessions

Abbreviation	Title	Notes	RFC number
RSVP	Resource Reservation Protocol	Protocol specification	2205
	RSVP applicability statement	Guide to deployment	2208
	Message processing rules		2209
RTCP	Real-Time Control Protocol	Part of RTP	1889
RTSP	Real-Time Streaming Protocol		2326
RTP	Real-Time Protocol		1889
SDP	Session Description Protocol		2327
UDP	User Datagram Protocol		768

the video viewed at the player is dictated by the transmitted frame rate. The delivery rate has to be controlled so that the video data arrives just before it is required for display on the player. The associated audio track or tracks must also remain synchronized to the video. IP data transmission is not a synchronous process and delivery is by best effort. To achieve synchronism, timing references have to be embedded in the stream.

The Internet Engineering Task Force issue Request For Comment documents (RFC) that become the de facto protocols.

Intimately linked to real-time delivery is the quality of service (QoS). To ensure the reliable delivery of packets the network bandwidth would have to be reserved for the stream. This is not generally the case with the Internet. One protocol that allows resources to be reserved by a client is Resource Reservation Protocol (RSVP). It allows the client to negotiate with routers in the path for bandwidth, but does not actually deliver the data. It is not widely supported.

Transport protocol for real-time applications (RTP)

Real-Time Protocol (RTP) is a transport protocol that was developed for streaming data. RTP includes extra data fields not present in TCP. It provides a timestamp and sequence number to facilitate the data transport timing. It allows control of the media server so that the video stream is served at the correct rate for real-time display. The media player then uses these RTP fields to assemble the received packets into the correct order and playback rate.

Sequence number. The value of this 16-bit number increments by one for each packet. It is used by the player to detect packet loss and then to sequence the packets in the correct order. The initial number for a stream session is chosen at random.

Timestamp. This is a sampling instance derived from a reference clock to allow for synchronization and jitter calculations. It is monotonic and linear in time.

Source identifiers. CSRC – this is a unique identifier for the synchronization of the RTP stream. One or more CSRCs exist when the RTP stream is carrying information for multiple media sources. This could be the case for a video mix between two sources or for embedded content.

RTP usually runs on UDP, and uses its multiplexing and checksum features. Note that RTP does not provide any control of the quality of service or reservation of network resources.

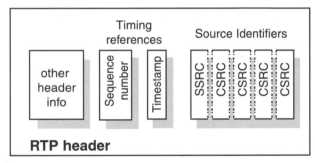

Figure 2.2 RTP header.

Proprietary private data formats are also used for data transport between the media server and the browser client. An example is RealNetworks Real Data Transport (or RDT).

Real-Time Control Protocol (RTCP)
RTCP is used in conjunction with RTP. It gives feedback to each participant in an RTP session that can be used to control the session. The messages include reception reports, including number of packets lost and jitter statistics (early or late arrivals). This information can potentially be used by higher layer applications to modify the transmission. For example, the bit rate of a stream could be changed to counter network congestion. Some RTCP messages relate to control of a video-conference with multiple participants.

Session Description Protocol (SDP)

SDP is a media description format intended for describing multimedia sessions, including video-conferencing. It includes session announcement and session invitation.

Real-Time Streaming Protocol (RTSP)

The Real-Time Streaming Protocol is an application-level protocol for the control of real-time multimedia data. RTSP provides an extensible framework rather than a protocol. It allows interactive, VCR-like, control of the playback: Play, Pause, etc. A streaming server can also react to network congestion, changing the media bandwidth to suit the available capacity.

RTSP was intentionally developed to be similar in syntax and operation to HTTP version 1.1. It does differ in several important aspects. With RTSP both client and server can issue requests during interaction – with HTTP the client always issues the requests (for documents). RTSP has to retain the state of a session, whereas HTTP is stateless.

It supports the use of RTP as the underlying data delivery protocol. The protocol is intended to give a means of choosing the optimum delivery channel to a client. Some corporate firewalls will not pass UDP. The streaming server has to offer a choice of delivery protocols – UDP, multicast UDP and TCP – to suit different clients.

RTSP is not the only streaming control protocol. Real's precursor, Progressive Networks, used a proprietary protocol before RTSP was developed.

MMS

Microsoft has a proprietary control protocol, MMS – the Microsoft Media Server. MMS handles client interaction, the controls like Play or Stop. MMS uses TCP as the delivery layer. The media data can be transmitted separately over UDP or TCP.

SMPTE time code

RTSP uses SMPTE time code as a time reference for video frames. This has a configuration setting called *drop frame*. To the reader from outside the television industry drop frame format may seem illogical. It has a background in the editing of composite NTSC videotape. To achieve a simple relationship between the color subcarrier of NTSC and the television line rate, the math arrives at a frame rate of 59.96 rather than the 60 Hz of the earlier monochrome system. In NTSC 60 frames will occupy slightly more than 1 second, so to maintain a fixed relationship between tape time and real-time over the duration of a program of say 30 minutes, designated frames are dropped from the counting sequence.

Note that RTP uses a different time reference, the Network Time Protocol (NTP), that is based on universal time (UTC). RTP uses the middle 32 bits of the NTP 64-bit fixed-point number to represent the time. The high 16 bits of the 32-bit NTP fraction are used to represent sub-second timing – this gives a resolution of about 15 μs, or about one quarter of a television line.

Multicasting

Suppose the CEO of an enterprise wants to stream an address to all the staff. Let us say there are 500 staff at headquarters on the West coast, 1,000 personnel work at the South coast plant, and another 500 at the East coast offices. The normal way to transmit an Internet presentation is to set up a one-to-one connection for each media player client. This is called unicasting. In this

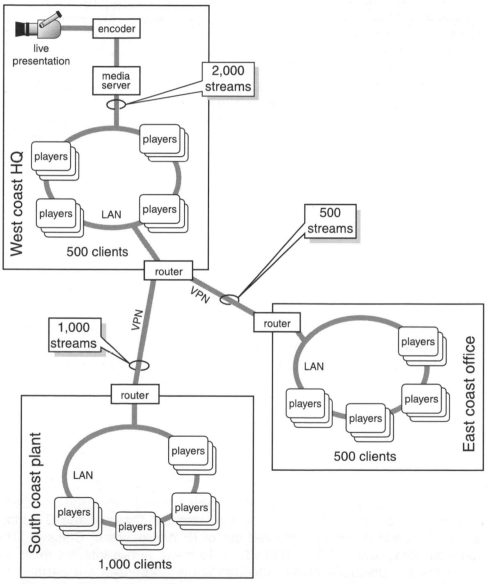

Figure 2.3 A unicast presentation.

example you would have to transmit 500 + 1,000 + 500 (= 2,000) separate content streams.

The webcaster can look with envy at the television broadcaster. With one transmitter and one tower the broadcaster can reach every resident living within his service area. In a metropolitan area he or she can reach an audience of several million people. As a webcaster you have to provide server resource for each viewer. Plus the bandwidth of the Internet has to be sufficient to carry all the streams that you want to serve.

Multicasting offers an alternative to conventional streaming or unicasting. A single stream is served to the Internet as a multicast. All the viewers can then attach to the same stream. The client initiates a multicast; the server just delivers the stream to the network. Further viewers just attach to the same stream. The server has no knowledge of where the stream is going, unlike the normal TCP client–server handshaking interactions of an Internet connection. A client will be made aware of a multicast by some out-of-band channel; it could be an e-mail or could be through publicity on a web site. The viewer then requests the multicast at the appropriate date and time. An alternative is to use the session announcement protocol.

Note that you can broadcast to a network, but it is not like a television broadcast. It is used by network administrators for control messages, and does not propagate beyond the local sub-net.

Multicasting sounds a very efficient solution to the resource problems of delivering a webcast to very large audiences. But there are catches. First, it can only be used for live or simulated live webcasting. You lose the interactivity of on-demand streaming. The second drawback is that many older network routers do not support multicasting. There are ways around this: multicast streams can be tunneled through legacy plant, and the multicast enabled backbone (MBone) can be used. Many of the problems have restricted its use to corporate networks (intranets). Large public webcasts have had to resort to conventional splitting and caching to guarantee delivery to all potential clients.

Note that multicasting is not limited to streaming; it can also be used for general data delivery (like database upgrades across a dispersed enterprise, or for video-conferencing).

Multicast address allocation

Most IP addresses fall into Class C, unless you are in a very large corporation or government department, where you may use the Class A and B address spaces. Multicasting uses a reserved set of IP addresses in Class D. They range from 224.0.0.0 to 239.255.255.255. To make public Internet multicasts you will need a unique address. Although some addresses are permanently allocated to hosts, they are usually transient and allocated for a single multicast

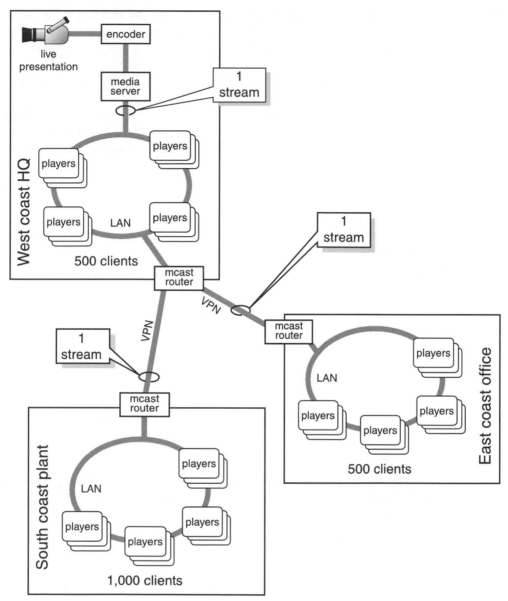

Figure 2.4 Multicast presentation.

event. There is a proposal to dynamically allocate the host group addresses, much like the dynamic allocation of client IP addresses. The permanent addresses have to be registered with the Internet Assigned Numbers Authority (IANA), or the designated proxy organization for your country (like the RIPE-NCC in Europe). There has been a certain amount of chaos in this area, and it is not unknown for an address not to be unique. Hopefully the upgrades to IP version 6 will help to solve that problem by making far more addresses available.

IGMP

Most of the complexity of a multicast lies with the routing, not the server and the client. Instead of the server sending individual packets to each client, a single packet is transmitted to a multicast group. This group is allocated a single IP address.

The primary mechanism for controlling the delivery of the datagram to multiple destinations is the Internet Group-Membership Protocol (IGMP). It is a session-layer protocol used by the client to join and leave a multicast. A multicast-enabled router uses this session information to set up the route from the server to the client. The router will only forward multicast datagrams if regular IGMP messages are received from downstream clients (typically at intervals of about 60 seconds).

Several routing options have been developed for multicast routing:

● Protocol Independent Multicast (PIM)
● Distance-Vector Multicast Routing Protocol (DVMRP)
● Core-based tree (CBT)
● Multicast Open Shortest Path First (MOSPF)

There are two ways of multicast routing, dense mode and sparse mode.

Sparse and dense routing

Dense mode floods the network then prunes back the unused branches. This assumes that the viewers of the multicast are densely distributed through the network. This could be the case for corporate communications over an intranet. It requires a generous bandwidth. DVMRP, MOSPF and PIM dense mode are all such protocols.

The reach of dense routing trees is limited by the time-to-live parameter (TTL). The value of TTL is decreased by one each time a datagram passes through a router. Once it reaches zero the router will discard the packets. This can be used to restrict the range of the multicast that could potentially propagate through the entire Internet. TTL is measured in seconds and usually set to a default value of 64.

The other type of multicast routing is sparse mode. This is used for applications where the clients are dispersed, possibly geographically, over a wide area of the network. In such a case the dense-mode flooding would cause unnecessary congestion on the network.

Table 2.4 Time-to-live initial values

Scope	TTL
Local area	16
National high-bandwidth sites	32
National sites	48
Continental sites	64
Intercontinental high-bandwidth sites	128
Worldwide coverage	192

The core-based tree (CBT) uses a core router to construct a distribution tree. Edge routers send requests to join the tree, and then a branch is set up. Network traffic will concentrate around the core, which can cause problems with congestion.

Mbone

The multicast-enabled backbone project (MBone) was set up in 1992 to enable the IETF (Internet Engineering Task Force) meetings to set up audio-conferencing to communicate with remote delegates. In 1994 the MBone was used to multicast a Rolling Stones concert to the public.

The term is used more now to refer to the general multicast-enabled backbone. This piggybacks onto the general unicast Internet backbone. The multicast datagrams are encapsulated as unicast packets and tunnel through unicast networks.

Telecommunications

Telecommunications networks were originally set up for telephony, but more than half the traffic is now data. The packet-switched networks used for data and telephony traffic can also be used to carry the Internet. The circuits are constructed in a hierarchy of bit rates designed to carry multiple voice circuits, with the basic unit being 64 kbit/s. Data is carried in a compatible form.

T-1 and E-1

If you have ever tried encoding multimedia content, you will have seen T-1 on the menu. T-1 is the basic digital carrier used in N. America. It transmits data at 1.5 Mbit/s in the DS-1 (digital signal) format. The European equivalent is E-1 at 2 Mbit/s.

US and international standards

There are two main telecommunications standards: the ANSI used in N. America and parts of the Pacific Rim, and the ITU-T standards used in the rest of the world. The ANSI hierarchy is based on a digital signal (DS0) of 64 kbit/s.

Plesiochronous Digital Hierarchy (PDH)

The early digital trunks circuits multiplexed a large number of voice circuits into a single high data rate channel. The systems at the remote ends were not absolutely locked together; instead, each runs off a local reference clock. These clocks were classed as 'plesiochronous'. Plesio- is a Latin term derived from the Greek for 'near', so plesiochronous refers to clocks that are in near synchronism. The early data circuits were asynchronous; the clocks were derived from simple crystal oscillators, which could vary from the nominal by a few parts per million. Large receive buffers are used to manage the data flows. In PDH networks, to cope with terminal equipment running on slightly different clocks, extra bits are stuffed into the data stream. This bit stuffing ensures that a slower receiver can keep up with the real payload rate by simply dropping the extra bits.

To extract a single voice circuit from a DS3, the channel has to be demultiplexed back to DS1 channels. To build trunk circuits in rings around a country, each city passed would have to demultiplex and remultiplex the data stream to extract a few voice circuits.

Synchronous networks (SONET)

To avoid the multiplexing issues and the overheads of bit stuffing, highly synchronous networks were developed. By referencing terminal equipment to a single cesium standard clock, the synchronism could be ensured to a high degree of accuracy.

Table 2.5 Plesiochronous Digital Hierarchies

ITU-T standard			ANSI standard		
Signal	Data rate	Channels	Signal	Data rate	Channels
			DS0	64 kbit/s	
E1	2.048 Mbit/s		DS1	1.544 Mbit/s	24 × DS0
E2	8.45 Mbit/s	4 × E1	DS2	6.3 Mbit/s	96 × DS0
E3	34 Mbit/s	16 × E1	DS3	45 Mbit/s	28 × DS1
E4	144 Mbit/s	64 × E1			

Figure 2.5 Voice circuit multiplexing.

The standard uses a byte-interleaved multiplexing scheme. The payload data is held in a fixed structure of frames. At a network terminal the signals can be added or dropped from the data stream, without the need to process the other traffic.

It is rather like a conveyor belt carrying fixed size containers at a regular spacing. As the belt passes a city, you take away the containers you want, and drop new ones into gaps. The other containers pass unhindered.

The Synchronous Optical Network (SONET) is a subset of the Synchronous Digital Hierarchy (SDH), an ITU-T standard. The SDH standard can accommodate both ITU and ANSI PDH signals.

Table 2.6 Synchronous Digital Hierarchies

Data rate	SDH		SONET	
	Signal	*Capacity*	*Signal*	*Capacity*
51.84 Mbit/s	STM-0	21 × E1	STS-1, OC-1	28 × DS1 or 1 × DS3
155 Mbit/s	STM-1	63 × E1 or 1 × E4	STS-3, OC-3	84 × DS1 or 3 × DS3
622 Mbit/s	STM-4	252 × E1 or 4 × E4	STS-12, OC-12	336 × DS1 or 12 × DS3
2.48 Gbit/s	STM-16	1008 × E1 or 16 × E4	STS-48, OC-48	1344 × DS1 or 48 × DS3

Frame relay

So far I have been describing voice circuits. When a voice circuit is set up you reserve a bandwidth slot for the duration of the call. If none is available you get the busy tone. The requirements for data are different. The bandwidth is not so important, it's delivery that is important. Data can use the spare capacity as voice traffic changes up and down. Data packets can be dispatched as capacity is available.

Frame relay is a standard for packet-switched networks that operate at layer two – the data link layer of the OSI model. A bidirectional virtual circuit is set up over the network between the two communicating devices. Variable-length data packets are then routed over this virtual circuit. A number of virtual circuits can share a physical link; the link bandwidth is shared dynamically, giving much more efficient use of the link.

This is called opportunistic bandwidth. As there is now a queue of data awaiting available bandwidth, quality of service becomes an issue. The advantage is that the toll rates can be lower than the reserved bandwidth of a voice circuit.

ATM

Asynchronous Transfer Mode (ATM) was developed for high-speed packet transport over optical networks like SONET. ATM uses small fixed-size data cells rather than the large packets of frame relay. Each cell is 53 bytes long, with a payload of 48 bytes. These small cells are more suited to voice and multimedia traffic, where low latencies are demanded.

Both permanent and switched (PVC and SVC) virtual circuits can be set up. The cell header carries the virtual channel and virtual path identifier that are used to identify connections within the network. ATM is linked to other network layers by the ATM Adaptation Layer (AAL). The packets are given one of five categories of priority by traffic class:

1. Constant bit rate
2. Real-time variable bit rate
3. Non-real-time bit rate
4. Available bit rate
5. Unspecified bandwidth or 'best effort'

Constant bit rate has the best QoS, with low cell jitter. It can be used for broadcast video contribution circuits, possibly a 34 Mbit/s data stream. The variable bit rate real-time can be used for standard voice circuits. IP traffic is usually allocated the unspecified bandwidth.

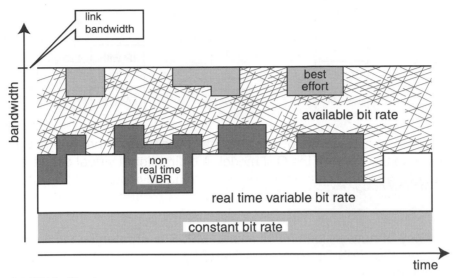

Figure 2.6 ATM traffic classes.

Some characteristics that make ATM particularly attractive for television distribution are the choice of uni- or bidirectional links; the two-way links can be asymmetric.

As network traffic increases the bandwidths grow to the point where optical switching becomes the only cost-effective way to handle the very high data rates of the network backbones. So the electronic processing of SONET and SDH will fall by the wayside.

There is a move to an all-optical infrastructure called photonic networking.

Photonic networking

As IP becomes the standard for data exchange, and voice-over IP becomes more used, the overhead of the ATM traffic engineering becomes more of a hindrance.

There are proposals to run IP directly over the Dense-Wave Division Multiplexed (DWDM) photonic network. This would greatly simplify the routing of traffic by stripping out two layers, ATM and SONET. To introduce this new concept, the capability of IP routing would have to be extended.

Generalized Multi-Protocol Label Switching (GMPLS)

Most of the telecommunications networks have evolved to carry voice traffic and general data packets. Neither of these models is really suited to the streaming of multimedia. IP routing has evolved to use label switching. This can improve

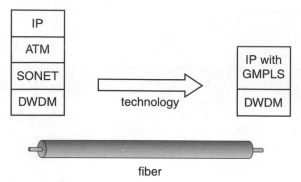

Figure 2.7 The technology migration to photonic routing.

the efficiency of network communications. MPLS is a potential technology that can improve the QoS of content delivery, by allowing traffic engineering of packet routing.

Generalized MPLS extends this capability to cover legacy ATM and SONET plant plus the new optical cross-connects, so that potentially IP can be transmitted directly over DWDM.

The local loop

There is a wide choice of connections to the Internet, split into the lower cost services for the consumer and higher capacity services for corporate systems.

Services tailored to the domestic consumer, for reasons of cost, usually use existing connections. Virtually all homes have a copper pair from the telephone company, and many in metropolitan areas have a coaxial connection to the local cable television system. Both of these connections can be used to carry Internet data alongside the existing services.

Wireless also offers connectivity, sometimes as a hybrid with a telephone back-channel.

The enterprise user

A corporate user with tens or hundreds of users will require a higher bandwidth and more reliable connection to the Internet. Traditional connections like a T-1 or E-1 circuit can provide a starting point, with T-3/E-3 where a higher capacity is required. Once a corporation moves to the use of streaming on a large scale, T-1/E-1 is unlikely to serve more than a handful of users. If you want to webcast, then outgoing capacity could be an issue. Serious consideration should be given to capacity planning. Will staff be allowed to watch streams from the public Internet, or will access be limited to the corporate intranet? Is streaming to be unicast or will multicast also be used?

Options for small businesses

Many small businesses have leased ISDN lines for telephony and data. These can also be used for connection to the Internet, but the capacity is limited for multimedia streaming to a single client. Alternatives include xDSL and T-1/E-1.

Consumer connections

Cost is the primary concern here, and usually takes precedence over the quality of service. Whereas business lines usually offer a guaranteed service, residential users are often provided with variable-rate access. At periods of high demand, network congestion increases and the service throttles back. Streaming media codecs incorporate design features to cope with these variable bandwidth conditions.

ISDN

The Integrated Subscriber Digital Network (ISDN) is a service offered by telcos that enables voice, data and multimedia to be carried over a single line to the central office or exchange. ISDN is often introduced to a business just for voice and fax services. It has also been generally adopted for the delivery of large data files in the desktop publishing environment. Video-conferencing systems can use ISDN for H320 or H323 connections. When streaming media first rolled out, ISDN seemed a natural vehicle to deliver content.

The basic service (basic rate interface or BRI) carries two bidirectional 64 kbit/s channels over two twisted pairs. The primary rate has a higher capacity of 23 or 30 channels. A separate data channel carries control information.

Table 2.7 ISDN bit rates

	Geographical area	B-channels 64 kbit/s	Data channel	Total data rate
BRI		2	1 × 16 kbit/s	192 kbit/s
PRI	N. America, Japan	23	1 × 64 kbit/s	1.544 Mbit/s
	Europe and rest of world	30	1 × 64 kbit/s	2.048 Mbit/s

The data rate of the BRI is more than sufficient for streaming audio, but for video is considered barely adequate. Note that the BRI includes two channels, which if used together can give a download of 128 kbit/s. This is often seen on streaming encoder configurations as 'dual ISDN'. ISDN offers a guaranteed data rate, unlike a dial-up modem, where a 56 kbit/s throughput is the maximum achievable, and lower rates are normal, especially over long or noisy lines.

Leveraging existing copper

The local telcos have a ready-made delivery pipe for media streams, the plain old telephone line. Copper pairs have virtually 100 per cent penetration to the home, so are an attractive carrier for content. The first use has been dial-up modems over an analog speech channel.

Dial-up modems

The use of an analog modem over a voice circuit is not really an option for the reception of video streaming unless the pictures are thumbnail size. However, it can be successfully used for streaming audio, where the bandwidth requirement is more modest.

The dial-up modem uses an analog voice circuit to the central office (CO); this is limited to a maximum speed of 56 kbit/s. In practice the best that can be achieved is more likely to be 40 kbit/s. This should be borne in mind when you are encoding content. A 56 kbit/s data stream will not pass through a dial-up circuit. A lower aggregate rate has to be chosen, for example Real recommend 34 kbit/s.

Much research effort has been devoted to exploiting the existing copper pair used by the analog telephone circuit. Although ISDN to the home has been successful in some countries (notably Germany), it is by no means in universal use. One drawback is that the bandwidth available (128 kbit/s) is insufficient for value-added services like video on-demand (VOD).

The digital subscriber line

ISDN could be considered the first digital subscriber line, but the focus now is on delivering higher data rates over the same copper pair used for the analog voice circuit, the plain old telephony service (POTS).

HDSL

The first development was high bit rate (HDSL). It uses the same four-level phase amplitude modulation as IDSN (referred to as '2B1Q'). By applying more sophisticated DSP technology and by using a wider bandwidth, HDSL can achieve the same, symmetric, rates as T1 or E1 (1.5 or 2 Mbit/s) over a range of 12,000 ft of 24 a.w.g. using two pairs (3 km of 0.5 mm). This range is the Carrier Serving Area (CSA): that is, the area served by the local exchange carrier or telco (or in the USA the RBOC) – often using Digital Loop Carrier (DLC) technology.

In many areas HDSL has replaced the original T-1, which required repeaters every few hundred yards. In Europe a variant of HDSL uses a single pair, but cannot achieve the same range. This is not a problem in countries like Germany and Italy, where the local loop tends to be shorter.

All the HDSL systems are loop powered (no local power requirement at the subscriber end) and they use the analog voice band for data.

ADSL

Asymmetric DSL or ADSL is designed to allow the plain old telephone service (POTS) to be used at the same time as the digital service. This means that the line can still be used for voice or fax while data transfer is taking place. Frequency division multiplexing is used to separate the channels. The data occupies the spectrum from 25 kHz up to over 1 MHz, leaving the low-frequency baseband clear for the POTS.

The downstream data capacity is much higher than upstream, hence the descriptor 'asymmetric'. Typical maximum downstream rates range from 1.5 up to 8 Mbit/s, and upstream up to 1 Mbit/s. The actual performance varies from supplier to supplier, and upon the local propagation conditions.

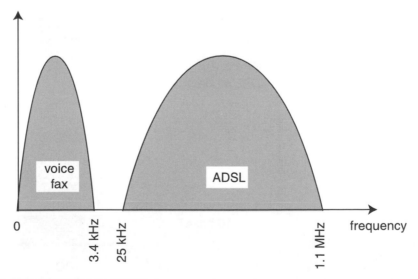

Figure 2.8 ADSL frequency multiplexing.

ADSL is good for large file downloads and receiving streaming files. The drawback is that the client can only transmit data at a lower rate (maybe 300 kbit/s), so it is not going to be suitable for a home webcasting station. For such applications the HDSL connection is a better option, albeit at higher cost. The ADSL splitter is a passive device, so the telephone service will still operate normally even when the modem is not powered.

Rate-adaptive DSL

Rate-adaptive DSL is an option where full specification DSL is not possible. The data rate adapts to the propagation conditions so bandwidth is not guaranteed but depends upon the distance from the CO.

Figure 2.9 ADSL connections.

G.lite

A key factor in providing low-cost ADSL circuits is to avoid a truck roll for installation. G.lite was developed from full specification ADSL (called 'g.dmt') as a system that could be installed simply by the consumer. G.lite does not require the installation of a splitter, so is often referred to as 'splitterless'. Many consumer systems do not give very good results with splitterless systems. The solution is the use of a low-cost filter in the line to each device.

Other DSL standards

You may come across a number of other abbreviations related to DSL.

Reverse ADSL. Doesn't work because low-level signals at the central office (CO) will be drowned by crosstalk from adjacent downstream circuits.

MSDL (moderate speed DSL). Does not achieve CSA range at T-1 rates but can satisfactorily offer lower rates (512 or 384 kbit/s), so still holds advantages over an analog modem or ISDN.

VDSL (very high speed DSL). Used for a final short-distance copper link from FTTC or FTTB systems. Can achieve T-3 data rates (45 Mbit/s) over 1,000 ft.

Cable modems

Cable TV is the other connection in many homes. Cable operators are updating older coaxial cable systems to provide wideband fiber networks, with coax for the final link to the home. Spare capacity can be utilized to provide Internet access alongside conventional television channels. This is referred to as data over cable (DOC).

The cable modem can be a PCI card fitted in the PC, or an external modem hooked up with Ethernet or USB. The modem uses one of the video channels for the downstream (head-end to consumer) connection. Between 27 and 56 Mbit/s of data can be carried over a single channel with a bandwidth of 6–8 MHz. This data is not for just one consumer but is shared between users on a node, much like an Ethernet network. Much like the digital cable networks, Quadrature Amplitude Modulation (QAM) is used. The upstream (consumer to head-end) channel uses the free spectrum under the video channels (5–24 MHz), with a bandwidth about 2 MHz and a data rate of 3 Mbit/s. QPSK or QAM modulation is used. Again it is a shared channel.

The telcos often make a point of saying that there is only one user on an ADSL line, so there are no issues of network contention. They cite this as an issue with cable systems. But the phone company will most likely hook up the ADSL termination equipment with an Ethernet, which also has a finite capacity. So treat these claims with care. How many cable modems are sharing a node, and how many ASL modems share the Ethernet?

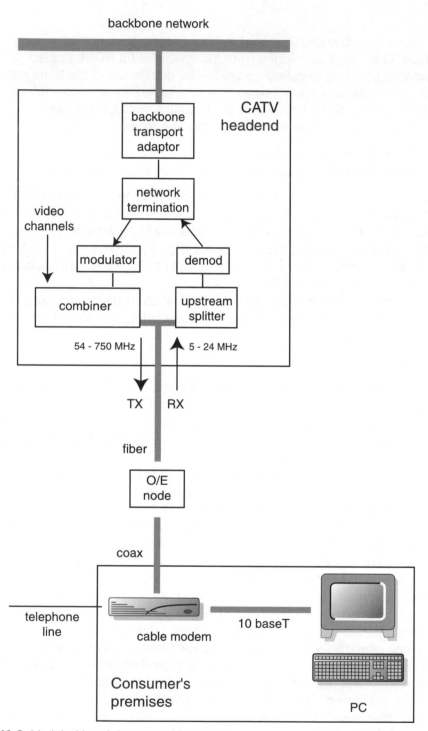

Figure 2.10 Cable television data over cable system.

Satellite

ADSL is fine if you live near the telco central office, cable modems are great if your neighborhood has cable television. If you live in rural areas, you will have to look elsewhere for broadband provision. The alternative to a copper or fiber connection is a microwave connection. This could be from a satellite or MMDS.

Very small aperture satellite antennae (VSAT) offer one-way and two-way links to the Internet. In North America the DirecTV satellites offer a data service called DirecWay. A similar service is offered in Europe by the Astra satellites.

Wireless

Wireless can be used to hook in to the Internet. You can get fixed links in many cities; these provide up to 1.5 or 2 Mbit/s over point-to-point microwave links. US Cables Warp Drive Networks are a typical supplier. To the user the terminal looks just like an Ethernet connection. An Ethernet standard covers many of these applications, 801.11b. It can carry data at rates in excess of 10 Mbit/s. It operates in the 2.5 GHz area of the spectrum.

Wireless can also be used for mobile applications; the third generation cellular radio devices will offer broadband access at rates up to 2 Mbit/s.

Always-on and client security

The domestic user of the Internet with a cable modem or DSL connection that stays permanently connected to the network is at a higher risk of attack by hackers than the user of a dial-up circuit who is only connected for short periods of time.

As a consequence the user with permanent connection will have to take greater security precautions, like the use of a firewall.

Summary

It is a demonstration of the flexibility of the OSI layer model of network communications that a system developed for the transfer of text and data files has been stretched to carry real-time multimedia. That is not to say everything is dandy. Anyone who has watched streams will know it is not always an enriching experience. Stalling video and distorted audio do not make for good viewing. Yet if we watch the same file when downloaded to a local disk, the quality is remarkably good.

The problem lies with a number of bottlenecks between the origin of the content and the player. These may be between the origin and the first Internet point-of-presence, across the backbone, or the last mile to the viewer (the local loop).

As broadband access extends to the home the problems with the local loop should be solved, but there are still issues with network congestion and the costs of edge serving. Traffic will only increase; there are other demands beyond streaming and rich media – voice-over IP and video-conferencing are two expanding markets.

Multicasting can help ease the demands on the servers and the network for live or scheduled (simulated live) webcasts. Interactive applications, like distance learning, still provide many challenges, not least stemming from their demands for low round-trip delays.

For the mobile user or remote communities, fixed wireless and satellite offer alternatives to copper and fiber. Wireless is rolling out to hand-held devices; only time will tell if the spectrum can cope with demand.

3 The WorldWide Web

Introduction

This chapter starts with a brief overview of the WorldWide Web and web sites, and then describes some of the key elements of a web page. This chapter covers the enhancements that have been added to web pages to add dynamic and graphical content: animated GIFs, dynamic HTML and Flash vector graphics.

The Web has, for many people, become synonymous with the Internet. The use of the Web has become ubiquitous, from the cyber-café in a backpackers' hostel to high bandwidth corporate intranets. But universal adoption of the web browser as the user interface has, for many, masked the fact that the Internet provides the communication fabric; the Web refers to the linked pages of content. The Web is only one of the several applications that use the Internet. The earlier applications popular in the academic community include gopher, TELNET and FTP. Streaming media came along later, and is also delivered over the Internet. However, streaming is intimately linked to the Web. Web pages often embed the pointers to streaming media, and the media player itself can be embedded in a conventional web page, so that video appears alongside the text and still images. The Internet is just one delivery channel; streaming can be delivered to a set-top box for display on a television or via cellular radio to hand-held wireless devices.

The original Web was text based. Great strides have been made by the more creative web designers to create dynamic sites without using streaming video. Vector graphics are great for many web applications, but they are clearly not suitable for many of the applications for which streaming is used. The corporate quarterly call to stockholders is not going to look too good with a cartoon CEO.

Thin clients and the web browser

In the old mainframe computing days, the client was usually a VDU running a basic Teletype emulation. The PC led to the development of distributed computing, but carried with it a maintenance nightmare for the IT department. To upgrade one application can involve visiting every PC across the enterprise. Remote administration is making this easier, but deployment is by no means universal. Users have a bad habit of installing their own applications, even games. When the PC crashes, IT then has to come and fix it. Again there are ways and means of preventing such behavior. In the 1990s, IT departments searching for solutions to these, and other problems, made moves to return to a more centralized model. In this a web browser replaces the VDU, albeit with far more facilities.

The database and the application server (the business logic) are presented through web pages on a web server. This migration makes it much easier for a corporation to use streaming, as the core infrastructure of web servers already exists. You may need to upgrade the network infrastructure to handle the wider bandwidths, but the web-enabled client workstations are ready to go.

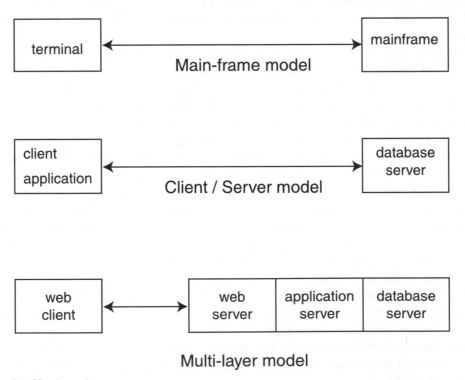

Figure 3.1 Clients and servers.

This same model has been adopted for general informational web sites. Rather than serving the conventional static HTML pages, the application server creates dynamic content on the fly, interacting with input from the browser.

The web browser is becoming the de facto thin client. So it has become the primary application for access to the Internet and corporate application servers (via an intranet). So, although a standalone media player can request files directly from the content server and play standalone, the players are most often embedded in the web client. This close association is also best suited to rich media content, where text, video and images are presented as a synchronized multimedia experience.

Some basic background knowledge of the Web is therefore required to fully understand the deployment of streaming media. Most enterprises will already have either a house web project team or an external agency maintaining a text site, so this chapter is an aid to interfacing with that team.

WWW

The WorldWide Web is the generic name for all the web pages that can be accessed via the Internet. The Web derives its name from the web-like structure constructed by the links between web pages.

At the heart lies the HyperText Markup Language (HTML) used to author the pages of a web site. Hypertext is electronic text that has cross-links within the document and between documents.

HyperText Markup Language – HTML

HTML is a language developed to describe how text, graphics and other information are formatted into documents, and how those documents are organized and linked together. The files contain only text – images and media files are referenced by links. An HTML page does not have to be a web page; HTML pages can be used just like word processor files, and never uploaded to a web server – just retrieved from disk, locally or over a network, and rendered by the browser.

An HTML page has a basic structure of a *header* and the *body* (which contains the content). The layout instructions are referred to as *tags*.

HTML is written in plain text, so can be authored using a basic word processor or text editor. The HTML standard has developed through several versions, with support for graphics and creative layout improving with each new release. The final version was HTML 4.0. HTML has outlived its usefulness, having grown in an ad hoc manner from its original design aim to enable the exchange and linking of text documents. Future revisions are to be as an application of XML

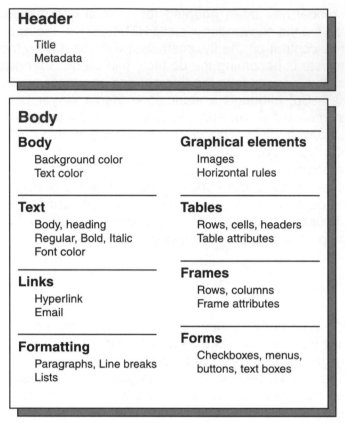

Header

Title
Metadata

Body

Body
Background color
Text color

Graphical elements
Images
Horizontal rules

Text
Body, heading
Regular, Bold, Italic
Font color

Tables
Rows, cells, headers
Table attributes

Links
Hyperlink
Email

Frames
Rows, columns
Frame attributes

Formatting
Paragraphs, Line breaks
Lists

Forms
Checkboxes, menus,
buttons, text boxes

Figure 3.2 HTML tags.

(eXtensible Markup Language), the first implementation being XHTML 1.0. This will ease the development of more complex multimedia applications. Examples of other tag sets include Synchronized Multimedia Integration Language (SMIL) and Scalable Vector Graphics (SVG).

XML

The eXtensible Markup Language (XML) is a structured set of rules for defining data. With XML you can separate structure and content from the presentation. So a file could be displayed on a web browser, much like HTML, but also on a wireless device or a television set-top box. The content can then be rendered to suit the display device.

XML is not just for delivering documents to displays, it can be used for generic data exchange between applications. Because XML is extensible, it can be used for yet to be developed applications, unlike HTML, which is now set in stone.

HyperText Transport Protocol – http

HTTP was developed for the delivery of HTML files. It is used for application-level communication between the browser and the web server in distributed, collaborative, hypermedia information systems. The communications consist of requests and responses.

The headers indicate the purpose of a request. The message uses the Uniform Resource Identifier (URI), in the form of the familiar URL or name (URN) to indicate the resource. In the response MIME-like information describes the format of the data to be transferred.

HTTP is also used as a generic protocol for communication between user agents and proxies or gateways to other Internet systems. This includes those supported by the RTSP, SMTP and FTP protocols. In this way, HTTP allows basic access level to multimedia content sourced from a diverse range of applications.

This protocol is important for streaming, as it is used to locate the content, plus it is often the only choice for a communication protocol in simple network installations. Some company firewalls prevent access to regular streaming media using real-time protocols, so HTTP is the only option for the delivery of media streams.

It is an application-layer protocol, and is usually used over a TCP/IP connection. It is a stateless protocol; that means each command is executed in isolation, with no knowledge of preceding commands. Cookies are used as a way around this so that web servers can more intelligently serve content to a browser by storing state information in the cookie.

This may be viewed as a disadvantage of HTTP, but it has great benefits. Because the protocol is stateless and connectionless the web server is relieved of the overhead of maintaining a connection to the browser. This characteristic leaves the resources of the server free to handle many, many, users simultaneously.

Web graphics

A basic web browser will render HTML files into a screen image. Text is sent as a straight ASCII-like format; the font properties are sent separately as tags and rendered by the browser to give the appropriate display. Text formatting codes give positional information for the text, and enable the author to use other devices like tables and forms.

The source files for bit-mapped images are potentially very large, which leads to long download times – unpopular with users. There are two ways around this. Line art can be sent as the very compact GIF and continuous-tone images can be compressed using the JPEG standard.

Graphic Interchange Format (GIF)

CompuServe released the original GIF format in 1987 as a means of encoding raster graphic images into a compact file. It is normally used for the placement of line art on web pages. It is not suitable for continuous-tone images. In 1989 the format was extended to include support for transparency and interlace (GIF89a). GIFs allowed web designers to liven up the rather dull text-only pages with graphic elements. The GIF format supports indexed color images with a maximum of 256 different colors. It uses the LZW algorithm for lossless compression.

Portable Network Graphics (PNG)

GIF is a copyright of CompuServe (AOL) and distributed under a royalty-free license for general use across the web. PNG was developed as an alternative open format, with additional features. It had limited support from the earlier browsers, so had a slow acceptance by web designers. It uses lossless compression, and can encode grayscale or color images, up to 24 bits per pixel. It carries an alpha channel to define the transparency.

JPEG

The Joint Picture Expert Group developed this extremely popular format for lossy compression of raster images. It has proved to be the forerunner for the techniques of video compression. JPEG compression is used for continuous-tone images, like photographs. It can be used for any image, but line art would exhibit artifacts at the high compression settings that give an equivalent small file size that a GIF image would give for line art.

Bit maps and vectors

There are two ways of coding an image: as a bit map or as vector graphics. The bit map is the familiar rectangular grid or raster of picture elements (pixels).

Table 3.1 HTML graphic formats

	Line art	Photos	Colors	Transparency	Compression	Animation
GIF	Y		8-bit	Y	Lossless	Y
PNG	Y		24-bit	Y	Lossless	N
JPEG		Y	24-bit	N	Lossy	N

Each pixel carries brightness and color values. The alternative representation is vector graphics. Objects are described by geometric characteristics. So an object could be made up of lines and curves. It could be a shape, a circle or a square, each filled with a specific color.

Vector graphic images are resolution independent. To display vector graphics, they are rendered to a bit map by the graphics adaptor. Similarly a raster image processor in a printer will convert the image to a regular grid of dots.

Vectors are more suited to line artwork, clipart or cartoons, whereas bit maps are used for continuous-tone objects, like natural video and photographs.

Animating pages

Animation is a halfway house to streaming. It has the big advantage in that well-designed animations use far less bandwidth than video streams. Macromedia's Flash animated vector graphics typifies such animation. This is not to ignore the fact that Flash file downloads can be lengthy through 28k or 56k modems.

There are three main ways to animate. A GIF object can be animated. DHTML allows objects to move and reveal. Flash is a step up, and allows fully animated and interactive graphic sequences.

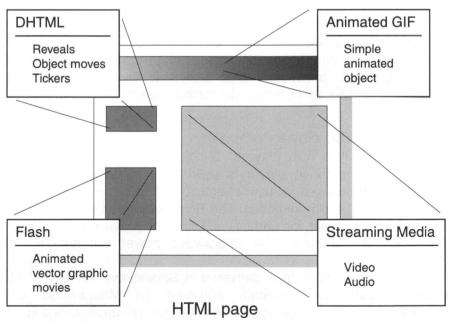

Figure 3.3 HTML page add-ins.

Animated GIFs

A number of GIFs can be played in rapid sequence, much like a cartoon flipbook, to produce a basic animation. It is only suited to short clips of a few seconds. It is much used on web pages as an attention seeker, like a flashing neon sign. The animated GIF is being replaced with Flash animation because of the vast capabilities of the format.

Dynamic HTML

A straight HTML page is static; once it has been downloaded it sits there until you select a new link and another page is downloaded. Dynamic HTML or DHTML allows the content of a page to change after it has been loaded. It is typically used for hidden menus that appear when the mouse passes over a button. It can also be used to move objects around the screen along a programmed path. Pages can be periodically refreshed; this is used for news tickers on web pages.

DHTML is a mix of technologies. The core is the Document Object Model (DOM). The DOM allows changes to be made to cascading styles sheets and to basic HTML. The changes are made with client-side scripts using JavaScript or VBScript.

Flash

Flash is an animated vector-graphic format that offers the advantages of dynamic graphics, without the large file sizes required by true video. It requires a plug-in to the web browser to play back the files. The player can be downloaded free of charge from the Macromedia web site.

Shockwave and Flash player comparison

Macromedia offers two web players: Shockwave and Flash. Each has a distinct purpose. The Flash player is used for fast-loading front-end Web applications. It can be used for user interaction, interactive online advertising, and short to medium form animation. The Shockwave player is used for long-form content. It is popular for games, and for interactive multimedia product demonstrations and training. The Shockwave player will also play Flash content.

Note that the Flash content is delivered in Shockwave file format (.SWF). Shockwave content is specifically authored on Macromedia Director, whereas Flash files can be generated by many applications (not just Macromedia).

Proprietary tools

It is often said that you can lay out a web page with a basic text editor like Microsoft Notepad. To improve productivity, especially with the more creative sites, a number of specialized products can be used. These high-level tools let you concentrate on the design and content creation, rather than the mechanics of HTML.

Web page editing. Macromedia *Dreamweaver* and Adobe *GoLive*.

Web animation. Macromedia *Director* and Adobe *LiveMotion*.

Plug-ins

Apart from the basic graphic formats supported by web browsers, other formats are viewed with a software application that plugs into the browser – a 'plug-in'. There is marked reluctance by users to install plug-ins. It may be that a corporate IT department does not want the maintenance issues. The public is suspicious, associating plug-ins with backdoors to their hard drive, possibly introducing viruses, and compromising confidentiality with unseen reporting to remote web servers.

For this reason it is unwise to step outside the most popular plug-ins if you want the widest audience for your web site. Many users have Flash, Shockwave, QuickTime, Real and Windows Media. Other plug-ins have not achieved the same level of market penetration and should be selected with care.

Web servers

At its most basic, the web server delivers a file in answer to a request from a browser.

- The user asks for a page using a URL
- The web server maps the URL to a file name
- The server reads the file from disk
- The server transmits the HTML file to the browser using http

The web server has to handle many hundreds or thousands of connections concurrently. To handle this high processing load a combination of multi-processing and multi-threading is used. Communication between the browser and server uses HyperText Transport Protocol or HTTP over a TCP/IP connection. The first version of HTTP required a separate TCP connection to be negotiated for each browser request. So a page with many graphic elements

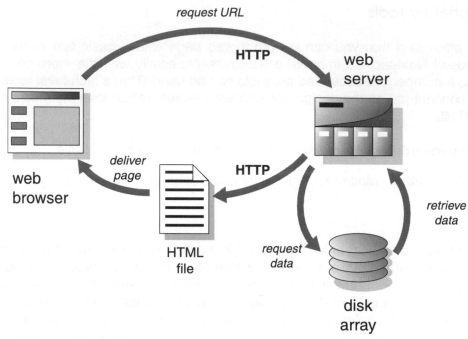

Figure 3.4 Requesting an HTML page.

needed a TCP connection to be set up for each element. HTTP 1.1 now maintains a persistent TCP connection during an HTTP session; this cuts down the communications overheads.

Content types, MIME

If the file is a web page, it will be HTML format, but the page may also have embedded graphics or media files. To instruct the browser how to handle these files correctly, the media content type is specified in the header using the Multipurpose Internet Mail Extension or MIME (RFC 1521). MIME types include audio, image, text and video. Subtypes beginning with /x- are private values, and require a proprietary application to view. The type 'message' is used for mail. The browser has several options for handling the file:

- The browser can handle the file internally
- The browser can call a plug-in
- The browser can pass the file to another application
- The browser can download the file to disk

The browser preferences define how each MIME type is handled. Table 3.2 gives typical examples.

Table 3.2 MIME types

Description	Extension	MIME type/subtype	Handling
Hypertext	htm, html	text/html	View with browser
Image	jpg, jpeg, jpe	image/jpeg	View with browser
GIF Image	gif	image/gif	View with browser
MP3 audio file	mp3	audio/x-mpeg	Listen with player
Real Media file	rm	application/vnd.rn-realmedia	View with plug-in or post-process with player
Windows Media	wmv	video/x-ms-wmv	View with plug-in or post-process with player

Server farms

If your web site handles large traffic volumes, one server is unlikely to cope with the demand. Several servers can be deployed to share the load. Special hardware or software balances the load of browser connections across the servers. Similar load balancers are also used with streaming media. Servers are sometimes split by content – one cluster for text, one for images and one for video files.

Tuning

A web server is usually tuned to optimize I/O connections, as the processor load is low. Contrast this with an application server that is probably tuned for high processor utilization. The tuning requirements vary from site to site; it depends on factors like the balance of static to dynamic content, and whether security, like SSL, is used. The streaming media server will also require tuning, but to satisfy a different set of requirements. The streaming files are much larger, and require continuous transfer. An on-demand server will require wide interconnections from the disk array.

Summary

The web has evolved a long way since Berners-Lee developed, at CERN, the concepts of linked and cross-referenced text documents. Under the auspices of W3C, XML now offers an extensible and flexible set of formats that can be used for the delivery of multimedia content, not just to web browsers but TV set-top boxes, cell phones and PDAs. As part of this rationalization HTML is evolving into the XML-compatible XHTML.

The HTML standards have developed into a format that can support innovative and high standards of graphic design. The main element that is missing is natural video and audio – streaming media.

The web server lies at the heart of access to streaming media content. The video content is often embedded in a web page and the links announcing content are normally placed in pages. For a content delivery system with a low level of streaming traffic this same web server may be used to source the media files. But for any system of size the advantages of using a separate streaming server are compelling.

4 Video formats

Introduction

The usual way to make a streaming video is to start with a conventional television signal, live from a camera or pre-recorded from videotape. This video signal is converted to computer file format before it can be processed by the streaming codec. This is called capture.

There are many similarities between television and computer video, but there are minor differences in the standards and formats that are relevant to capture. This chapter gives an overview of the broadcast television standards for the reader who may be more familiar with computer formats like AVI and QuickTime. This chapter also covers the many tape formats you will encounter, and the different interconnections that can be used between the tape deck and the encoding workstation.

Although we live in a digital world, there is still much legacy analog equipment in use in video production. We must not forget that the majority of television viewers still watch an analog transmission, and the changeover to digital reception may not happen until 2010, varying from country to country. The pioneers in digital transmission have been the satellite operators, where the driving force for the deployment of digital transmission (using the MPEG-2 standard) has been the emission of four to six times the number of channels within a given transponder bandwidth. So any overview has to start in the analog domain.

Essentially, television is the reproduction of a moving two-dimensional image by the transmission of a regular sequence of color bit maps. Television started as a monochrome system, with color added later. The color information was interleaved into the luminance channel without requiring any additional bandwidth. How this was achieved is a precursor to modern compression techniques.

Analog television uses several techniques to lower the bandwidth requirements without causing unacceptable visual artifacts. Some of these artifacts may today be considered as obvious distortions, but it must be remembered that the engineering compromises were made half a century ago, and were implemented with a handful of vacuum tubes. The methods used include scan interlace, color space conversion and chrominance band limiting.

Scanning

The scene captured by the camera lens is projected onto a planar sensor. The early tube cameras scanned the light-sensitive sensor layer in lines, generating a varying voltage proportional to the incident light. Analog television is specified in terms of lines and frames, rather than the regular pixel grids familiar to computer users. There are two picture dimensions for standard definition television, one the NTSC system used in North America, and the PAL and SECAM systems used in Europe and Asia. The NTSC system was developed from an earlier monochrome standard: RS-170.

Table 4.1 Analog picture resolutions

	Line duration (μs)	Picture height (lines)	Line rate (Hz)	Frame rate (Hz)	Active picture area	
					Width (μs)	Height (lines)
RS-170		525	15,750	30		486
NTSC	63.49	525	15,734.26	29.96	720	486
PAL, SECAM	64	625	15,625	25	52	576

The transmitted signal includes vertical and horizontal blanking intervals, used for synchronization of the receiver and to allow flyback time of a scanning electron beam in the CRT display. As a consequence the signal is split into the active picture area and synchronization information.

The brightness values of each pixel are read out from top left to bottom right, always reading left to right. Why not alternate the direction of the scan from line to line, a serpentine scan? That would remove the need for the line flyback in the CRT. Unfortunately any non-linearity in the scan drivers would mean misalignment of left-to-right lines relative to the right-to-left.

Interlaced scan

The developers of television had many problems to grapple with, not least the difficulty of driving the scans at high writing speed, and the limited transmission bandwidth that was then possible. To give a display without apparent flicker, it had long been known from the motion picture industry that the frame rate had to be greater than 48 per second. Although movies are shot at 24 frames per second, the projector displays each frame twice. It was not possible for the early television receiver to display each frame twice, which would have needed a picture store. Such developments had to wait for affordable digital memory.

The compromise was to transmit a frame as two halves or fields, one field of the even lines, one of the odd lines. Thus the transmitted signal is a 250- or 300-line picture, but the final display has 500 or 600 lines. This is called an interlaced scan, as opposed to a simple top to bottom scan, called progressive. To avoid a line-by-line flicker the phosphors used in the CRT continue to emit light after the stimulation by the electron beam. The persistence time for the light output to decay is chosen to maintain emission until the next writing cycle. Interlaced scans had another benefit; the bandwidth required for transmission was halved.

Drawbacks of interlaced scanning

Interlacing gave a very acceptable picture when the source of pictures was the television camera. The combination of the modulation transfer factor of the taking lens (which acts as a low-pass spatial filter) and the finite scanning beam size of the early tube camera meant that picture detail was filtered of high-frequency vertical detail, a natural anti-aliasing.

Once computer graphics equipment was introduced, it became possible (if there was no vertical filtering) to generate very hard vertical brightness transitions. These did produce visible flicker on horizontal edges at the frame rate (25 or 30 Hz). The workaround was for the character generator manufacturers to apply spatial filters to the original image. These softened the edges and lowered the incidence of visible flicker. This vertical filtering means that an interlaced scan has a lower vertical resolution in practice than a progressive scan.

The second drawback is that television post-production uses many special effects that transform the scene geometry (squeezes and zooms). These have to be processed as a complete picture of the odd and the even field. After the mathematical transforms, the new frame then has to be converted back to the two interlaced fields.

Frame rates

Video equipment is sold in two standards, 25 or 30 frames per second. These are a hangover from the early days of television. The receivers had poor power supply regulation, so line-related hum was evident throughout the processing.

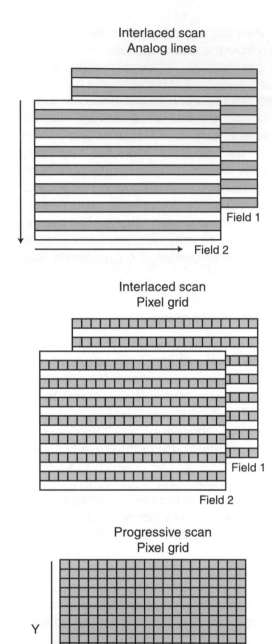

Figure 4.1 Progressive and interlaced scanning.

To avoid 'hum bars' scrolling through the picture, the field rate was chosen to be the same as the power line frequency, 50 Hz in Europe and 60 Hz in the USA. This was not a big issue until international program exchange started; but by then the standards were entrenched.

In all probability all your production can be done in one standard. The problem arises if you want to edit together material shot at two different frame rates. For example, something shot at the headquarters in the USA and an insert shot in a European office. The best way round this is to have the foreign tape converted to the standard that you use for editing. It is best to go for a high-quality conversion, it should be motion compensated. A low-quality conversion will exhibit motion artifacts, juddering or softness around moving objects. These artifacts will give your encoder a hard time, and lower the final streaming video quality.

If you have the opportunity to plan ahead, it is best to shoot an entire production in one format.

Color space conversion

Human vision has two types of sensor: the rods, sensitive to light level, and the cones, sensitive to level within three spectral bands – red, green and blue. To give realistic color reproduction the television system is based on these three spectral bands or primary colors. A requirement of the original NTSC system

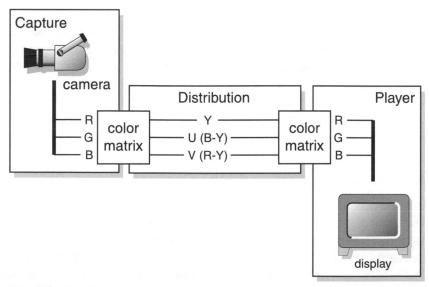

Figure 4.2 RGB and YUV.

was backwards compatibility of the legacy monochrome system. To that end the RGB color space is mapped to a luminance signal (used by a monochrome receiver) and two color or chrominance signals. By a reverse conversion, the original RGB signals can then be derived by the color receiver.

The luminance component is called Y, the color components R-Y (or V) and B-Y (or U). The user of bit map imaging programs like Photoshop will be familiar with different color spaces.

Table 4.2 Color spaces

Designation	Name	Notes
RGB	Red, Green, Blue	The native format
CYMK	Cyan, Yellow, Magenta, blacK	For color printing
HSB	Hue, Saturation, Brightness	Related to human perception
L-a-b	Luminance, a (green to red) and b (blue to yellow)	The CIE model

Color television is most similar to the CIE (Commission Internationale d'Eclairage) model of color with a luminance and two color-related components.

Additive and subtractive color

The computer color displays use the additive system of color to represent the different hues we perceive. The light emitted by red, green and blue pixels add to give the wanted color. All three together add to give white light. Contrast this with subtractive systems, like color printing. Here the ink or pigment subtracts or absorbs part of the visible spectrum to give the desired color. The pigments are the secondary colors cyan, yellow and magenta. The three together at maximum density subtract all light, so appear black.

Chrominance band limiting

It was also known, when NTSC was developed, that the human eye perceives color detail at a lower acuity than luminance detail. This meant that the color channels could be transmitted at a lower resolution than the luminance signal without an apparent loss of picture detail. In the NTSC system the two chroma channels, I and Q, are limited to bandwidths of 1.3 MHz and 400 kHz respectively. Contrast this with the luminance bandwidth of 4.2 MHz. The PAL

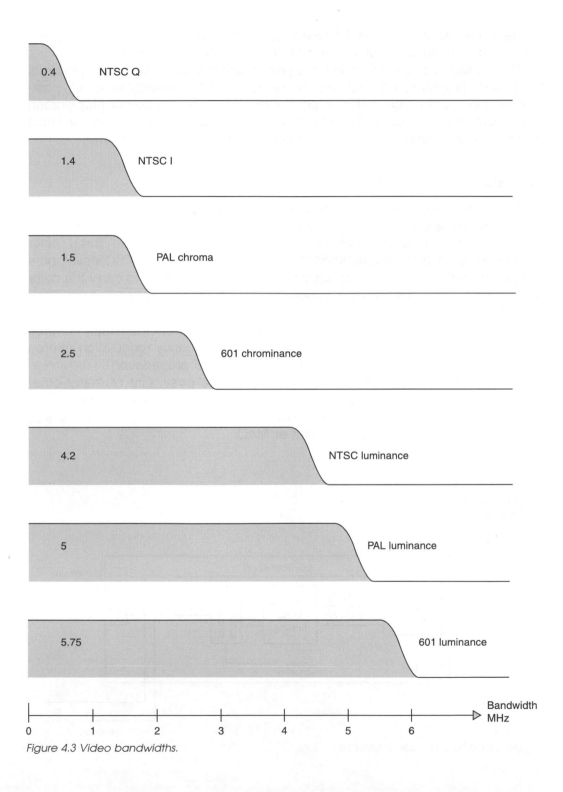

Figure 4.3 Video bandwidths.

system has slightly larger bandwidths, 5 or 5.5 MHz for luminance, and symmetrical bandwidths of 1.5 MHz for the U and V color channels.

This limitation of chroma detail has proved acceptable for final distribution of television programming, but the more demanding requirements of post-production require more detail. A good example is chroma key or blue-screen compositing. If PAL or NTSC sources are used, the chroma mattes (or keys) have very soft edges, too soft to produce a realistic composite scene.

Component and composite

Although your workstation has three cables carrying RGB to the display monitor (and possibly a sync channel), such an interconnection is only feasible for a short distance of a few meters. For general distribution the three color components have to be combined to a single channel. The NTSC developers had open to them a number of possible modulation schemes to carry the color information within the existing bandwidth of the monochrome system. They opted for quadrature amplitude modulation of the two color components onto a subcarrier. This is not the only possible method; the SECAM team later adopted frequency modulation of the color components. Frequency modulation offered potential advantages for videotape recording and RF propagation.

The advent of digital processing opened up the possibility of many other systems. One short-lived analog standard used time-division multiplexing of the three components, with temporal compression of each component – this was called Multiplexed Analog Component or MAC.

Figure 4.4 Composite video coder.

The advances in multiplexing really began with the adoption of digital distribution. A number of proprietary bit-parallel schemes existed for short-range interconnection of computer graphics equipment, but it was long recognized that a cost-effective solution had to use serial transmission so that standard coaxial cable and connectors could be used.

Drawbacks of analog composite

When analog composite video is encoded, the luminance and the modulated color components are simply added together. It is the job of the receiver to separate the color information. The simplest decoders exhibit two main artifacts. Cross-luminance is the interpretation of color information as luminance detail. This is visible as dot-crawl or 'hanging dots', especially in areas of saturated color. The other effect is cross-color, where high-frequency luminance detail is interpreted as color. This is most commonly seen in patterned fabrics, like check shirts and jackets. The fabric has a rainbow effect.

Many decoder designs have been developed to counteract these effects, based in the main on the comb filter. A comb filter can very effectively separate the interleaved frequency components of the luminance and chrominance information for static pictures. Unfortunately, if the subject is moving, this no longer holds true. To get around this manufacturers can use a motion-adaptive filter. The other problem that arises is limited to low-cost VCRs. The playback signal has timing jitter, so it is not possible for a comb filter to effectively separate the two components.

S-Video

S-Video is a workaround, to avoid the cross-luminance and cross-color artifacts of the composite system and the playback jitter problems that prevent the use of comb decoders. It uses the same quadrature amplitude modulation system, but carries the chrominance component as a separate circuit. It requires two coaxial cables so is only suited to short-range local interconnections.

Digital composite

Digital composite was another short-lived, but very successful, standard. It acted as a stepping-stone from analog composite to digital component. It was developed as a spin-off from the D-2 digital composite tape format. D-2 offered the advantages of digital recording (error correction, cloned copies) in an analog composite environment. If you used analog recording you were limited in the number of generations of copying before picture degradation became unacceptable, somewhere around four generations. This constraint caused limitations in post-production, where the program-makers demanded complex special effects. Digital composite simply sampled the analog composite waveform at four times subcarrier.

Digital component coding

A number of proprietary digital formats evolved for special effects and computer graphics equipment. These early developers established some of the ground rules that could support realistic pictures.

- Three color channels
- Eight bits per channel
- Around 700 pixels per television line

601

The standard, ITU-R BT601 to give its full designation, has proved to be a solid foundation for much of the later developments in digital video technology. 601 was intended to be used for program production, so offered a high picture quality, with sufficient resolution to be used for special effects. One specific example is chroma-keying or matting. This is where the talent is shot in front of a blue or green screen. In post-production the colored screen is replaced with another picture. Much loved by weathermen, it also has many applications for the corporate and training productions that may well be encoded for streaming.

Sampling

Much as the NTSC standard uses band limiting for the I and Q color components, the 601 standard also exploits the feature of the human visual system that color is perceived at a lower acuity. The color information is sampled at a lower spatial resolution than the luminance. There are several schemes, but the 601 standard uses half the sampling frequency. Early digital systems used four times color subcarrier as the sampling rate. The luminance signal is close to this frequency, hence 4 $\times$ sampling. The chrominance channels are sampled at half this, so the nomenclature for the YUV sample is 4:2:2. The vertical resolution for luminance and chrominance is the same. If chrominance is sampled every other line, we arrive at symmetric color sample spatial scaling. This is called 4:2:0 sampling, and was adopted for MPEG-1 and later used for

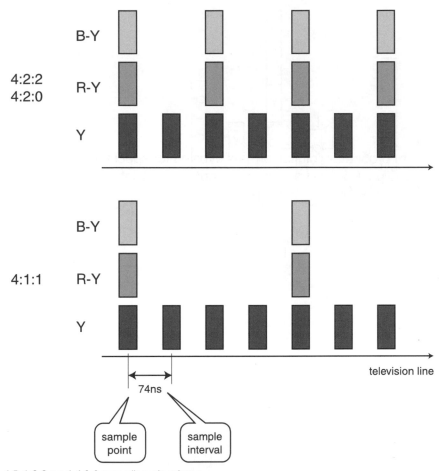

Figure 4.5 4:2:2 and 4:1:1 sampling structures.

MPEG-2 MP@ML. The alternative is to sample color at one-quarter the luminance rate, 4:1:1. This has been adopted for the DV format. The color resolution is still as good as analog composite, but is not suitable for high-quality chroma key matting operations.

Coding range

Computer video uses the full gamut of codes to specify colors. So black has a value of zero, white is 255 (8-bit coding). Video uses a restricted range, giving headroom above white level and below black. If the original source is analog this headroom avoids clipping of the video signal (in the case of DC offsets or analog-to-digital converter misalignment). So the actual range is from 16 to 235, a range of 220 values, as opposed to the 256 values of computer graphics. You

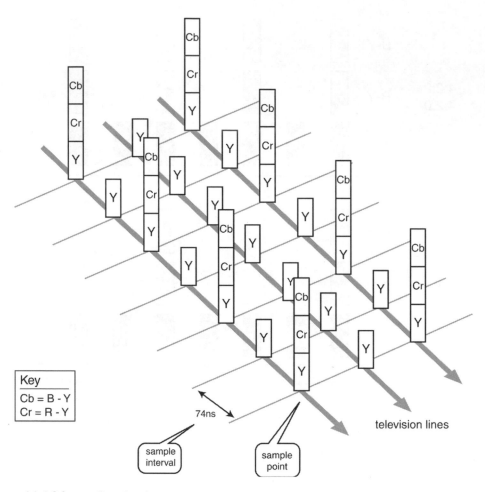

Figure 4.6 4:2:0 sampling structure.

can convert from one range to the other, but this will introduce rounding errors, so should be applied with regard to the number of conversions.

Eight and 10 bits

The 601 standard originally specified 8-bit sample values. This proved insufficient for extensive video processing. For example, keying processes could cause visible banding on graduated tones. To ease this problem the standard was extended to support 10-bit samples, although most equipment only supports 8-bit interfaces. The two least significant bits (of the 10) are truncated or rounded.

For streaming applications 10-bit interfaces are a luxury, 8 bits are fine.

Gamma

If you are used to computer video, you may well be familiar with the display gamma, 2.2 for Windows and 1.8 for Macintosh. Television has a fixed gamma, so all the receivers should be the same.

Scanning resolutions

There are two picture dimensions for standard definition television, one the NTSC system used in North America, and the PAL and SECAM systems used in Europe and Asia.

Computer displays use a plethora of scanning rates and screen resolutions. The frame rates vary from 60 Hz up to 120 Hz.

Table 4.3 Digital picture resolutions

	Active picture area		Total including sync interval		Frame rate (Hz)
	Width	Height	Width	Height	
NTSC	720	486	864	525	29.96
PAL, SECAM	720	576	864	625	25

Table 4.4 Computer monitor resolutions

Designation	Resolution	
VGA	640 × 480	Video graphics array
SVGA	800 × 600	Super video graphics array
XVGA	1024 × 760	Extended video graphics array
	1280 × 1024	
	1600 × 1024	Wide aspect ratio

Square and rectangular pixels

Computer paint programs that use bit maps rather than vector graphics (like Adobe Photoshop) all use square pixels. That means a circle 10 pixels high is also 10 pixels wide. Digital television does not use square pixels. The horizontal resolution is chosen to have a sensible mathematical relationship to sampling frequencies, line rate and frame rate. Simple geometry was not an overriding concern for analog systems. The television pixels depart from a square by about 10 per cent; NTSC is higher than wide by 11/10, PAL wider than high by 59/54.

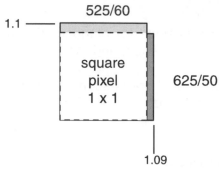

Figure 4.7 Pixel aspect ratios.

Does it matter? Usually the scaling algorithms in the video codecs should convert from one aspect to another. So you should not have to worry about it – unless a circle is no longer circular by the time it is displayed on the player. In that case an investigation is called for.

Videotape formats

The newcomer to video recording might well ask 'why are there so many formats, and which should I use?' Videotape formats seem to grow with a geometric progression. They were originally developed as all-encompassing formats, but are now optimized for specific applications. Formats may be developed for the highest quality – for studio recording and high-definition work – or for the low-cost, low-weight demands of newsgathering and consumer camcorders. There have been about 100 formats developed over the last 50 years, but less than 20 have been successful in the marketplace. The SMPTE has standardized many of the tape formats, using letters for analog formats (type 'C') and numbers for the digital formats (D-1).

Many formats have evolved to give backwards compatibility with legacy formats. This allows broadcasters to use the same deck to play back new digital recordings and archive analog recordings, saving cost and space (that several decks would occupy).

The enabling development for videotape recording was the flying head. This gave a fast enough writing speed to record the high frequencies of the video

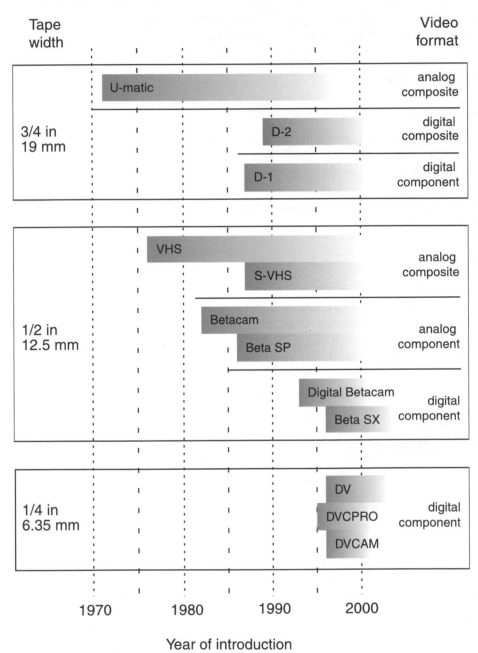

Figure 4.8 Evolution of videotape formats.

waveform, while retaining a low linear tape speed. Initially released in the transverse-scan quadruplex format by Ampex, it soon evolved into the helical scan system that video recorders use today.

Analog formats

One-inch C-format

This was the most successful of the open-reel 1-inch formats and was the workhorse of the edit bay until the production quality cassette formats were developed. A consequence of its success is that there is much archive material still lying in vaults that was recorded on this format. To use this for streaming content it is probably best to have it dubbed to a digital format and then encode from the digital copy.

U-matic

A consortium of JVC, Matsushita and Sony developed the U-matic format in the late 1960s, originally as a domestic format. It was soon adopted for industrial and professional use, and also by television networks for early electronic newsgathering trials. Sony only ceased manufacture in 2000, so there is a lot of material out there in this format, especially corporate and industrial content.

The format used 19 mm tape, with color-under recording. It used a 110 mm diameter head drum rotating at 1,800 rpm. Contrast this with the DV recorder, which has a drum diameter of 21.7 mm turning at 9,000 rpm. There were several implementations, including hi-band and SP.

VHS

Dating from 1976, this has been the most successful tape format to date. It was developed for the domestic market for single generation recordings. It does not offer acceptable multi-generation performance that is required for professional editing applications. As an analog format it does exhibit visible picture noise, an artifact that impairs the potential quality of streaming video. It is best avoided for capture of new material; you should opt for one of the DV formats.

S-VHS

A development of VHS to offer improved record quality. Noted for the adoption of the S-video interconnection, where the modulated chroma is kept separate from the luminance channel as opposed to being combined in to composite video (NTSC, PAL).

Betacam and Beta SP

This format used compressed time division multiplexing of the R-Y and B-Y chroma channels, making it a true component recorder as opposed to the Y-C recorders previously available (U-matic records a single modulated chroma channel). Broadcasters rapidly adopted this for general production recording as well as ENG use. The SP version offered improved performance.

MII

Another 1/2-inch format, this time from Matsushita, it used very similar design principles to Betacam. It replaced the largely unsuccessful M-format. Several major networks around the world adopted MII. Probably had the best performance of any analog format.

Digital formats

Digital formats split into composite and component.

Digital composite

D-2 was developed as a replacement for ageing robotic cart machines that for 20 years played out television commercials 24 hours a day. Being a cassette format, it was easily handled by machinery rather than a human tape jockey. The digital format meant that tapes could be cloned as repeated plays caused tape wear. It was also used as a general-purpose replacement for the C-format open reel machine. Although a digital format, the recorder was usually used with analog plant.

D-3 was a Panasonic product, using 1/2-inch tape. It was used in a similar way to D-2, with analog composite interconnections.

Digital composite has been largely replaced by component VTRs, giving the many advantages of component processing.

Digital component

The first digital component VTR was D-1. This was the pioneering digital component format, much loved for film transfer and high-end commercial production. It does not use compression, and was designed to use the new BT601 sampling format. It uses 19 mm tape with 8-bit words per color channel. Panasonic later developed the D-5 format, using 1/2-inch tape, similar to the D-3 machines. It offered 10-bit recording of 270 Mbit/s video, or 8-bit for the little-used 16:9 360 Mbit/s format.

Most component formats now use 1/2- or 1/4-inch tape. The basic choice is between the Betacam derivates (1/2 inch) or the DV format (1/4 inch), although there are several other formats.

Sony manufactures three 1/2-inch formats, Digital Betacam, Betacam SX and IMX.

Digital Betacam

A general purpose, high-quality digital recorder intended as a replacement for the Betacam SP analog format. It uses modest DCT compression, and can be considered essentially transparent. It is very popular for all forms of teleproduction, from field shooting to studio recording and editing.

Betacam SX

Based on 18 Mbit/s MPEG-2, this format is optimized for ENG applications.

IMX

Uses MPEG-2 recording at rates up to 50 Mbit/s. The coding is the studio profile with 4:2:2 sampling and I-frame only compression.

Note that the digital Betacam is essentially a closed system with regular video interconnections. SX and IMX can exchange video as the compressed data files, either to other VTRs or to disk recorders.

DV

A group of different professional and consumer camcorder formats, all based on the DV 1/4-inch format cassette. The format specifies two tape cassette sizes, the standard for VTRs and the miniDV for camcorders. The compact size lends it to the implementation of very small camcorders, the so-called palm-corders. The DV format samples video at 4:1:1 (525/60) or 4:2:0 (625/50), then uses DCT intraframe coding with a 5:1 reduction in data; this gives a final data rate of 25 Mbit/s for standard definition pictures. It is often referred to as DV25 compression. It has two digital stereo audio channels. The normal tape stock is metal evaporated.

When broadcasters expressed interest in these compact and lightweight DV camcorders, Panasonic and Sony developed two new formats based on the DV tape, but achieving a better performance (the DVCPRO and the DVCAM respectively). Panasonic also offer enhanced professional formats, also offering 50 Mbit/s recording (DVCPRO-50). This uses 4:2:2 sampling and milder compression (3.3:1).

Most manufacturers have adopted the IEEE 1394 interface as the general port on their products to allow users to download the DV compressed files to the video editing system in the native format, as an alternative to regular video interconnects.

DV comes in several flavors from different manufacturers:

DV
The original consumer format, also known as DVC.

DVCPRO (SMPTE D-7)
A high-quality format from Panasonic, much liked for professional field use. Uses nearly twice the linear tape speed of the consumer versions and uses the more reliable metal particle tape. This improves performance in editing applications and lowers the bit error rate. It is also available in a 50 Mbit/s version.

DVCAM
This is the Sony professional format based on the DV cassette. Like DVCPRO it uses a higher linear tape speed and it uses metal particle tape.

Others

There are many other formats, these are just a few of the more common ones:

D-5
Uses a similar transport to the D-3 digital composite recorder, but offers 10-bit 4:2:2 component recording. The video is not compressed so it is popular for high-end uses in post-production.

D-9 (Digital-S)
Uses a metal particle tape in a VHS footprint cassette. D-9 decks can potentially play back VHS, S-VHS and Digital-S tapes.

Table 4.5 Analog tape formats

	Format	Tape width (in.)	Max. playing time (min)	Composition
Analog composite	C-format	1	94	Ferric oxide
	U-matic	3/4	60	Ferric oxide
	U-matic SP	3/4	60	Metal particle
Analog component	Betacam	1/2	300	Ferro-chrome
	Betacam SP	1/2	90	Metal particle
	MII	1/2		

Table 4.6 Digital tape formats

	Format	Tape width (in.)	Max. playing time (min)	Composition	Compression	Sampling
Digital composite	D-2	3/4				4 fsc
	D-3	1/2				4 fsc
Digital component	D-1	3/4				4:2:2
	D-5	1/2				4:2:2
	Digital Betacam	1/2	94		DCT 2.3:1	4:2:2
	Betacam SX	1/2			MPEG-2 10:1	
	Betacam IMX	1/2			MPEG-2 4:2:2P@ML	4:2:2
	Digital-S (D-9)	1/2	104		DCT 3.3:1	4:2:2
	Digital 8		Mini 60	Metal particle		
	DV/DVC	1/4	Standard 300	Metal evaporated	DV 5:1	4:1:1/4:2:0
	DVCPRO	1/4	120	Metal particle	DV 5:1	4:1:1/4:2:0
	DVCAM	1/4	180	Metal evaporated	DV	4:1:1/4:2:0
	DVPRO-50	1/4	60	Metal particle	DV 3.3:1	4:2:2

Video compression

The compression used in Digital Betacam is a closed system, optimized for recording on tape. The DV format is more general purpose, and can be interchanged between units in the native format – this avoids unnecessary decompression and recompression stages that would degrade the signal. The SX and IMX formats have adopted MPEG-2 compression.

The compressed formats can often be copied between devices at higher than real-time, typically four times. This can be very useful for cutting down the capture time from tape to disk storage systems.

DV and MPEG I-frame

MPEG-2 at main profile/main level is ideal for program distribution, satellite DTH and DVB transmissions. But the long group of pictures does not lend it to editing. The ideal for editing is to be able to cut to the frame. DV does not use inter-frame coding so meets the requirements for editing. The alternative for MPEG-2 is to adopt a profile that does not use inter-frame coding, or 'I-frame only'. It does not use the B or P frames (bidirectional and predictive). The drawback of the avoidance of inter-frame coding is that for a given video quality the data rate is much higher than regular MPEG-2. ENG users have adopted 24 or 25 Mbit/s, and 50 Mbit/s is used for studio use. Compare this with the maximum rate used by MP@ML of 15 Mbyte/s. So DV and MPEG-2, I-frame only, deliver a similar level of video quality for a given bit rate, yet still allow freedom to edit at random frames.

What format of VTR deck should I purchase?

If you are setting up an encoding station from scratch, the question always comes up as to which formats to use. There is no straight answer to this. A video dubbing facility may well have at least one of each format – but that is their core business. Of course the choice may be restricted – suppose you have decided to use a DV-based desktop editing system. It would make sense to opt for a DV format. Alternatively you may have a large archive of Betacam tapes. In that case one of the Sony 1/2-inch decks would be a better choice. The later models can play both analog and digital tapes. It is always useful to have a deck that can play VHS and S-VHS – there is a huge amount of corporate material that is available in these old formats.

You could standardize on one format and outsource interformat dubbing to a video facilities house, but remember that this will add to turnaround time, which could give problems with rush jobs.

Time code

Computers usually count time in 'x' millisecond increments from a certain date. Television uses a system more suited to reading by humans. Since program tapes rarely exceed 3 hours in length, the time code only needs to resolve up to 1 day or 24 hours. The resolution needs to be to one frame. The SMPTE have a standard used throughout the television industry, that counts each frame in frames, seconds, minutes and hours.

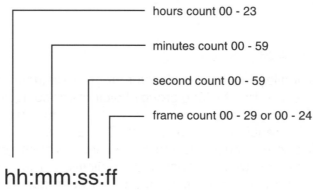

hours count 00 - 23

minutes count 00 - 59

second count 00 - 59

frame count 00 - 29 or 00 - 24

hh:mm:ss:ff

Figure 4.9 Time code format.

Drop-frame time code

The NTSC standard further complicates the problem, with relation to program durations. The line and frame frequencies are derived from color subcarriers, rather than the arbitrary line and field rate values of PAL. The new line scanning frequency was defined as 2/455 times the subcarrier (3.579545 MHz) or 15,734.26 Hz, while the frame rate was defined as 1/525 times the line frequency, or 29.97 Hz.

With this frame rate of 29.97 Hz (rather than exactly 30 Hz), 30 frames last 1.001 seconds rather than precisely 1 second. This means the time code registering the frame count is not the same as the studio clock (probably locked to GPS). If the duration of a clip is calculated from the time codes, over a period of time this error will accumulate. This can be ignored for short clips like commercial spots, but for a 2-hour movie the error amounts to a 7-second overrun. This may not sound much, but with the tight scheduling of television commercials, 7 seconds is potential revenue. To get around this, the SMPTE standard specifies an algorithm for dropping certain time code values. This drops the first two frames (00 and 01) of every minute, except every tenth minute. This amounts to dropping 108 frames per hour. This is 3.6 seconds, which effectively corrects the error.

You will notice that most editing equipment has configuration settings for time code, to select drop-frame (29.97 Hz) or non-drop-frame (30 Hz). Note that this setting is not required for PAL (625/50) as the frame rate is exactly 50 Hz.

Interconnection standards

Television companies have always preferred simple, robust interfaces that use coaxial cable and connectors. This is different from the computer industry, that has migrated towards the use of twisted pairs. Broadcasters prefer a single circuit, whereas computer interconnects frequently use multiple pairs. Any standard that departs from the single coaxial cable tends to be used for short interconnects, a few meters. This policy is partly due to cost; coax can be terminated very easily and quickly, and partly due to a vast legacy of coaxial cable around the television plant.

- Analog composite
- S-Video or Y/C
- SDI (BT601)
- IEEE 1394

Analog composite

Analog composite uses the familiar 75 Ω coaxial format, with BNC connectors. Some consumer equipment uses RCA connectors. Analog composite is the de facto standard interconnect – even today many low-cost video monitors only feature composite inputs.

S-Video, Y/C

S-Video is a spin-off from the S-VHS format. The chroma component, modulated on the subcarrier, is carried on a separate circuit from the luminance. This is to avoid the artifacts that result from the frequency interleaving of composite video. It uses a small four-pin connector.

BT601

Again uses 75 Ω coaxial cable, but the high frequency (data rate 270 Mbit/s) demands better quality cable than analog composite. Belden makes cable designed especially for 601.

IEEE 1394

Originally developed by Apple as FireWire, it was adopted by IEEE as a standard and is now used by many other manufacturers. Sony uses the trade name i.LINK. There are two versions of the connector, a six-pin and a four-pin. The cable uses two pairs for data and one for power. The system can be daisy-chained around up to 17 devices. Each device regenerates the signal. If any device in a chain is turned off, the internal IEEE 1394 buffer is powered from the cable. The four-pin does not carry power and is used on self-powered cameras.

Figure 4.10 Video and audio connectors.

It can be hot-plugged, and it can be likened to a high-speed USB connection in its simplicity of use. The data rates that are supported are 100, 200 and 400 Mbit/s, with extensions planned to over 1 Gbit/s.

The interface not only carries audio/video data but also remote control. So the capture card can stop, start and cue the VTR over the IEEE 1394 cable. This makes for a very simple interconnection between the recorder and the encoding workstation.

Note that IEEE 1394 is not DV, although often called such, but it can carry DV compressed signals from a DV format camcorder.

Which interface to use

The priority for streaming interconnects should be as follows:

1. BT601
2. Analog S-video
3. Analog composite

If the source were using DV compression, then IEEE 1394 would be the first choice for a file interchange or streaming.

High definition

Everything in this chapter so far relates to standard definition or SD television. Although standard definition is great for small and medium-sized displays, once the screen diagonal gets above 750 mm the lines become very visible. Projection receivers and home theater systems demand higher resolution to equal the experience of watching 35 mm film.

The Advanced Television Systems Committee (ATSC) set about defining a new standard for high-definition television. The end result was a family of possible resolutions, leaving the broadcaster to make the choice. Both progressive and interlaced scanning are supported.

At the same time, studios were using digital processing for special effects sequences in movies. Often using 4,000 by 4,000 pixels per frame, such sequences can be seamlessly composited with the film stock. There had long been a demand to shoot productions on videotape rather than using film – electronic cinematography. Rather than shoot at 30 frames per second the same rate as film is used, 24 frames per second.

What has all this to do with streaming? – well not much. An ATSC transmission uses a data rate of 18 Mbit/s, a long way from the requirements of a streaming file for less than 1 Mbit/s. If you are given HD source material you will have to convert the material to SD for encoding, a process called 'down-rezzing'.

Maybe one day we will be able to view HD streaming, but that will have to wait for fiber-to-the-home and improved compression techniques.

Summary

Video formats have evolved from the standard definition color format developed by the NTSC in the late 1940s. This standard established the interlaced scan and the composite color encoding. Later, videotape recorders were developed. The pace of new formats has quickened, but by the year 2000, the DV family has proved very popular for streaming video production.

Analog television is being replaced by digital formats, although analog composite is still the most used delivery format for the terrestrial receiver. The defining standard is BT601; this set the rules for the sampling structure that we see in MPEG compression.

Digital capture has a great advantage for streaming: there is less noise than analog systems. This makes for a better picture quality at a given bit rate. The compression codec and noise do not mix.

Domestic television formats are moving to higher definition standards, up to 1080 lines. Electronic cinematography is adopting a frame rate of 24 to be compatible with film. So there is ever increasing diversity in standards and in tape formats. For the streaming video producer, this means cross-format conversion is likely to be part of the production workflow.

5 Video compression

Introduction

Compression reduces the number of bits used to represent each pixel in the image. The algorithms used to compress the images introduce, to a lesser or greater extent, visible artifacts. In general the more complex algorithms introduce fewer of these artifacts. The processing power available to us increases with time, so more sophisticated algorithms are always being introduced into the codec products. This has to be done in a way that uses realizable computation, and has a short processing delay. The processing should not distort the image so that visible artifacts are generated.

As the level of artifacts decrease, so does our acceptance of the distortions. Once we were happy to watch monochrome television, now it must be color. Families were thrilled with the flickering home movies shot on 8 mm film, now a DV camcorder produces almost broadcast quality results. Even so the acceptable level of artifacts will depend on the application. If you paid to go to a movie theater to see the 70 mm print with Dolby Digital, and they showed you a projection from a VHS tape, you would consider the picture unacceptable.

Compression systems exploit the mechanisms of human visual perception to remove redundant information, and yet still produce a compelling viewing experience. A typical example of the process is the persistence of vision. This is where an instantaneous view of a scene (for example, through a shutter) fades over about one-tenth of a second. This allows us to portray the continuum of time by a series of discrete pictures or frames. As an example, viewing a motion picture shot at 24 frames per second (fps) gives a good approximation of motion in the original scene.

Now there are artifacts – the classic is the wagon wheels of the stagecoach appearing to turn backwards. This is called aliasing. Another potential artifact is flicker – where the brain is conscious of the discrete frames. If the refresh rate of the display drops below a certain threshold, the viewer will observe flicker.

Below 60 fps this begins to become noticeable. To avoid flicker in the movie theater each film frame is shown twice, giving a display rate of 48 fps. The perception of flicker is reduced at low luminance levels. At the low levels of light used for projection in the theater flicker is not a problem, even though it is lower than the optimal rate.

At the higher luminance levels used with television and VDU displays, refresh rates of at least 60 Hz have to be used to avoid flicker. Television uses a similar system to film, but rather than repeating each frame twice it splits each picture into two, one half of the odd lines and the other of the even lines. These half pictures are called fields; two fields make a picture of frame. The process is called interlaced scanning. Because European television systems use a 50 Hz field rate under certain viewing conditions the flicker can be apparent.

Compression is always a trade-off – between the level of artifacts and the bandwidth. Note that the shooting or encoding rate (which is chosen for realistic motion portrayal) can be different from the final display rate. We watch a film shot at 24 fps on a television receiver at either 25 or 30 Hz frame rates (50 or 60 Hz field rates).

Compression basics

A video clip is a sequence of pictures or frames. Each picture can be processed in isolation, much like a still image. A typical example is the JPEG standard.

Still images – JPEG

The JPEG format is widely used to compress continuous-tone grayscale and color images. JPEG compresses the file size by selectively discarding picture data. This is called lossy compression. The final picture is a representation of the original, but the original can never be restored from the JPEG file. The standard also supports a lossless compression with about a 3:1 reduction in data, but it is more usually used in the lossy mode with ratios of 20:1 or greater. JPEG compression is based on a technique called the discrete cosine transform.

A lower compression ratio results in less data being discarded, but the JPEG compression algorithm will degrade any fine detail in an image. As the compression is increased more artifacts become apparent. Wave-like patterns and blocky areas become visible, and there is ringing on sharp edges. The levels of artifacts that are considered acceptable depend upon the application. A picture reproduced in a magazine should have no visible artifacts, whereas minor distortions are to be expected with a thumbnail on a web page. It is more important to have a small file size with a short download time.

Intra-frame compression

This compression of a single image in the spatial domain is called intra-frame – within the frame. Video editing systems have used an extension to JPEG called motion JPEG where the video sequence is compressed as a sequence of frames. When you are editing you need random access to each frame, and the ability to reorder the frame sequence.

Once the material has been edited into the final clip and is ready for dissemination, we no longer need the ability to freely cut a sequence on any frame. A streamed clip is delivered in a fixed order of frames. We can now take advantage of the redundant information in scene content that repeats from frame to frame.

Video and inter-frame compression

A sequence of video images has little change from one picture to the next, except at scene changes. This redundancy can be exploited by transmitting only the difference between successive pictures, by this means a large reduction in the data rate can be achieved. This temporal or inter-frame compression allows the data rate for video sequences to be reduced much more than a sequence of unrelated still images. It typically allows a further 3:1 reduction over any initial spatial (intra-frame) compression.

Visual perception

The human retina and visual cortex together process the visual scene in a way that detects edges and lines. This allows objects (like potential prey or predators) to be rapidly separated from the background. A consequence of this is that codecs that destroy or create edges will be viewed as creating perceptible distortions. Another feature is that fine detail near the edges of objects is not perceived with great acuity. So there are opportunities for perceptual redundancies, and potential pitfalls where distortions are easily noticed. A good compression architecture has to exploit the mechanisms of visual perception.

Compression algorithms

Compression algorithms aim at lowering the total number of parameters required to represent the signal, while still delivering a reasonable quality picture to the player. These parameters are then coded into data packets for streaming.

There are four main redundancies present in the video signal:

- Spatial
- Temporal
- Perceptual
- Statistical

Compression can be lossless or lossy. If all the original information is preserved the codec is called lossless. A typical example for basic file compression would be PKZIP. To achieve the high levels of compression demanded by streaming codecs, the luxury of the lossless codecs is not possible – the data reduction is insufficient.

Spatial redundancy occurs where neighboring pixels in a frame of a video signal are related; it could be an object of a single color. If consecutive pictures are also related there is temporal redundancy. The human visual system has psycho-visual redundancy; not all the visual information is treated with the same relevance. An example is lower acuity to color detail than luminance.

Finally, not all parameters occur with the same probability in an image. This statistical redundancy can be used in the coding of the image parameters. For example, frequently occurring parameters can be coded with fewer bits (Huffman coding).

The goal with compression is to avoid artifacts that are perceived as unnatural. The fine detail in an image can be gently degraded without losing understanding of the objects in a scene. As an example we can watch a 70 mm print of movie or a VHS transfer and in both cases still enjoy the experience. If too much compression is applied, and the artifacts interfere with the image perception, the compression has become unnaturally lossy.

Table 5.1 lists some of the more popular technologies that have been used for encoding streaming files.

The techniques may be combined within codecs, for example MPEG-2 removes spatial redundancy using DCT, then run-length encodes the coefficients. MPEG also uses motion prediction to remove temporal redundancy.

Table 5.1 Compression techniques

Spatial compression	Other techniques
Vector quantization	Frame differencing
Block Discrete Cosine Transform (DCT)	Motion estimation/compensation
Discrete Wavelet Transform (DWT)	Run-length encoding (RLE)
Fractal image compression	
Contour-based image coding	

Intra-frame coding or spatial compression

Each pixel can be quantized separately – spatial quantization – but this would lead to posterization artifacts with any continuous-tone images. An alternative is vector quantization, where a group of pixels are quantized together. This offers theoretically the most efficient compression, but in practice it is computationally intensive and has a long processing delay. The alternative is transform coding, where a block of pixels is transformed to the frequency domain, and then quantized. Entropy coding can then be used to further reduce the data rate. The result can be as efficient as vector quantization, but without the processing overheads.

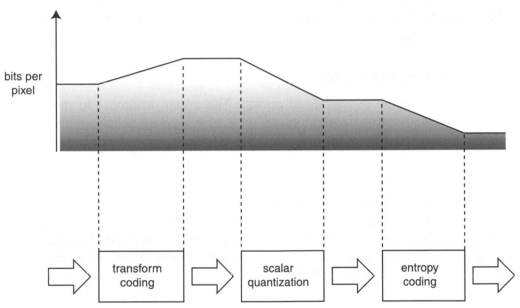

Figure 5.1 Compressing the bits.

Transform coding

Transform coding converts the spatial array of pixel blocks, a bit map, to the frequency domain. Although several different transforms have been proposed, the discrete cosine transform has been the most widely adopted for video codecs. Some other transforms investigated include the following: Discrete Fourier (DFT), Karhunen Loève (KLT) and Walsh–Hadamard (WHT).

The DFT was ruled out because it suffers discontinuities at the block boundaries. For typical real-world images, the DCT outperforms the WHT and DFT in the energy compaction. The KLT has the optimal decomposition but requires a very large number of operations, so has the longest processing time. The DCT has been generally adopted because it approaches the performance of the KLT, but with a lower processing overhead. Any encoder that is to be used for video-conferencing or other live applications must have a short processing delay. So the DCT was chosen as the best compromise.

Wavelet compression

Although the DCT has been very successful, there has long been a demand for other compression schemes that do not suffer from the, often visible, blocking artifacts inherent in DCT compression. Wavelet compression has often been cited as an alternative. It has been employed in desktop video-editing systems, as an alternative to motion JPEG. It is becoming a more mainstream technology since it has been adopted as the core technology for the JPEG2000 format for still image coding.

Model-based compression

This is an alternative to waveform coding. The codec attempts to model the scene and then transmit descriptors, rather than a representation, of the spatial image.

Fractal

The fractal compression technique relies on the fact that, in certain images, parts of the image resemble other parts of the same image. So similar sections of an image are located then the fractal algorithm is applied. Patents have restricted its use, and since wavelet compression offers better efficiency it has been the focus of more intense development effort.

Object-based

Object-based coding has been adopted for MPEG-4 coding. A scene – which can be in two or three dimensions – is represented by a number of video objects. Each object is described by its shape, texture and motion. Conventional algorithms like the DCT and wavelet can be used to compress the objects.

Entropy coding

Entropy coding can yield a much shorter image representation with average content by using short code words for more likely bit sequences, and longer code words for less likely sequences. One of the first examples of entropy coding was Morse code.

Discrete cosine transform

This has formed the basis of all the popular video compression codecs. The picture is divided in to regular blocks, and then the transform is applied block by block.

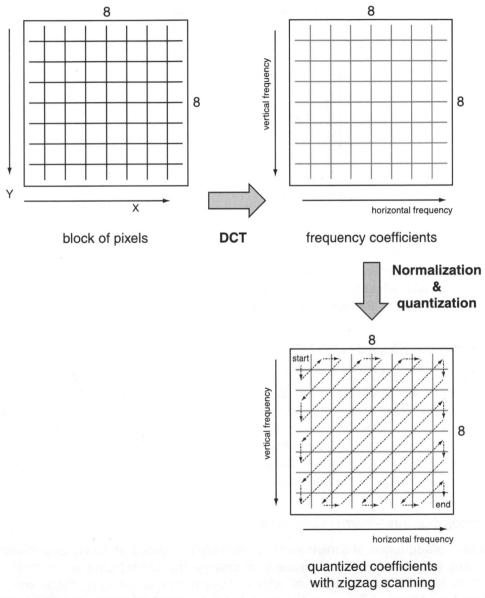

Figure 5.2 Discrete cosine transform.

Each 8 × 8 block of pixels is transformed to another 8 × 8 block of transform coefficients. Vertical edges in the picture transform as a horizontal frequency, and horizontal edges as vertical frequency coefficients. At this stage there has been no compression of the data. The goal is to gain a representation of the video signal in a form where perceptual and statistical redundancies can be used to reduce the data rate.

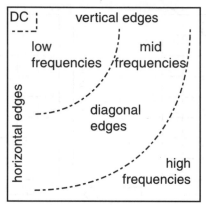

Figure 5.3 Spatial frequencies.

The coefficients are normalized and quantized. The quantization process allows the high-energy, low-frequency coefficients to be coded with a greater number of bits, while using fewer for the high-frequency coefficients. So as we go from top left to bottom right, the coefficients tend toward zero.

Variable-length coding (VLC)

By scanning the coefficients in a zigzag the result is long runs of zeros. The coefficients are then converted to a series of run-amplitude pairs. Each pair indicates the number of zero-value coefficients and the amplitude of the non-zero coefficient. These run-amplitude coefficients are then coded with a variable-length code. This uses shorter codes for commonly occurring pairs and longer codes for less common pairs – a form of entropy coding. These can be run-length encoded to reduce to the overall data rate.

Temporal or inter-frame compression

Video is a sequence of similar images, with step changes at scene boundaries. In many sequences there is virtually no change frame on frame to the next. In scenes with subject motion, or where the camera is moving, there will be differences from one frame to the next, but there are many areas of the picture that do not change. This redundancy of information from one frame to the next can be exploited to lower the data rate. The basis of the compression is to transmit the only the difference between frames – *frame differencing*. The player stores the entire picture in a frame store, and then reconstructs the picture from the previous frame and the difference information.

Since most of the difference between frames is from moving objects, there is further potential to reduce the data. The player already has the information to reconstruct the object; it is just in the wrong position. If a motion vector could be sent to say this block has moved from position A to position B then the block would not have to be retransmitted.

Of course it is not that simple. We are looking for a coding gain, where the total data rate is reduced with no apparent change to the picture quality. Motion vectors are additional data that have to be transmitted to the player. As an example a scene with considerable subject movement coded to MPEG-2 at a rate of 6 Mbit/s can comprise 2 Mbit/s of motion vectors. That represents one-third of the total data.

Another problem is the reveal. As an object moves, what is revealed in its previous location?

Motion estimation

To generate motion vectors the encoder has to estimate the movement of picture elements. There are many ways to do this, some more complex than others. Since codecs like MPEG define the decoder rather than the encoder, the method used for vector generation is left to the encoder designer.

In a typical encoder, the motion prediction compares a previous frame with the current frame, and then estimates how blocks of the picture have moved. A local decoder generates the previous frames, rather than using the original frames before intra-frame compression. This is so that the predictor is using the same information that the player's decoder has available for computation.

The motion predictor makes trial moves of a block of pixels to establish the best match for the position of any moving elements. This match is then used to create a motion vector. Block matching is not the only technique for motion estimation, but it is one of the simplest to implement.

Compression codecs

Compression codecs fall into three families:

- International standards
- Proprietary formats
- Open standards

Evolution of international standards

The video codecs we use today come from two backgrounds: the first is the telecommunications industry and the second is multimedia. These are some of the most used codecs.

H.261 – video-conferencing

This was the original video codec, and was the starting point for the MPEG-1 standard. H.261 was formulated under the auspices of the ITU for videophones and video-conferencing over ISDN lines. Even today we await a commercially successful videophone, but video-conferencing has long been a key communication medium for business. One of the demands of both applications was real-time operation, so the codecs had to have a short processing delay.

The standard defines screen sizes of the Common Interface Format (CIF), 352 × 288, and Quarter CIF (QCIF) of 176 × 144 pixels. It uses progressive scan and 4:2:0 sampling. Data rates from 64 kbit/s up to 2 Mbit/s are supported by the standard. The compression is DCT-based with variable-length coding. As an option, intermediate predicted (P) frames could be used with integer-pixel motion-compensated prediction.

MPEG-1

This was the first successful standard developed by the multimedia community for audio-visual coding. The standard has long been used for video presentations on CD-ROMs. The normal resolution is source or Standard Input Format (SIF). Unlike the common interface format of H.261, the spatial resolution differs for PAL and NTSC systems (352 × 288 at 25 fps for PAL, and 352 × 240 at 30 fps for NTSC). It uses progressive scanning. The video compression, like H.261, uses the discrete cosine transform with variable-length coding. The motion prediction was improved over H.261 with sub-pixel motion vectors and the introduction of bidirectional predicted (B) frames.

It was designed for storage-based applications like the CD-ROM, at data rates up to 1.5 Mbit/s, and does not support streaming.

H.263

H.263 is a development of H.261 aimed at low bit rate applications. It dates from 1992. H.261 did not have a data rate low enough for operation at 28 kbit/s, so could not be used for videophone applications on analog phone circuits. For lower data rates a thumbnail size picture can be coded; the H.263 standard supports SQCIF, QCIF, CIF, 4CIF and 16CIF resolutions.

H.263 is now the baseline standard for MPEG-4 natural video coding.

MPEG-2

A higher resolution, high-quality system for broadcast television. It is intended to replace analog composite systems (NTSC, PAL) for digital transmission systems. It is also used for DVD encoding. Its primary applications use channel bandwidths greater than 4 Mbit/s. The main profile at main level (MP@ML) is a standard definition television frame rate and resolution with data rates up to 15 Mbit/s. The standard was extended to support high-definition television bit rates (up to 80 Mbit/s) and an I-frame-only studio profile (50 Mbit/s). MPEG-3 was to be a separate high-definition standard but was dropped in favor of extensions to MPEG-2.

MPEG-4

MPEG-1 and MPEG-2 were developed for specific applications. MPEG-1 is for multimedia CD-ROM presentations. MPEG-2 is for broadcast television. The spawning of so many potential multimedia applications, from hand-held wireless devices though to high-definition home theaters, led to demands for a much more flexible coding platform. The support of the very low bit rates used for streaming is one example of the new demands.

MPEG compression

MPEG compression divides a video sequence into groups of pictures. Each picture in the group is then divided into slices of macroblocks. A macroblock

Table 5.2 Summary of compression formats

Compression format	ISO/IEC Issue date	Target bandwidth (bits/s)	Typical resolution (pixels)	Application
H.261	1988–1990	384k–2M	176 × 144 or 352 × 288	Video-conferencing, low delay
H.263	1992	28.8k–768k	128 × 96 to 720 × 480	Video-conferencing
MPEG-1	11172	400k–1.5M	352 × 288	CD-ROM
MPEG-2, MP@ML	13818 1994	1.5M–15M	720 × 480	Broadcast television, DVD
MPEG-4	14496 1998	28.8k–500k	176 × 144 or 352 × 288	Multimedia

Figure 5.4 MPEG picture hierarchy.

comprises four luminance blocks and one U and V color block each. The block is the basic unit for the spatial compression.

The slice was first introduced in the MPEG-1 standard. It divides up the picture, so that if a fatal data error occurs within one slice, the rest of the frame can still be decoded.

Motion prediction

The temporal compression is arranged in groups of pictures. MPEG defines three types of frame within the group:

- **Intra-frame or I-frame**. These are coded spatially solely from information contained within the frame.
- **Predicted frame or P-frame**. These are coded from previous I- or P-frame pictures. The decoder uses motion vectors to predict the content from the previous frames.
- **Bidirectional frame or B-frame**. These pictures use past and future I and P pictures as a reference, effectively interpolating an intermediate picture.

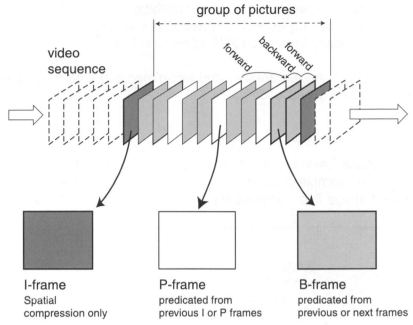

Figure 5.5 I, P and B frames.

I-frames provide reference points for random access to a stream. The number of pictures between I-frames is set by the encoder, and can be varied to suit subject material. The data in a typical P-frame are one-third that in an I-frame, and B-frames are half that of a P-frame.

So that the decoder can make backwards prediction from a future frame, the natural frame order is re-sequenced. The B-frames are transmitted after the next and previous pictures that each references.

MPEG-4 natural video encoding

MPEG-4 is the first MPEG system that supports streaming as part of the standard. The ability to stream is not related to the method of compression, but to the way that the video sequence is time-referenced. This is so that the media server can control the delivery rate to the player.

The requirements for the standard were for a flexible multimedia encoding format designed to support a very wide range of bit rates, from 5 Kbit/s up to 50 Mbit/s. This is sufficiently flexible to cover low bit rate wireless data through to HDTV applications. Version 1 MPEG-4 supports the following formats and bit rates:

- Bit rates: typically between 5 kbit/s and 10 Mbit/s
- Scan formats: interlaced as well as progressive video
- Resolutions: typically from sub-QCIF to beyond HDTV

MPEG-4 broke from the rectangular and two-dimensional bit map of previous coding, and adopted object coding.

Video objects

If we consider the cartoon as an analogy – cartoons are produced by cel animation. As an example consider a downhill skier. The animators deconstruct the storyboard image into components: the background and the characters.

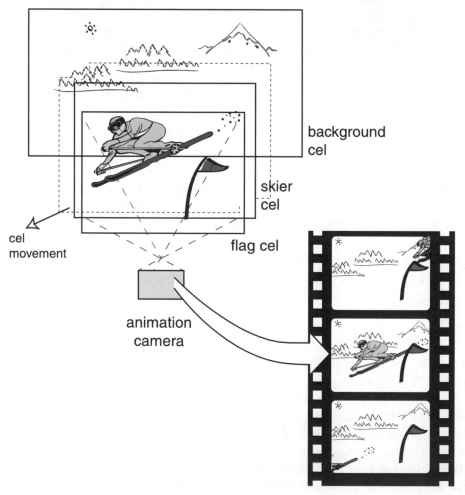

Figure 5.6 Cel animation for animated cartoons.

Each scene consists of a single background drawing, with a number of characters and foreground objects. Each is drawn separately on a clear sheet of acetate called a cel. Then each frame of a scene is photographed, with the cels stacked in the appropriate order. The skier cel can be moved for each exposure, or more likely a sequence of cels will represent the movement of the skier. So a great deal of drawing effort has been saved. Only one background has been drawn, and only one flag for the foreground. The saving over drawing each frame in its entirety is immense.

This deconstruction of a video sequence into different components or objects is the basis of MPEG-4 video coding.

This is the big difference between MPEG-4 and earlier standards. Rather than the restrictions of coding a single two-dimensional rectangular video image, MPEG-4 allows both two-dimensional and three-dimensional objects to be mixed in a synchronized presentation. So MPEG-4 breaks way from the cinematic representation and moves towards the virtual reality world of video games. This paradigm shift leads MPEG-4 to be a natural vehicle for rich media presentations. Immersive and interactive presentations can combine synthetic three-dimensional objects with two-dimensional stills and conventional video images.

An object has shape, texture and motion. The object texture is equivalent to the information that was intra-frame encoded in blocks by the earlier MPEG standards by the discrete cosine transform.

Consider a downhill racer again. The skier is moving, but the background is essentially a still image. If the skier could be separated from the background, the background could be sent once, and the skier alone could be transmitted as a moving image. This would potentially save a large amount of data. The background is called a sprite.

A sprite is defined as a large video object, possibly panoramic, and it is persistent over time. The media player can crop and spatially transform (warp) the sprite, for example as a camera pans around the foreground objects.

Rendering a number of video objects together in the player is relatively easy. Separating video objects from a two-dimensional scene within the encoder is non-trivial. This process is called video segmentation and is a subject of ongoing research.

The concept is a natural process for the human brain; we look at a scene and immediately decompose it into a number of objects. So, although the idea of object coding may seem foreign to a video engineer, to the neural physiologist it must seem like the obvious way to encode visual images. The scanned raster that we are familiar with is an engineering convenience.

In practice, a rectangular video image is encoded in much the same way as the earlier H.263 and MPEG-1 and -2 encoders. There are simple ways of extracting objects that are suited to rich media presentations. The speaker could be shot on a blue-scene set, then extracted as an object.

original scene

background sprite

video object

video object

Figure 5.7 MPEG-4 video objects.

Figure 5.8 The MPEG-4 media player.

The arrangement of the objects within a scene is described by the scene descriptor, the Binary Format for Scenes (BIFS). Both natural video (pixel based) and synthetic two- and three-dimensional objects can be encoded. The player stacks the object layers together to render a two-dimensional representation of the scene.

Shape coding. A video object can be coded as an arbitrary shape. In the example the foreground flag could be coded as a separate video object. The shape of the object is defined by an alpha channel. To reproduce a complex edge structure the shape can be coded as a grayscale, giving an 8-bit resolution. A simple shape can be represented as a binary object (present or absent).

Texture coding. The texture of a video object is conventionally coded by the DCT. The codec is similar to H.263, and MPEG-1 and -2. The texture of static objects can be coded using the wavelet transform.

Motion coding. The motion coding adds a global motion prediction. If an object is moving as a whole (like a camera pan), rather than code the motion vectors for each macroblock, the motion parameters of the entire object are transmitted. This can be very compact data.

Video encoder

Just like MPEG-1 and MPEG-2 the standard for MPEG-4 defines a standard player or *terminal*. The details of the encoder are left to the vendor – as long as the encoded bit stream can be played back on an MPEG-4 terminal.

A typical MPEG-4 encoder is shown in Figure 5.9. The texture and shape coding are new components. The basic encoder architecture is similar to MPEG-1 and -2 encoders. The enhancements to the coding do offer a small increase in efficiency over MPEG-2, typically 10–15 per cent for typical material. So claims for some MPEG-4-based codecs to offer DVD quality (MPEG-2) at one-tenth of the DVD data rate seem hard to believe.

MPEG-4 has a number of different profiles for natural video content.

- **Simple** for low-bandwidth wireless applications
- **Core** profile for interactive rich media applications
- **Main** for broadcast television

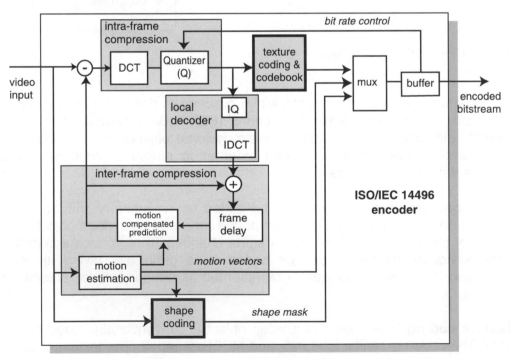

Figure 5.9 MPEG-4 encoder system.

Table 5.3 Subset of MPEG-4 profiles

Profile and level		Typical scene size	Bit rate	Maximum number of objects	Total macroblock memory
Simple profile	LI	QCIF	64 Kbit/s	4	198
	L2	CIF	128 Kbit/s	4	792
	L3	CIF	384 Kbit/s	4	792
Core profile	L1	QCIF	384 Kbit/s	4	594
	L2	CIF	2 Mbit/s	16	2376
Main profile	L2	CIF	2 Mbit/s	16	2376
	L3	ITU BT601	15 Mbit/s	32	9720
	L4	1920 × 1088	38.4 Mbit/s	32	48960

Other MPEG standards

MPEG-7

This is a standardized system for describing audio-visual content. This enables fast and efficient searching. You can compare this with the facilities provided with a search engine to locate textual content. Images and sound could be described in many abstract ways: textures, text descriptions of content, color. Much of this is open to interpretation. Consider somebody searching for a clip of a happy person. Happiness is an emotion that is not obvious from a description of the shape, color and texture of the images. Content description is not a trivial task, but essential to the efficient utilization of audio-visual archives.

MPEG-21

MPEG-21 is a framework for integrating multimedia resources across a wide range of platforms and services. Streaming media is an important part of this framework. One focus of MPEG-21 is in value exchange, typically the sale of content. Key to this is the management of intellectual property rights.

MP3 misnomers

MP3 is the file extension for MPEG-1 and -2, layer 3, audio files, and not MPEG-3. This was a proposed standard for HDTV that was dropped in favor of MPEG-2 high level. There are also proposals for support for high definition by MPEG-4.

Proprietary architectures

The proprietary architectures have been the most popular platforms for streaming. In the year 2001 MPEG-4 architecture was immature, but Windows

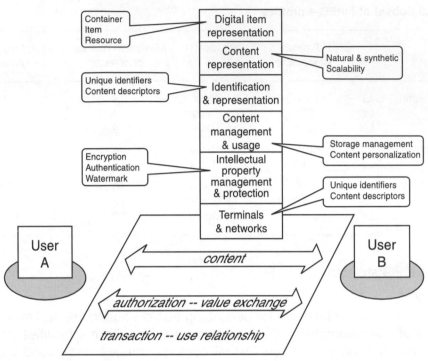

Figure 5.10 MPEG-21 framework.

Media and Sorenson both support the MPEG video encoding standards. There is the usual issue of proprietary versus international standard. Both vendors claim that a proprietary solution brings higher quality encoding to the market quicker that the standards-based. Video codecs are a fast-moving product area. This list that follows gives the status as of 2001. It pays to use the latest versions of the encoders, as the quality is improving all the time. The only drawback with the improved encoders is the general rule of thumb that the better the video quality, the more processing power the encoder needs. If you want to do live webcasting, which needs a real-time encode, do not expect to use an old 486.

Apple QuickTime

QuickTime supports a large number of video formats, including uncompressed, but came late to streaming. Most of the codecs are for authoring CD-ROMs. As a general-purpose multimedia production tool in an editing environment, QuickTime can be used to wrap DV content and motion JPEG. Apple does not offer their own streaming codecs, but has partnered with Sorenson. If you want to use QuickTime the primary choice would be Sorenson Video 3 codec, with H.263 as an alternative – albeit at a lower quality.

QuickTime does not support multiple bit rates. Instead, using 'movie alternates', you encode a high, medium and low bit rate file. The QuickTime player then selects the correct movie file for the link bandwidth.

Sorenson video

Sorenson 3 video codec is used with Discreet's Cleaner 5.1 to prepare QuickTime movies for streaming. Sorenson 3 supports two-pass variable bit rate encoding, but it is only recommended for progressive download. As part of the QuickTime encode a hint track is generated for the streaming server to control the stream delivery. This is not required for progressive download encodes.

RealNetworks

The RealVideo 8 codec replaces the earlier G2 codec. It was co-developed with Intel using the principles of MPEG-4 encoding. The G2 codec can still be selected, the player requires less CPU resource, and so may be an option if you know that the audiences are using older PCs.

Real 8 uses frame rate upsampling with data from motion vectors to interpolate frames. The scalable video technology allows a file to be delivered at different frame rates; more powerful PCs get the frame rate as encoded, less powerful machines can use a lower frame rate.

SureStream allows the content files to include video and audio encoded at different bit rates. The streaming server can optimize the delivery rate to suit the network conditions. Variable bit rate encoding can be used to maintain a constant video quality level. Two-pass encoding can be used for pre-recorded video files (not live encoding) to give the optimum processing. This provides improved encoding quality with both constant and variable bit rates, but does of course lengthen the encoding time.

Windows Media Encoder 7.1

Microsoft offers the Windows Media user a choice of codecs. The primary codec is the Windows Media Encoder 8. It is similar to MPEG-4 video but claims improved video quality. The Windows Media encoder gives a choice of the following video codecs:

- Windows Media Video 8 codec
- Windows Media Video 7 codec. For encoding stations with more modest CPUs. It is also useful for content that is to be played on legacy codecs (prior to codec 8)

- Microsoft MPEG-4 version 3.0 codec (a legacy format that is compatible with Windows Media Services 4.1)
- ISO MPEG-4 video codec version 1.0. This is based on the video coding of the MPEG-4 standard

The video component can be encoded at multiple bit rates for intelligent streaming over congested networks.

Windows Media 8 supports two types of variable bit rate encoding. The first encodes to a preset quality level; the bit rate goes up and down to maintain a constant video quality. The second encodes to a specified bit rate. This requires two passes of the content, the first is to analyze and establish the necessary parameters to meet the requirements. The second pass is the real encode. Note that Windows Media Services do not support streaming of variable bit rate files, they are to download and play.

Summary

Which codec offers the best compression? This is a moveable feast – codecs are improving all the time. Choosing a codec depends upon many factors. First there is the audience for your streams. What players do they have installed and what speed of connection do they use? You can make tests to see what codec gives the best quality at the required bit rate.

There are commercial concerns, what is the cost of an end-to-end solution? Then the producer may have a view. Does the architecture support all the rich media content that he or she may want to use? Only you can answer these questions. To recommend a codec for a specific task depends upon many factors.

Codecs are often compared to existing video formats – for example, VHS quality. It is difficult to sensibly compare an analog tape format with DCT compression. We quite happily watch the poor quality of VHS (compared to broadcast television) because of the constant level of artifacts like noise. The brain ignores continuing distortions. DCT-based coding produces changing levels of artifacts. This means that stationary pictures with low levels of fine detail look better than fast-moving fine detail. So the picture quality changes as the picture content changes. This is visually disturbing as the blockiness comes and goes. So it is meaningless to compare DCT coding with VHS. To achieve a constant video quality you have to resort to variable bit rate encoding, as adopted with the DVD format. That way the fast-action sequences get a higher bit rate than the stationary scenes. This is now an option with some streaming codecs.

Compression will always be a trade-off between bit rate and artifacts, but the use of perceptual coding now allows compelling viewing over broadband circuits like DSL and cable modems.

6 Audio compression

Introduction

Audio is the first streaming media to gain public acceptance. The first applications of streaming media that have been widely used by consumers are the audio-only webcasts, or 'Internet radio'. The other driver for interest in PC audio has been the universal acceptance of the MP3 format for low-data-rate audio files. Although not a streaming format (it is for download then play), most popular codecs can be used to wrap MP3 files for streaming. There are the audic-only codecs: Shoutcast, Winamp, Audion, and the multimedia architectures: Windows Media, QuickTime and Real.

To stream audio you have to go through three processes:

- Digitization
- Encoding (or compression)
- Packetization

The professional digital audio format, AES-3, is often the basis for digitization. The AES standard has a data rate of over 3 Mbit/s for stereo audio sampled at 48 kHz. To transmit this over a 28 kbit/s dial-up circuit, the data would have to be reduced by a factor of 100:1, and that excludes the overheads of packetization and error resilience.

The compression schemes split between the speech or voice coding developed by the telcos and the military, and the general audio or waveform encoders developed for multimedia applications. The speech coding algorithms generally use a model of the vocal tract and transmit voicing parameters for reconstruction by the decoder into intelligible speech. Much of the 'Internet radio' delivers music over a 28 or 56 kbit/s voice circuit, but there is a big difference in fidelity between voice telephony and an acceptable system that can be used for the enjoyment of music. This has led to the development of a number of sophisticated compression schemes for general audio. They are based upon the concepts of *psychoacoustics*, that is, the study of the mechanisms used by the human ear for the perception of sound. The problems for the developers of codecs stem from the very different waveforms generated by, for example, the piccolo or the castanets.

The quest to squeeze maximum fidelity from a channel started in the analog era before digital processing.

Analog compression

The compression schemes of analog audio were originally developed to counter the limited dynamic range of magnetic tape recorders. A typical recorder could have a range between peak level and the noise floor of 70 dB. High-quality recording demanded at least 90 dB.

Dolby A

This was the first commercially successful noise reduction product to be used by professional recording studios. It dates back to 1965. It established the principal of splitting audio into sub-bands for processing, a system still used by MPEG codecs and by audio pre-processors. Multi-channel recording added to the demands from recording studios for noise reduction. In a final mix-down, 40 or so tape tracks could be combined into a stereo signal. The noise from each channel adds, and without Dolby, the result would have been unusable. To get around the noise problem the dynamic range of the input audio was compressed before recording on tape, then expanded back on replay. This process is commonly referred to as companding.

To make the process inaudible was not trivial, especially using analog computing elements. Earlier proposals for noise reduction systems had suffered from noise modulation and poor transient response. The Dolby system made use of psychoacoustics to mask the effects of compression. With the low-cost digital processing available now, much more complex algorithms can be used.

Dolby B, C

This was a low-cost noise reduction system aimed at consumer products like the compact cassette. At the low tape speeds used, the frequency-dependent noise – tape hiss – was a big problem. It could be reduced to acceptable levels with Dolby noise reduction. It used a single, sliding, frequency band for companding.

Digital audio

Natural sounds are captured as an analog signal by a microphone. To convert the signal to a streaming format it passes through several processing stages.

- Pre-emphasis (optional)
- Sampling
- Analog-to-digital conversion
- Compression
- Packetization and wrapping

PCM

The basis of digital audio is pulse-code modulation or PCM. The microphone generates a voltage proportional to the air pressure (or velocity). This is sampled at regular intervals. The sample value is turned into a digital code word. The key parameters of the coding are the sampling rate and the resolution or bit depth.

analog waveform   *pulse amplitude*   *pulse code*

Figure 6.1 Analog-to-digital conversion.

Sampling

The sampling rate is set by the desired frequency response. Sampling theory dictates that the sampling frequency should be greater than twice the highest frequency that is to be captured (the Nyquist criteria). The sampling rate is a compromise: the higher the rate, the more sample data is generated.

Human hearing extends from 20 to 20,000 Hz, but speech uses a limited range in the center from 500 to 3,000 Hz.

Resolution

The digital coding converts the analog waveform, with essentially a continuum of values, to a number of discrete levels – a process of quantization. The number of levels used determines the resolution.

Table 6.1 Main audio sampling rates

Sampling rates	Frequency response	Application
8 kHz	200 Hz–3.3 kHz	Telephony
16 kHz	100 Hz–7 kHz	Wideband speech
32 kHz	50 Hz–15 kHz	Broadcast distribution
44.1 kHz	20 Hz–20 kHz	Consumer (CD)
48 kHz	20 Hz–20 kHz	Professional and broadcast
Max. 192 kHz	Up to 96 kHz	DVD-A
2.8224 MHz	DC to 100 kHz	SACD (uses bit stream coding)

The minimum step value sets the noise floor of the converted signal. In most conversions, each step has the same value – called linear PCM. Less demanding applications typically use 16-bit sampling. Professional users will demand a higher resolution of 20 or 24 bits. Table 6.2 indicates the potential dynamic range. In practice this will not be reached, as some noise will be present in the analog-to-digital conversion and in preceding stages between the microphone transducer and the converter.

The introduction of digital storage and transmission allowed the dynamic range to be increased when compared with analog systems. Even a 16-bit bit depth digital system potentially offers a better dynamic range than an analog tape recorder.

The conversion stage is prone to distortions. The conversion process may be non-linear, there may be circuit noise, and the sampling clock may have jitter. All these will impair the conversion process. A basic sound capture card may exhibit all of these problems to a lesser or greater extent. Any distortions introduced will impair the later compression codecs and lower the quality of the audio delivered to the consumer's player.

Table 6.2 Dynamic range versus bit depth

Code word length (bits)	No. of levels	Minimum step vs. full-scale* (dB)
8	256 (2^8)	−48.16
16	65,536 (2^{16})	−96.33
20	1,048,576 (2^{20})	−120.41
24	16,777,216 (2^{24})	−144.49

*Note. The ratio of the minimum step to the full scale in decibels = $-20 \log_{10}$ (No. of levels).

value (V)	0.65	3.00	1.31	1.68	1.46	1.37	1.50	*pulse amplitude*
binary level	54	255	111	142	124	116	127	*pulse code*

Figure 6.2 Pulse-code modulation.

In practice you would allow headroom between the maximum positive and negative excursions and the peak values. If the excursion reaches the peak values the waveform will be clipped. This produces unpleasant distortion, usually heard as a cracking sound.

The ADC is usually a unipolar system, although the sampled waveform is bipolar, representing positive and negative sound pressure variations. The pulse code will often use signed notation to represent the bipolar waveform. It is possible for a DC offset to occur between the analog waveform and the digital code. This means that silence does not have a value of zero. Some codecs exploit periods of silence to lower the data rate. So it is important to remove DC offset before compression.

Non-uniform coding

Linear PCM uses a fixed step value for the quantization levels. It is possible to use non-uniform steps, for example a logarithmic scale.

G.711

G.711 is the international-standard encoding format for telephony set by the ITU. Two versions exist, μ-law (used in the 'Bell' area) and A-law (used for international circuits).

The audio is sampled at 8 kHz (realizing a bandwidth up to a frequency of 3.3 kHz) with a linear 16-bit conversion. The 16-bit sample is coded to 8 bits using a logarithmic table. A 13-bit dynamic range is achieved, with three least significant bits dropped. Both of the encoding schemes approximate to a logarithmic transfer function. This ensures that low-amplitude signals are sampled at a higher resolution, while maintaining enough dynamic range to encode high amplitudes. The output data rate is 64 kbit/s, the standard for a voice channel.

G.711 sets a baseline standard for speech encoding. It provides a reference fidelity that the listening public can use when assessing the acceptability of a codec.

The actual encoding doesn't use logarithmic functions, however. The input range is broken into segments, each segment using a different interval between decision values. Most segments contain 16 intervals, and the interval size doubles from segment to segment. Figure 6.3 shows three segments with four intervals in each.

Figure 6.3 G.711 segments.

Both versions are symmetrical around zero. μ-law uses eight segments of 16 intervals each in each of the positive and negative directions, starting with an interval size of 2 in segment 1, and increasing to an interval size of 256 in segment 8. A-law uses seven segments. The smallest segment, using an interval of 2, is twice the size of the others (32 intervals). The remaining six segments are 'normal', with 16 intervals each, increasing up to an interval size of 128 in segment 7. Thus, A-law is skewed towards representing smaller signals with greater fidelity.

As the levels are compressed, then expanded, this technique is often referred to as *companding* PCM (as opposed to linear PCM).

Floating-point coding
Some older computers were more efficient at floating-point arithmetic, rather than integers. Audio sampling for these machines reflect this, using 32- or 64-bit floating-point sample values. Integers are used with AIFF and WAV formats.

Sampling rates

The sampling rate chosen determines the frequency range that can be reproduced. Telephony has an upper limit of 3.2 kHz; a sampling frequency of 8 kHz is used. Broadcast audio is usually limited to 15 kHz; this requires a sampling rate of 32 kHz. High-fidelity reproduction extends to at least 20 kHz, requiring sampling rates of 44 kHz or greater.

AES-3

This is the international standard digital audio interface. Its full title is 'Serial Transmission Format for Two-channel Linearly Represented Digital Audio Data'. In simple terms that means it is stereo and uncompressed. It was a joint development by the Audio Engineering Society (AES) and the European Broadcasting Union. The standard is based on balanced, shielded twisted pair cable, and for transmission distances up to 100 meters. Three sample rates are supported.

Table 6.3 AES sampling rates

Sample rates (kHz)	Audio channels	Aggregate data rate (bit/s)
48	2	3,072,000
44.1	2	2,822,400
32	2	2,048,000

The AES rates are those most generally used for the capture of streaming media; 48 kHz is the popular professional recording rate.

Table 6.4 gives some other popular sampling rates that are in general use.

Mono, stereo and multi-channel

Audio can be transmitted as a single channel (monophonic) or can carry spatial information in a multi-channel format. Stereo is very popular, most PC audio systems use two loudspeakers for reproduction. Although streaming codecs support multi-channel audio, for most applications it pays to stick to mono. It saves valuable streaming bandwidth, and the luxury of stereo is lost on PDAs and laptop computers.

A halfway house is to remove stereophonic irrelevance, that is redundant information in both left and right channels. Human hearing does not use stereo

Table 6.4 Computer audio sampling rates

Sample rates (kHz)	Description	MPEG-1	MPEG-2
8	The G.711 telephony standard (μ-law and A-law encoding)		
11	Half the Mac sampling rate		
16	Used by the G.722 compression standard. Also specified for MPEG-2		Low
18.9	CD-ROM standard		
22.05	Half the CD sampling rate		Low
22.254	Mac rate		
24	One-half 48 kHz rate		Low
32	Used in digital radio, and for TV audio distribution by the EBU	Y	Y
44.1	The CD sampling rate	Y	Y
48	The standard professional audio rate, AES-3. Used for DVD and DAT (Digital Audio Tape)	Y	Y

hearing below around 2 kHz, so the lower registers can be transmitted as mono with no detriment to directional information at higher frequencies.

Cinema and home theater have introduced the public to surround sound, usually in the 5.1 format. The 5.1 refers to five channels plus a low-frequency effects channel. This can be reproduced through the main speakers or through a separate sub-woofer.

The ear and psychoacoustics

Many of the characteristics of human hearing are exploited as part of perceptual encoding. The study of hearing is called psychoacoustics. The factors that are exploited by audio codecs include the following:

1. Threshold of hearing
2. Critical bands
3. Frequency or simultaneous masking
4. Temporal masking
5. Stereophonic irrelevance

Threshold of hearing

The human ear is relatively insensitive to low- and high-frequency sounds when listening at low sound pressure levels. The 'loudness' button on consumer stereo equipment provides a partial compensation for this effect by boosting the high and low frequencies. Fletcher and Munson published typical sensitivity curves some 60 years ago. Note that the dynamic range at mid-frequencies is 120 dB.

Figure 6.4 Fletcher–Munson curves.

Note also that the dynamic range falls off at lower frequencies and to a lesser degree at high frequencies. This means that less resolution is required of a codec to faithfully reproduce the bass registers.

Sub-bands

Studies of the mechanisms of hearing within the cochlea arrived at a model based upon a number of critical bands of frequencies. There are typically

24 critical bands from 20 Hz to 15 kHz. A unit, the bark, is used for this perceptual pitch scale, 1 bark representing the width of one critical band.

Masking

A characteristic of hearing is that, within one of these critical bands, a loud tone will mask low-level tones. The amount of masking is dependent upon the frequency and level of the tone. The greatest masking occurs closest to the masking signal. The second harmonic of high-level mid-frequency tones also has a masking effect (this indicates a non-linearity within the ear).

Figure 6.5 shows a loud tone of 500 Hz. The threshold of hearing is modified at frequencies near the tone. Sounds within the gray area are masked by the tone. This effect is called *noise masking* and is exploited by most general audio codecs to remove the masked audio information.

There is another, similar, phenomenon called temporal or non-simultaneous masking. After a masking tone is removed, the masking effects gradually decay for about one-fifth of a second. There is a short pre-masking, less than 50 ms before the masking tone.

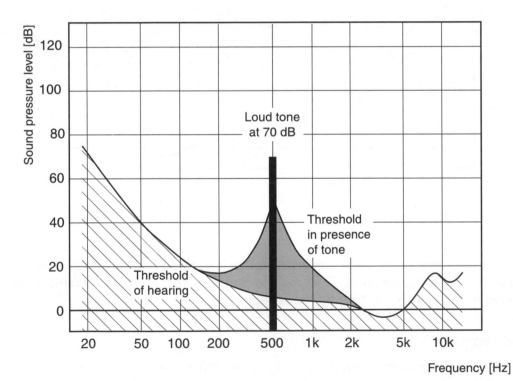

Figure 6.5 Noise masked by a loud tone.

Figure 6.6 Noise masking threshold.

The human voice

Psychoacoustics apply only to hearing so are equally applicable to speech or general audio coding.

The other human characteristics that are used in compression are the modeling of the vocal tract. It was established by research undertaken in the 1950s on speech models. If speech was broken into short frames (about 20 ms long), it could be considered as steady-state sound. This sound could than be modeled by a combination of a 'buzz' generator for voiced sounds and a white noise generator for unvoiced sounds. A filter bank then reproduced the effects of the resonant cavities of the mouth, nose and throat.

The vocal chords produce a buzzing noise. The fundamental is about 100 Hz for adult men and 200 Hz for women. The tone is rich in harmonics (overtones). The vocal tract then acts as a filter on this tone, producing vowel sounds (consonants or 'plosives' are formed by controlled interruptions of exhaled air). The vocal tract has three cavities, the pharynx, or back of the throat, the nasal cavity and the oral cavity (mouth). The resonant frequencies, or formants, are

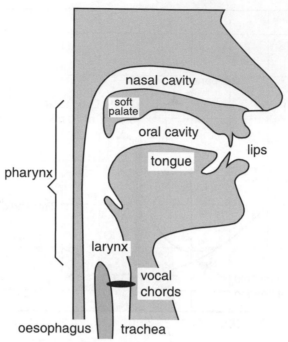

Figure 6.7 The human vocal tract.

changed by muscle actions in the jaw, tongue, lips and soft palate. This gives voicing to the basic tones from the vocal chords. The nasal cavity acts as a parallel filter.

This is called the source-filter model of speech. These proposals were used to develop voice coders or vocoders that could be used to synthesize speech. The vocoders use the model to analyze speech to produce a parameter set for this model.

Figure 6.8 The source-filter speech model.

Lossy compression

Lossless audio codecs offer limited opportunity to radically lower the data rates. To achieve the rates demanded by streaming applications, developers have moved to lossy codecs. A lossy codec throws away data that can never be recovered. There are two ways this can be achieved. The first takes advantage of statistical redundancy in the data; the second exploits our knowledge of psychoacoustics to remove information that is perceived as irrelevant to the hearing process. Of course there are levels of judgment involved in this. What is considered irrelevant to a narrow band speech circuit is not going to be redundant for a broadband codec delivering music.

The fidelities delivered by speech codecs are classified by the application:

Broadcast. This would be used for radio and television broadcast contribution circuits. The channel would have an audio bandwidth extending to 15 kHz with a minimum sampling rate of 32 kHz. The dynamic range would exceed 90 dB. Data rates exceed 64 kbit/s.

Toll. Toll or network quality is equivalent to the speech quality for a regular analog telephone. The frequency range is 200–3,200 Hz; the data rate is over 16 kbit/s.

Communications. Typified by cellular phones, this is a degraded version of toll quality where a lower data rate is demanded by the channel. Communications speech still sounds natural but has more audible distortions.

Synthetic. A good example is LPC-10; although intelligible the voice sounds unnatural. Used for low data rates below 4 kbit/s.

Music coders all fall into the broadcast category, and generally use higher bit rates than speech to support an increased sampling rate and larger sample word size.

Statistical redundancy

Lossy compression can use statistical redundancy in the audio waveform, with no regard to psychoacoustics. The best examples are DPM and ADPCM.

Differential PCM (G.726)

In Adaptive Differential PCM (ADPCM), 4 bits are used to quantize the prediction error sample, giving a bit rate of 32 kbit/s. This is found in ITU-T Recommendation G.726.

Perceptual compression

This uses knowledge derived from the study of the psychoacoustics of human hearing. Redundant information that can be called perceptually irrelevant is removed from the sample data.

Compression schemes split between those developed specifically for speech using very low bit rates (sometimes referred to as vocoders), and the more general-purpose or waveform codecs that can be used for any material – especially music. The success of a speech codec is measured by how natural and intelligible it sounds.

General audio codecs

Compressing general audio is far more complex than speech. A speech codec is encoding a single voice, and can use the human voice-tract model to represent that voice. A general audio codec has to reproduce a wide gamut of sounds. Consider musical instruments; these range from the almost sinusoidal tones of the flute, through to the complex spectrum produced by percussive instruments. This could be a harpsichord, castanets or bells. Then there are the many non-musical sounds: explosions, audience applause, the wind. Some have harmonic relationships, others are completely atonal. A general codec should perform reasonably with any such source.

The input to codecs is a time-varying voltage, represented by a regular series of discrete samples. Perceptual codecs generally sample a finite-length frame of samples, and then perform a time–frequency analysis of that frame. Frames are typically a few milliseconds long. A coarse time frame is optimum for long pure notes; a fine resolution is more efficient for percussive transients.

Sub-band coding

Designers of waveform codecs do not have the luxury of the model for speech generation used in the vocoder. Instead, they look to the perceptual irrelevancies identified by the study of psychoacoustics. The core for general audio coding is the masking effect – a consequence of the critical bands of human hearing.

Sub-band coding is the basis of most general audio codecs. The audio spectrum is split into a number of sub-bands that approximate to the critical bands. Within each sub-band, information that is masked by louder components can be discarded. Although this is a lossy compression, if suitable algorithms are used, the final listener will be unaware of the missing information.

The filter banks have to meet a number of criteria, not the least being a fast processing algorithm. Desirable characteristics are perfect reconstruction (in the decoder), good stop-band attenuation and constant group delay.

The filter banks convert the frequency spectrum of input waveform into time-indexed coefficients representing the frequency-localized power within each of the sub-bands.

The Pseudo-Quadrature Mirror Filter (PQMF) was adopted for the MPEG-1 algorithms. Later codec designs have used the Modified Discrete Cosine Transform (MDCT) to decompose the frequency components into the sub-bands.

Avoiding pre-echo

One problem that can arise with transform codecs is pre-echo distortion. If a transient occurs near the end of a sample frame, a pre-echo can be heard. MPEG-1 used four different windows (short and long), switched as appropriate to the signal content.

Rating codecs

To select a suitable codec algorithm with so many to choose from requires the identification of some key parameters. These are some that are usually considered.

1. Compression ratio achieved
2. Processing power required by encoder (MIPS)
3. Coding delay
4. Audio fidelity

In general, the more compression offered, the more processing power is required. The codec's cost is related to the processing power, so there is a direct cost/benefit relationship.

Codecs

Codecs fall into three groups: those defined by internationally agreed standards, proprietary systems and open source. Each has their proponents and supporters. If you are trying to decide which route to take, many factors have to be considered beyond the obvious one of audio quality. Different codecs will have different licensing costs; there is interoperability to think about, and then the level of support offered by the vendor.

The key technical parameters are the number of bits per sample, the encoding delay and the processing power required for encoding (MIPS). The encoding delay is very relevant for any two-way working. A natural conversation becomes more difficult as the delay increases. We have all seen television anchors interviewing a contributor over a satellite feed.

Table 6.5 Summary of codec algorithms

Organization/family	Algorithm	Codec
MPEG		MPEG-1, layers 1, 2, 3 MPEG-2, layer 2 and AAC MPEG-4, layer
ITU-T	PCM ADPCM	G.711 PCM (μ-law, A-law) G.726 ADPCM at 16, 24, 32 and 40 Kbit/s (replaces G.721 at 32 Kbit/s and G.723 for 24 and 40 Kbit/s)
Interactive Multimedia Association	ADPCM	IMA/DVI
US DOD Federal Standard	Linear predictive CELP	LPC-10E (1015) (1016)
ETSI	Linear predictive	GSM 06.10 (global systéme mobile)
Proprietary	ACELP ACELP ATRACS ADPCM	Voiceage Sipro Sony ATRAC3 Microsoft ADPCM

The processing resources required primarily impact mobile and telephony applications. Mobile applications have limited power resources and telephony demands low-unit-cost encoders. For the general encoding station for streaming, cost is only a small factor.

Codec standards

Military vocoders

The US DOD has developed low bit rate speech coders for use with secure telephone units (scrambled phones). The reason I mention them is that Code Excited Linear Prediction (CELP) has been adopted by MPEG-4.

LPC-10E

LPC-10E stands for Linear Prediction Coder (Enhanced) with 10 predictive coefficients. It is a US DOD Federal Standard (No. 1015). The bit rate is 2,400.

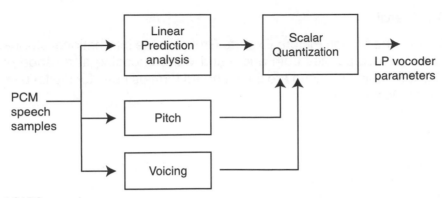

Figure 6.9 LPC vocoder.

Linear Prediction uses a simple model of the vocal tract. The speech is fitted to this model. The result can be understood, but sounds somewhat 'robotic'. The main disadvantages of LPC are the 'buzzy' sound from the parameter updates and the poor modeling of nasal sounds – but in practice the results are satisfactory. It is not suited to mobile applications, as it does not work well with high ambient noise levels.

CELP

The US DOD Federal Standard 1016 defines Code Excited Linear Prediction (CELP). Sometimes LPC and CELP are taken to mean the same thing, but the CELP standard is much more sophisticated. It does the same simple speech analysis as LPC, but compares the result with the original speech, and transmits a compressed form of the errors. This uses a code book for compression, hence 'code excited'. The result is a much higher quality of speech. It has a data rate of 4,800 bit/s, but the intelligibility has been compared to an ADPCM codec at 32 Kbit/s (G.721).

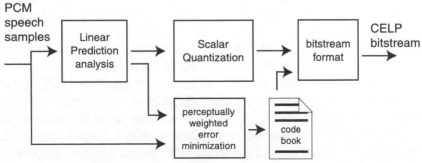

Figure 6.10 CELP vocoder (simplified).

MPEG general

MPEG (from the Motion Picture Experts Group) is the international standard for multimedia. It incorporates both audio and video encoding at a range of data rates. MPEG audio and video are the standard formats used for digital television (along with Dolby audio).

MPEG-1

The work undertaken to develop the MPEG-1 audio compression standards forms the foundation stone for the technology of streaming audio. The ubiquitous MP3 standard set the benchmark for good quality music encoding at low bit rates. Figure 6.11 shows the basic MPEG-1 encoder.

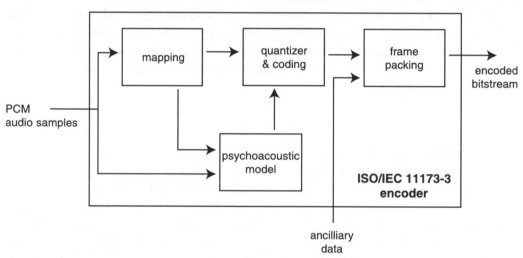

Figure 6.11 MPEG-1 encoder.

There are three types of MPEG-1 audio encoding, layer 1, layer 2 and layer 3, in order of improving sound quality and increased encoding time. This is to cover a wide range of different applications. MPEG codecs are asymmetric, which means that the decoder is simpler than the encoder. This is ideal for consumer products, where the player is the most used application.

Layer 1 evolved from the PASC compression used in Digital Compact Cassettes and layer 2 is based on the 'MUSICAM' compression format. The lowest data rate supported for MPEG-1 mono audio is 32 Kbit/s. Sample rates of 32, 44.1 (audio CD) and 48 kHz (Digital Audio Tape) are supported. Consumer equipment that supports recording requires a basic encoder that can be at a low cost for compact, battery-powered products. The lowest layer,

Figure 6.12 The evolution of MPEG audio formats.

layer 1, is used for such applications; a typical example is the Digital Compact Cassette (DCC).

Layer 2 uses a more complex encoding algorithm based on the MUSICAM system. The data rates from a typical layer II encoder are around 192 Kbit/s.

Layer 3 (usually called 'MP3') has recently become very popular on the Internet due to its combination of high quality and high compression ratio.

Table 6.6 Summary of MPEG audio

	Bit rate range (Kbit/s)	Target bit rate (Kbit/s)	Typical compression ratio
Layer 1	32–448	192 (mono)	1:4
Layer 2	32–384	128 (mono)	1:6 to 1:8
Layer 3 (MP3)	32–320	64 (mono) 128 (stereo)	1:10 to 1:12

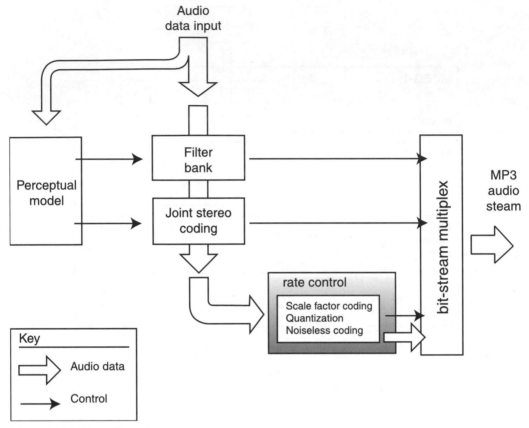

Figure 6.13 MP3 audio coder.

MPEG-1 decomposes the input into 32 bands, an approximation to the 24 critical bands of the human ear. The filter bank is a pseudo QMF. A Fast Fourier Transform is used for the psychoacoustic analysis. Layer 2 has several enhancements to lower the data rate.

MPEG-1 layer 3 (MP3) uses a more sophisticated hybrid filter bank with a modified DCT following each polyphase filter. This gives better high-frequency resolution and improved pre-echo control. Huffman coding is used to remove redundancy in the data stream.

MPEG-2

MPEG-2 provides broadcast quality audio and video at higher data delivery rates. MPEG-2 standard added to the original work on MPEG-1 to provide a high-quality audio format for digital television. In some applications, Dolby AC-3 has been used as an alternative to accompany an MPEG-2 video stream. The original MPEG-2 standard (ISO/IEC 13838–3) supports a Low Sampling Frequencies extension (LSF, 16, 22 and 24 kHz) and multi-channel audio (MPEG-1 is mono or stereo). The original standards were backwards compatible with MPEG-1. To take advantage of newer coding algorithms, backwards compatibility was abandoned. This led to the definition of the Advanced Audio Coding scheme (AAC), ISO/IEC 13838–7.

Advanced Audio Coding (AAC)

The original goal was to produce a coder that could compress CD format audio (44.1 kHz sampling, 16-bit sample, more than 2 Mbit/s) to less than 384 Kbit/s, yet be indistinguishable from the original. This represents about 3 bits per sample.

AAC was based on layers 1, 2 and 3 but introduced several new tools.

Filter bank window shape adaptation. The MDCT filter bank can switch between two alternative window shapes depending on the spectral characteristics of the input. This maximizes the coding gain. The filter banks approximate more closely to the critical bands than the original MPEG-1 filter banks.

Spectral coefficient prediction. For redundancy elimination with steady-state signals.

Bandwidth and bit rate scaling. The rate-control feedback loops are more complex. These control the quantization process through the exploitation of psychoacoustic irrelevancy.

Noiseless coding. The entropy coding of the quantized coefficients has been improved with the use of 12 Huffman codebooks. Much like video coding, the grouping maximizes runs of zero-value data.

MPEG-4 scalable audio profile

The MPEG-4 standard departs from the simple structure of the MPEG-1 and -2 audio coding. The MPEG team wanted to give a much wider flexibility. MPEG-4 was designed for use in a much wider range of applications than the focused remits of MPEG-1 and -2. Rather than adopting a number of levels, each more complex than the layer below, MPEG-4 offers a number of profiles.

The first departure is that two groups of codecs are used, one for general audio coding, or waveform audio, and the other for speech. The speech coding is based on the vocoders developed for secure voice communication by the military. The general audio is based more on the previous work of the MPEG-2 team.

Figure 6.14 MPEG-4 audio coding algorithms.

MPEG-4 uses the following algorithms for encoding at different bit rates:

1. HVCX
2. CELP
3. Twin VQ
4. AAC

Speech coders

Harmonic Vector eXcitation Coding (HVXC). The HVCX is a parametric vocoder operating at 2 and 4 kbit/s, and offers a good speech quality for the low data rate.

Code Excited Linear Prediction (CELP)

The CELP speech coding tools offer encoding from 6 kbit/s (for a narrow audio bandwidth of 3.5 kHz) up to 18 kbit/s at a higher sampling frequency for wideband speech.

The MPEG-4 speech coding tools differ from legacy standards such as ITU-T G.723 in that they offer three new functionalities: multiple bit rate coding, bit rate scalable coding and bandwidth scalable coding (the latter for CELP only). This variable rate is important for support of streaming applications to cope with network congestion, and for the wide variety of playback devices.

General audio coders

Advanced Audio Coder (AAC)

This is based on the MPEG-2 AAC low complexity audio coding algorithm. It includes an additional tool called PNS (Perceptual Noise Substitution) to lower the data rate. MPEG-4 AAC has been designed with full backwards compatibility with the low complexity profile of MPEG-2 AAC. You can use an additional object type with long-term prediction.

Twin Vector Quantization (Twin VQ)

Twin VQ is a general audio coder that is optimized for encoding music at ultra-low bit rates, typically 8 kbit/s. It uses an interleaved vector quantization of the same scaling factors and spectral data that are used in the AAC processing. It has a higher coding efficiency than AAC, but the drawback is that it always suffers a minimum loss in the audio quality. The break point in audio quality (with AAC) is about 16 kbit/s.

The general audio coder has many similarities with original MPEG-1 architecture. The psychoacoustic model is used to generate control parameters for the spectral processing tools. The output of the spectral processing is then quantized.

MPEG-4 tools

Long-term predictor (LTP)

The long-term predictor tool reduces the redundancy between audio frames for stationary harmonic signals with AAC and Twin VQ. It is a new feature for AAC, and introduced with MPEG-4.

Perceptual noise substitution (PNS)

Since one noise sounds like another, it is not necessary to transmit the fine grain structure of noise. The coder substitutes the actual spectral components of a

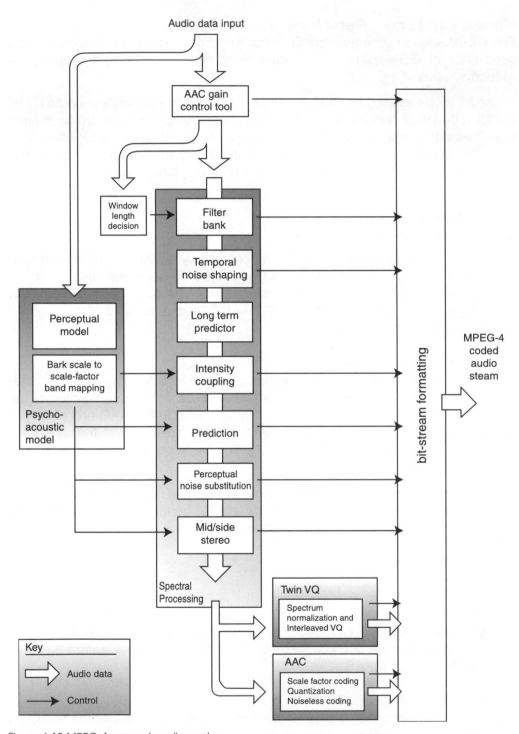

Figure 6.15 MPEG-4 general audio coder.

noise signal with data that represents a noise-like signal. The tricky part is determining which part of the input signal is noise.

Joint stereo coding

Rather than transmitting a stereo audio signal as two separate channels, left and right, the two signals can be matrixed into mid and side signals, much as FM radio uses a mono signal (for compatibility) and a difference signal (modulated on a subcarrier). Since there is a great similarity between left and right for typical audio material, the side or difference signal carries much less information than the mid signal. By this processing the redundancy in information between left and right is eliminated.

MPEG-4 levels

The following four levels are defined for MPEG-4 audio:

1. Maximum 24 kHz of sampling rate, one mono object.
2. Maximum 24 kHz of sampling rate, one stereo object or two mono objects.
3. Maximum 48 kHz of sampling rate, one stereo object or two mono objects.
4. Maximum 48 kHz of sampling rate, one 5.1 channel object or multiple objects with at maximum one integer factor sampling rate conversion for a maximum of two channels.

Note that a stream can consist of several audio objects. As an example this could be a speech object giving commentary and a music object. Different objects could carry different languages.

Proprietary codecs

There are three popular multimedia compression architectures: Apple Quick-Time, RealNetworks and Windows Media. Each supports a choice of different codecs for speech and music. There are also a number of audio-only systems for 'Internet radio', notably Shoutcast.

Microsoft Windows Media

The Microsoft Windows Media Player control acts as a universal player for rendering most standard multimedia formats. The player can decode live and interactive streams or play back local content that may have been downloaded at some earlier time.

Codecs supported by version 7 of Windows Media include the following:

- Windows Media Audio Codec v. 8 is a scalable codec that provides high-quality mono or stereo audio content over a wide range of bandwidths at different sampling rates

- Fraunhofer IIS MP3 is a high-quality audio codec that is particularly good for mono music encoding
- Sipro Labs ACELP.net is a low bit rate vocoder that provides excellent speech compression

RealNetworks

The RealAudio streaming audio players used CELP compression for the original version 2.0 audio codec for 28 kbit/s delivery, but they have since concentrated on codecs that are patented, proprietary methods.

The RealAudio format started as Progressive Networks Audio (PNA). It was the first compression format to support live audio over the Internet and thus gained considerable support. It requires proprietary streaming server software in order to provide the real-time playback facility. The server also supports repositioning during real-time playback. Version 2.0 offered two encoding algorithms; the original 8 kbit/s data rate and a higher data rate to give higher audio quality for music using higher sampling rates (11, 22 and 44 kHz).

Real 8

The release of Real 8 saw two new codecs to the RealAudio family. Real jointly developed with Sony the ATRAC3 codec for high-quality music encoding, and launched their own codec for low bit rate general audio encoding. The ATRAC encoder gives a 105 kbit/s bit rate for stereo music. These two cover bit rates from 16 up to 352 kbit/s. Stemming from their partnership with Sony, Real players can be used to download music in a format compatible with Sony portable players.

Apple QuickTime

Apple QuickTime supports a large number of codecs. Only a few are streamable formats. The following are the main choices:

- QDesign Music codec. A high-quality music codec. It claims to offer better performance to MP3 at lower rates. Typical stereo audio bit rate is 24 kbit/s.
- Fraunhofer IIS MP3 audio codec. This is the high-quality standard for compression and particularly good for music encoding.
- Qualcomm PureVoice for speech encoding at low bit rates, typically 6.8 kbit/s. Based on CELP coding.

Open-source codecs

The alternative to the licensed formats, like MPEG, and proprietary formats like Windows Media and RealAudio, is to use an open-source standard like the Ogg

Vorbis codec. This has been developed by a team with roots in the academic community at MIT, under the general umbrella Xiphophorous. Vorbis is a waveform coder for general audio applications and uses MDCT coding. The bit stream is in Ogg format. Data rates supported range from 16 up to 128 kbit/s, with sampling at 44.1 or 48 kHz. It claims to offer a better audio quality than MPEG-1, layer 3 coding, comparable with MPEG-2 (AAC). The format can be streamed in real-time using the Icecast server. This is another Xiphophorous project and is an open-source streaming server for the Vorbis audio codec. I suggest you look at their web sites for further details, and for downloads of the source code if you are interested.

Summary

There is no one-size-fits-all outfit for audio encoding. At the very least when you stream you will want to choose between speech and music. Speech can use one of the super-efficient vocoders, whereas music will use a general audio or waveform coder. The MPEG-4 standard recognizes this reality, and offers a number of different technologies to cover data rates from 1 to 64 Kbit/s and higher.

Streamed audio has been able to exploit speech-processing algorithms developed for secure military communications and for cellular radio. These codecs feature the low coding latencies required for a two-way conversation and the efficient processing demanded by compact, battery-powered hardware.

General audio coding has undergone similar developments. The consumer audio industry needs high compression ratios for the portable audio products. These have very limited storage capacity, for reasons of the limited space for magnetic and optical storage, and the cost of solid-state memory.

The latest audio codecs utilize the full resources of our understanding of psychoacoustics to remove perceptual irrelevancies in the audio waveform. Redundancy in the data signal then allows further reductions in bit rates.

We now have a wide range of codecs available to use, some vocoders, some for general audio. Bit rates vary from a few kbit/s for speech up to a few hundred kbit/s for multi-channel audio. So the compressionist can choose the optimum codec to match the quality requirements and the bandwidth available.

Section 2

Streaming

7 Introduction to streaming media

Introduction

Less than 10 years after its initial development, streaming has joined the mainstream of communication media. The ubiquity of the Internet led many multimedia content owners to search for a way to deliver media over an IP network. Because it is seen as the most natural way to communicate, content creators wanted to use video and audio. We only have to look at the overwhelming success of television.

The first multimedia applications just used the Internet for file transfer to the PC. Once the entire file had been downloaded, it could then be played back locally – much like a CD-ROM. This is called download-and-play.

True streaming is media content that is delivered to the viewer's media player in real-time. That means that it is transferred at the same rate as it is displayed. So a 10-minute clip will take 10 minutes to download over the network. There is no intermediate storage or caching of the content between its origin and the player. The data is processed as it arrives at the player, and then discarded.

Three developments introduced this seed change in media delivery: the streaming server, advances in compression algorithms and the improvements to the 'last mile'. Progressive Networks developed a way to control the delivery rate of a file, so that it could be transmitted in real-time. The ongoing developments in audio compression led to codecs that could deliver a reasonable quality music stream at 28 Kbit/s. Alongside this evolution of the streaming architectures, the telcos and cable service providers were rolling out broadband Internet to the home. The cable modem and ADSL could now offer download speeds higher than 1 Mbit/s. The delivery of video over IP now becomes a reality.

There have been many startups with innovative codecs but, from a plethora of technologies, three architectures now dominate the streaming business. RealNetworks showed it was possible, and have developed a comprehensive range of products for producing, serving and playing rich media content. Microsoft developed their Video for Windows multimedia platform into Windows Media – focused now on the streaming of video and audio. It has strong support for integrated presentation graphics for the world of corporate communications. Apple came from the QuickTime multimedia world. A favorite for CD-ROM production, it was later extended to support streaming. It now offers support for a wide variety of media formats, from 3-D to audio and video, and is moving towards compatibility with the MPEG-4 standard.

All these products have developed from a background of the traditional rectangular picture that we know from film and television. The focus has been delivery to the PC, but that is not the only possible display.

The world of multimedia is expanding into new platforms, and finding new ways to use old platforms. The production community has requested international standards for the delivery of multimedia content unrestrained by the platform. MPEG-4 has been the outcome of this work. Interactive content can be authored for a whole range of platforms: hand-held wireless devices, games consoles, interactive television. The PC is just one of many means to view content.

MPEG-4 has broken away from the traditional methods of audio/video coding as a two-dimensional rectangular raster. These were largely based on MPEG-1 and the H.261 video-conferencing standard. MPEG-4 supports new types of media objects: synthetic video and audio, and three-dimensional. It is highly scalable and covers resolutions from a thumbnail size image for mobile applications up to high definition for digital cinema.

Audio- and video-conferencing

Video-conferencing has much in common with streaming. Much of the streaming codec development started with the H.261 and H.263 video-conferencing standards. The real-time protocols are also shared by conferencing and webcasting. But there are also major differences. Video-conferencing demands very low latency so that natural conversations can be held; for webcasting the propagation delays and processing latencies are not important – if it takes 3 or 4 seconds for a live webcast to arrive it is of little concern. Another difference is the connection. Video-conferencing is peer-to-peer between at least two participants. In contrast, webcast streaming is server–client.

What are the applications of streaming?

Streaming media can potentially be employed wherever the CD-ROM or videotape has previously been used for content distribution. The initial

Figure 7.1 Streaming media applications.

applications very much followed the functions of the CD-ROM: training, corporate communications, marketing and entertainment.

Legacy formats

Before streaming media was developed, if you wanted to distribute a live broadcast to a multiple-site corporation, the main option was to rent a satellite transponder for the duration of the presentation. The cost for the distribution is not inconsiderable. As well as the satellite time, there is the rental of the uplink truck. The next problem is that most businesses do not have many television receivers. How many times have you taken a VHS tape home, because it was the easiest way to view it?

The alternative for pre-recorded content is the videotape cassette or CD-ROM. The tape is fine for linear programming (except for the above-mentioned lack of receivers), but is totally unsuited to random access. This was the strength of the CD-ROM. First, it can be played back on a PC, ubiquitous in the office. Second, the viewer could use interactive navigation, essential for applications like training.

The drawback with tape and CD is the duplication and distribution costs. There is also the delay while material is shipped out, so it always lacks the immediacy of a live broadcast.

Figure 7.2 Streaming media as an alternative to videotape, satellite and the CD-ROM.

The other form of distribution was on-demand. You want a training presentation, so you look up a suitable tape in a catalog, and then order a VHS tape for overnight delivery. The next day it arrives, you preview the tape and find it is not what you want. Three days could elapse before you have the correct tape in your hand. With streaming media you can browse the online catalog, preview a clip, then once satisfied, download the stream. The whole procedure may have taken 15 minutes.

Which is the most productive? Which has the highest distribution costs? Streaming can replace the videotape cassette and courier, just as the PDF file has replaced the wait for a catalog in the mail.

If you were to adopt streaming, it is quite possible that the corporate wide-area network can be used. If it does not have the capacity, the Internet infrastructure can also be used. One of the big advantages is that most of the audience can watch from their desktop PC. Home-workers or the field sales force can even dial up a company extranet server to watch on a laptop.

Corporate communications

Streaming opens up a whole new way to communicate. Until the advent of streaming, if a company executive wanted to communicate to the organization, the options were limited. A group e-mail could be sent out but it lacks impact, and will be buried in all the other messages. The alternative was to hire a conference facility in a suitable venue and make a stand-up presentation. While being effective, the cost of the latter option is considerable, both in time and money.

Using streaming media a webcast can be made from the CEO's office direct to all the staff, over the corporate WAN/LAN. The VP of Sales can address customers using the company extranet – the opportunities are endless.

The more natural feel of video and audio can be used as an adjunct to press releases, to give a more direct communication of important news. Investor relations can benefit greatly from streaming. It is becoming *de rigueur* to stream the quarterly earnings call.

Distance learning

Distance learning, often called e-learning, takes a big step forward when you can add video and audio content. One problem that distance learning has always suffered from is a high drop-out rate. In the past it has been limited to e-mail communication and voice over IP. Streaming now presents the opportunity to add video to help to convey facts and information in a far more compelling way. Video can help the student to relate to the tutors, giving a boost to the success rates of the courses.

Product and sales training

This is rather different from distance learning, in that it is more likely to be aimed at a group of staff or customers, as opposed to the one-to-one interaction of e-learning. For product training, streaming can replace the traditional slide presentation with a rich media show – slides, video audio and text – plus the opportunity for interactivity with web meetings. Of course it could also be a one-to-one training session – the boundary between e-learning and e-training is blurred.

Advertising

Many surveys have shown that streaming media users spend more online, so they are suitable targets for Internet delivered advertising. Streaming ads are one step on from the banner ads of the web page. The technology has to be applied with care. Viewers will not be best pleased if the result of a stalling download is a commercial for a loan they do not want.

One of the first major applications for advertising was the movie trailer. Streaming is an obvious vehicle, offering on-demand video teasers for upcoming films. The music business has also adopted streaming as part of interactive rich media promotions for new albums.

Entertainment

In some circles streamed entertainment has gained notoriety after the blatant abuses of intellectual property rights practiced by peer-to-peer content distribution systems like Napster. The widespread distribution of entertainment calls for an industrial-strength rights management solution to protect the potential revenues. Entertainment did get off to a slow start. Who wants to pay to watch a jerky, fuzzy video over a dial-up modem? The advent of broadband to the home changes all that. With high-performance content delivery networks and ADSL or a cable modem, the viewer can now watch at a quality that stands comparison with the VHS. Pay-per-view becomes a viable proposition.

The streaming architecture

There are four components to a streaming architecture:

- Capture and encoding
- Serving
- Distribution and delivery
- Media player

Capture and encoding take the raw audio and video from the microphone and camera and process them into a compressed computer file. These files are then stored on a content server, which has special software that can control the real-time delivery of the stream.

The distribution channel connects the server to the player. This may involve many interconnected networks and cache servers. The network may be anything from a local area network to the Internet.

The media player, usually a plug-in to a web browser, receives the stream and decompresses back to regular audio and video, where it can be displayed on the PC.

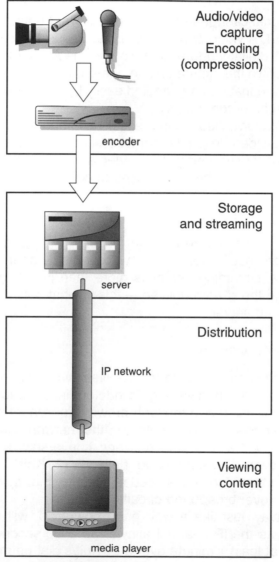

Figure 7.3 The four stages of streaming.

Capture and encode

The capture and encode processing takes regular audio and video signals in a television format and converts them to a streaming file. There are a number of stages to this:

- Capture to computer file format
- Compress the media data
- Packetize data with hints or index

A straight video signal cannot be handled by software until it is in a compatible format, typically AVI. A video capture card installed in the capture workstation converts analog or digital video and audio into the AVI format. The card most likely also scales down the picture size to one-quarter of the original resolution. This gives a data rate that can be handled easily by the processor and ease the storage requirements for the final file.

A software application called a compressor-decompressor, or *codec* for short, takes the raw audio/video file and compresses it down to a size that matches the bandwidth available for streaming. The codec also wraps the data with special hint or index metadata that the server uses to control the real-time delivery.

Serving

The encoded file is uploaded to a server for delivery out to the network. The server is a software application, like a web server, rather than the physical server hardware. A streaming server is more than just a fancy file server, it controls in real-time the stream delivery – this is what sets it apart from similar products like the web server.

Streaming versus download

Downloading was the normal way to receive files over the Internet. We are used to requesting a web page, then waiting an indeterminate period while all the files for the page are downloaded to the web browser for rendering. The recall of a page places no special requirements for the network bandwidth. A high-bandwidth network will allow rapid delivery; conversely, a large file will be delivered slowly over a narrow band network (28 Kbit/s). The process is asynchronous. The term bursting is used to describe the rapid download of low bit rate media files over broadband circuits.

Download-and-play, just like a web page download, will use best effort to download as fast as the IP channel allows. So a 30-second clip encoded at 56 Kbit/s will take at least 1 minute over a 28 Kbit/s dial-up modem or could be less than 2 seconds over a high-speed 1 Mbit/s link.

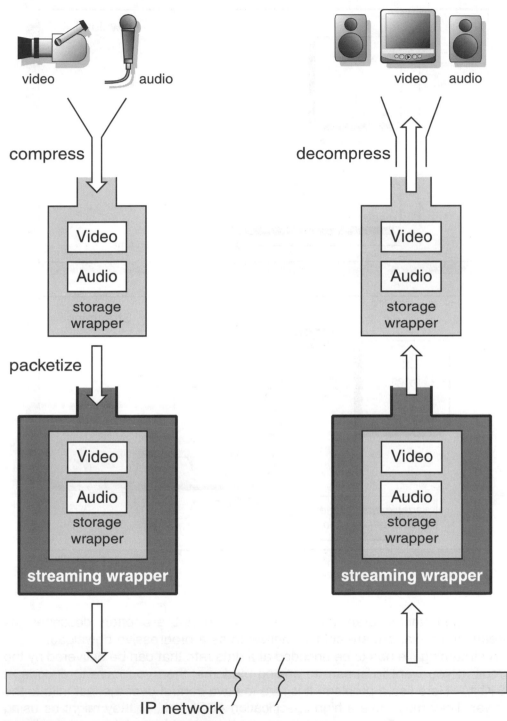

Figure 7.4 Compression and decompression.

Figure 7.5 Download versus streaming.

Animated vector graphics in the Flash format are often described as streaming media, but are actually delivered as a progressive download.

A streaming file has to be encoded at a data rate that can be delivered by the circuit. If you want to stream to analog modems, then you have to encode at 28 Kbit/s. Here lies a problem. It is rare to have control over the last mile to the viewer. They may have a high-specification ADSL link, or they might be using the 28K modem. The user who is paying the monthly rental on a broadband circuit wants to see a higher bit rate – that is why he or she is paying the extra cost.

The way around this adopted by the early codec architectures is to encode several copies of the clip at different bit rates. The server and media player negotiate to select the optimum file for the prevailing network conditions and available bandwidth. That does solve the problem, but at a price. Encoding has to be done several times over, and additional file space is needed on the content servers. Both add to the costs of serving content.

Progressive download

Progressive download is an intermediate step between download-and-play and true streaming. Rather than waiting for the complete file to be downloaded to the local disk before playback, the file can be opened while the remainder is still downloading. The difference from streaming is two-fold. The first is that the server is not delivering the file in real-time, so the player can run out of material if the transfer is slower than the encoded rate. How many times have you watched the race with the progress bar on a progressive download? If the player catches up with the download, the screen goes black – there is nothing to do but wait for more of the file to download. The second difference is that the entire media file is stored locally to the player.

Live and on-demand

Streaming can be used in two ways. Media can be pushed to the viewer, much like a regular television channel. This is live streaming. The alternative is for the viewer to pull, or request, the media from a content server, just like using a library. This is called on-demand.

A special case of live streaming is 'simulated-live', where the content is delivered by a server-side request. This can be mixed at will with a live presentation. So a speaker could be introduced with a promo, speak live to camera, and then afterwards show a pre-recorded clip from the server.

Streaming requires a persistent client-to-server connection and continuous data flow. Contrast this with the burst transmissions of a web server connection.

On-demand and interactivity

One major delineator of streaming from regular television is the interactivity. The viewer can interact with on-demand content files. The player has VCR-like controls (PLAY, STOP, FF, REW) and random access to any part of the clip. Hotspots on the video screen can take the viewer to another part of the file, or to a different file, at the click of a mouse – hypervideo replaces hypertext.

Live streaming

On-demand streaming

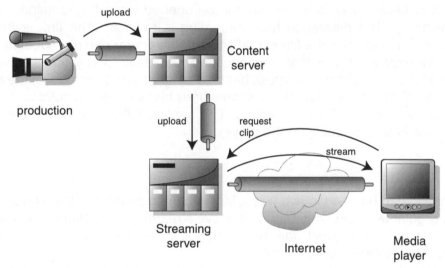

Figure 7.6 Live and on-demand.

To support this functionality a special streaming server is used, rather than a regular web server. The streaming file is time indexed to enable the random access. This means that a long program can be split into 'chapters' with random access by the viewer to any chapter at will.

Distribution

In principle, the distribution is simple. As long as there is IP connectivity between the server and the player/client the requested packets arrive at the player. In practice it is not that easy. No doubt you have seen a stalled media file; the video is distorted and blocky, the audio has silent passages. The problem is that the Internet was not originally designed to support continuous streams over persistent connections. It is basically a packet-switched system for asynchronous data.

Several different developments are aiding improvements to the delivery quality. First is increased bandwidth for the last mile to the consumer. Through either the cable modem or DSL, downloads of 1 Mbit/s or higher can be achieved. The next development is the Content Delivery Network (CDN). These use a smart overlay on the Internet to provide content-aware routing. The final development is the quality of the Internet. More and more fiber is installed, and QoS protocols help differentiate priority traffic.

The catch is that as quality improves, more companies will use streaming. This creates more traffic and potential congestion – the race that never ends.

Player

A regular web browser can only render text and images in JPEG, PNG and GIF formats. A special media player is required to render streaming files. Players are usually supplied as free downloads, or are pre-installed with the operating system. Some vendors also have a fully featured player available for a small charge.

Plug-in, player or portal

The player can be used as a plug-in to a web browser. The alternative is to use a standalone player. These players have been developed into media portals, with navigation to popular material and often offering unique content specific to a given architecture.

Download versus streaming

Download-and-play is what it says. The file is downloaded to the local hard drive. Once the entire file has been delivered, then the viewer can play the file locally. In contrast, streaming is processed chunk by chunk as it arrives and rendered directly to the display, then the data discarded. So there is no waiting, if you do not like what you see you can quit the stream immediately, rather than downloading the entire file before you decide. Note that there is no local copy of the file stored on the hard drive. This greatly eases the protection of content from illegal copying, although it is not proof against the determined hacker.

Download-and-play

Streaming

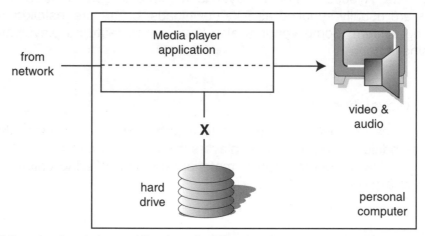

Figure 7.7 Download-and-play and the streaming player.

Bandwidth, bits and bytes

Throughout this book the units 'bit' and 'byte' occur. Although you know that a byte is 8 bits, it is very easy to get the two mixed up. Most of this stems from the abbreviations:

B = byte and b = bit.

To avoid confusion it is always best to spell out the abbreviations in full. Have you ever purchased eight times more disk storage than you needed because b and B were swapped around? Alternatively, midway through a live webcast the disk archive is completely filled. In general bits refer to streams and bytes to memory and storage. So a 10-second clip at 80 Kbit/s (that is 10 Kbyte/s) needs 100 Kbytes of storage. The other point is that the computer industry does not use the standard multiplier of kilo- to mean 1,000, but instead 1,024 (or 2^{10}). The two are abbreviated to k and K, respectively. If they are mixed up the error is only going to be 2 per cent.

1 byte = 8 bits
1 kbit = 1,000 bits
1 Kbit = 1,024 bits

Media	Stream rate	Notes
streaming media	30 kbit/s to 1 Mbit/s	
Audio CD	2.8 Mbit/s	uncompressed stereo
DVD video	< 10.7 Mbit/s	average rate 4.7 MBit/s
DV	25 Mbit/s	
studio inter-connections	270 Mbit/s	uncompressed standard-definition

28K modem

T-1 1.5 Mbits/

Figure 7.8 Media bandwidths.

Bandwidths and file sizes

Streaming is very different from other media in the shear range of bandwidths that can possibly be encoded. Whereas television is essentially a fixed bandwidth (although the bit rate can vary within close limits), streaming may be delivered down anything from an analog phone line to a high-speed local area network, or 28 kbit/s to 2 Mbit/s or higher.

The starting point for uncompressed audio is a bit rate of nearly 3 Mbit/s from a CD. For video the studio interconnection standard is 270 Mbit/s. Even the compressed 1,394 output from a DV camcorder has a video data rate of 25 Mbit/s (it can be transferred at different rates).

The streaming media has to be compressed to match the capacity of the user's connection. These vary widely; an analog modem will have a maximum rate of 56 kbit/s, although many users still use 28k or 14k modems (although the latter are not adequate for video streaming).

Table 7.1 Typical carriers for delivery of streaming

	Maximum	Actual	Notes
Dial-up modem	56 kbit/s	35 kbit/s	
Dual ISDN	128 kbit/s	128 kbit/s	
Cable modem/DSL	1–8 Mbit/s	300 kbit/s–2 Mbit/s	Rate varies with supplier
T-1	1.5 Mbit/s	1.5 Mbit/s	
10 base-T LAN	10 Mbit/s	3 Mbit/s	Typical

Most connections quote a maximum rate, but this is not usually achieved, except for ISDN and T-1, where the data rate is guaranteed. The dial-up modem will be limited by propagation conditions on the line, factors like noise pickup. The cable modem uses a shared fiber back to the head-end from your local node. If everyone on the block tries to watch high-bandwidth streams simultaneously the contention for the available bandwidth will cause degradation of the streams. DSL, much like the analog modem, will be limited by line conditions.

The rule is always to encode at a lower rate than the maximum the circuit is specified to carry. If you are using standard encoding tools these will have headroom already built in to the encoding templates.

Proprietary codec architectures

There are three popular codec architectures, Apple's QuickTime, Microsoft's Windows Media and RealNetworks. Each product supports a number of different compression codecs, although there is more choice of audio over video codecs.

Apple QuickTime

QuickTime is Apple's multi-platform, multimedia software architecture. It was originally used by content creators to author and publish CD-ROMs. It also offers virtual reality with 3-D views of objects and panoramas. The initial support for IP delivery was by progressive download. It was extended to support true streaming in version 4, utilizing the RTSP framework. As QuickTime has an established position in multimedia authoring there is a large community of users.

Some of the features of QuickTime include the following.

- Multiple delivery channels: WWW, CD-ROM, DVD, broadband, kiosk, presentations
- Mac and Windows are equally well supported
- Powerful interactive capabilities
- Includes synchronized graphics, sound, video, text, music, VR, and 3-D for rich media production

QuickTime is the dominant architecture for CD-ROM video. It enjoys an impressive market share due to its cross-platform support, wide range of features and free licensing. For these reasons QuickTime is used on the vast majority of CD-ROM titles.

The MPEG-4 team has adopted the QuickTime stream serving methodology (with the use of a hint track and RTSP/RTP) as the basis of MPEG-4 streaming.

Scalability

QuickTime offers multiple bit rate delivery through its alternate movies feature. At the beginning of playback, the QuickTime Plug-In requests an alternate version according to the settings the viewer has configured in their QuickTime Settings control panel. Content creators may create as many alternates as they need when they are encoding the movie, and specify complex criteria for when particular versions will be displayed. This allows for delivery of content based on: bandwidth of the user's connection, playback platform (Mac or Windows), QuickTime version and language (to select different audio tracks) or the CPU speed.

RealNetworks

RealNetworks pioneered streaming as a usable communication medium under the name Progressive Networks. Before the Real player, audio-visual content was delivered as a download, to be played later from the local drive.

RealSystem G2, incorporating RealAudio® and RealVideo®, is a network-oriented, streaming media architecture developed by RealNetworks. G2 is the second generation of RealVideo and represents a major improvement in quality, supported media types and features over the initial product.

RealSystem G2 is a streaming architecture, offering both server-based 'true streaming' and serverless 'HTTP streaming' (also known as 'progressive download'). There are performance and scalability advantages with the server, but you can get started without one. However, high volume sites definitely need a server for improved delivery performance.

RealSystem G2 is most appropriate for network delivery of audio, video and other media types, such as text and Flash animations. It is less suitable for CD-ROM or DVD delivery due to the high CPU requirements at greater bandwidths. Real files cannot be edited or re-compressed once they are encoded into the Real format.

Users can view RealSystem G2 movies with the RealPlayer, a free client application available from RealNetworks. The enhanced 'RealPlayer Plus' provides additional features, and must be purchased from RealNetworks. A Netscape plug-in is also available.

RealSystem G2 supports SMIL ('Synchronized Multimedia Integration Language', pronounced 'smile'). This language enables the content creator to synchronize media and actions within a web page to the video and audio tracks. For example, SMIL can control the loading of multiple movies at given times, URL page flips, transitions, text tracks and advertisement insertion.

Scalability

RealSystem G2 offers dynamic stream switching called SureStream. During playback, the RealPlayer and RealServer continually communicate and can repeatedly switch between versions to deliver the highest-quality stream that the viewer's connection can support at any given time. This real-time switching effectively handles changing network conditions, such as congestion. Switching of audio and video is handled independently, and you can indicate whether the video or audio should be given preference as the viewer's throughput drops.

In addition to the SureStream feature, the RealPlayer can also drop frames and/or degrade the image quality to maintain real-time playback over slower connections. If the available bandwidth drops very low, the RealPlayer can omit the video track entirely and simply play the audio track.

See RealNetworks web site for comprehensive background information.

Windows Media

Windows Media Technologies is Microsoft's complete solution for delivery of Internet multimedia. The architecture includes a number of products for encoding, serving and distribution, and an integrated and fully featured rights management system. An SDK allows integration into wider systems.

The Windows Media tools include the Windows Media encoder 7.1, which uses versions 7 and 8 codecs. A command-line encoder utility can be used to create on-demand content. The server (Windows Media Services) supports both live and 'on-demand' video. It is part of Windows 2000 and can be downloaded for NT. This can potentially offer a low-cost media server solution.

In 2001, Microsoft released Windows Media Player 7.1 for Windows XP and a player for Macintosh Mac OS X. Players are also available for legacy Windows and Mac operating systems, plus Solaris. A lightweight player is offered for several different handheld PCs for viewers who want streaming on the move.

The rights management allows content creators to set up a full e-commerce system to sell or rent streamed content. It can also be used for delivery of confidential media clips.

Scalability

Windows Media Server offers scaling of the transmitted data rate through the use of multiple video tracks called 'intelligent streaming'. At the beginning of playback, the Media Player and the Windows Media Server negotiate to select the video track which best matches the viewer's connection. If the network's performance degenerates, the server will automatically send a lower rate video stream. If the amount of available bandwidth decreases more, the server will degrade video quality further, until only the audio is left. This ensures that the clip can be followed even during excessive congestion.

Promised enhancements to the servers (called Corona) include a fast-start, thus avoiding the usual long buffering before a stream starts to play. The latest free downloads, as well as more information, are available at Microsoft's Windows Media web site and through the Microsoft Developers Network.

Summary

The development of the streaming file format and the associated streaming server has been the driver for the technology. Sophisticated compression algorithms have been the enablers for the transmission of video and audio over very modest bandwidths. The Internet is ubiquitous glue that connects the far corners of the world, so that we can send the video and audio long distances without resorting to the expensive medium of television – affordable only for mass market programming.

One of the drawbacks often cited for HTML is the need to design pages that render effectively with different browsers. Although the experienced web designer will get to know all the tricks, there are many pitfalls for the novice. The end result is the many unpredictable page views that we chance across on the Internet.

Unfortunately, streaming media has perpetuated this rather chaotic position, with the coexistence of a number of proprietary architectures. Although there are ways around this, that involve authoring in a number of formats, the problem is exacerbated if you want to use interactive rich media. The three main architectures do not have exactly complementary feature-sets.

You must never forget that content is for the users, not the creators. So it is vital that the complex technology application is transparent to the potential consumer. The early viewers of streaming media may have overcome any technical obstacles, but the bulk of the public will not tolerate quirks or unpredictable behavior if streaming is to be a mainstream media. It must be as easy as watching television or a DVD.

With careful HTML design you can make smart decisions about which file format to direct a browser to by detecting the plug-ins installed in the browser.

Standardization is often put forward as the answer to some of these issues. If there was one player that could render any media format, perhaps using proprietary plug-ins, all would be simple. After all, we can receive a television broadcast from any station without needing a special receiver. The flip side to this is that it is extremely unlikely that streaming could have developed from inception to be a mainstream communication medium in the period of only 5 years. The proprietary architectures can continuously improve without the constraints of standards, and are spurred on by intense competition.

Whether this situation continues as streaming moves out of the PC environment into general consumer devices remains to be seen. There is far more pressure to standardize when streaming is deployed to set-top boxes or wireless devices. The life of a television receiver or set-top box can be 10 times that of a software release, so there will be a drive to standardize.

8 Video encoding

Introduction

Encoding is the conversion of a video signal into a streaming media file. The video signal has first to be compressed, then packetized and finally encapsulated within a streaming wrapper. This chapter covers the encoding stage from a video signal through to the point where the streaming file is transferred to the streaming server.

The encoding takes place in several stages. The first stage is to capture a conventional video or television signal, then convert that to a file format that can be processed by computer software. The second stage is data rate reduction, by scaling and compression, to a bit rate that can be delivered over dial-up or broadband circuits. The third stage is to wrap the compressed video in a packetized format that can be streamed over an IP network.

The enabling developments that have led to the rapid adoption of streaming media lie mainly at the second stage – compression.

There is no 'standard' way of encoding; there are many different ways to get from video to a streaming format. The route that you choose will depend upon the hardware platform that you have selected, the required throughput of encoded material and the final viewing quality that you require. This chapter describes some typical architectures, but is not intended to be prescriptive.

To find the optimum solution for your application you may want to undertake comparative trials between some different solutions. It is quite possible to assemble your own system from PCs, video capture cards and suitable choice of software. Alternately a shrink-wrap solution can be purchased. Do you require the best quality at very low bit rates? Do you encode a few hours a week, or do you have a large archive to put online? All these factors have to be considered before deciding upon an encoding solution. Broadly speaking the price will rise with performance and with the convenience of operation. Some high-end applications allow automated batch encoding. If the system is to be used with a digital asset management system, consideration should be given to the ease of interfacing with the encoding process. The asset management systems use streaming video to preview content.

Distribution channels

Until the advent of high-definition (HD) television, a broadcast teleproduction was usually a single format. Now the producers may have to create in two formats. In contrast, the norm when encoding media for streaming is to produce multiple output formats. You may be called upon to encode up to 20 different versions of a video clip. These are files at different bandwidths, all repeated in a number of different streaming architectures.

First I will look at the different delivery channels – the prime cause of the need to encode multiple files.

Table 8.1 Typical distribution channels

	Channel data rate	Guaranteed bandwidth	Notes
601	270 Mbit/s	Yes	Uncompressed, standard definition video
Digital television	4–6 Mbit/s	Yes	Variable bit rate
T-1 (E-1)	1.5 Mbit/s (2 Mbit/s)	Yes	
DSL	144 kbit/s–8 Mbit/s	No	
Cable modem	128 kbit/s–1 Mbit/s	No	
Dual ISDN	128 kbit/s	Yes	
ISDN	64 kbit/s	Yes	
Dial-up modem	56 kbit/s	No	Typical capacity 35 Kbit/s

In the table the digital television example is the standard definition television that is broadcast to the DVB standard, and uses MPEG-2 MP@ML. It is very similar in quality to DVD video.

Some channels offer a guaranteed bandwidth; others are dependent upon the capacity of the local loop, plus the contention ratios within distribution nodes. Typically the local ends offered to the consumer do not have a guaranteed quality of service (albeit they are at a much reduced cost compared to the traditional telecoms circuits).

Table 8.2 Channel data parameters

	Uncompressed video source	Broadcast television	ADSL, cable modem	Analog modem
Target data rate	(270 Mbit/s)	4 Mbit/s	500 kbit/s	35 kbit/s
Data reduction required to meet target rate		40:1	330:1	4700:1
Frame size	720 × 480	720 × 480	192 × 144	160 × 120
Frame rate	30	30	15	5
Color sampling	4:2:2	4:2:0	YUV12	YUV12
Uncompressed data rate (Mbit/s)	166	124	5	1.15
Fraction of original data rate		1:1.33	1:33	1:144
Compression required to reach target rate		30:1	10:1	30:1

To encode video for all these different applications, the video is delivered with a range of basic parameters. Table 8.2 shows some typical data rates for the video alone, excluding audio and control data.

The table shows how scaling down before encoding reduces the uncompressed data rate. A thumbnail video for a dial-up modem requires that the data rate is reduced to nearly 1/5,000 of the original. This is accomplished by scaling down by a factor of 144:1, and then compressing by a further 30:1.

Figure 8.1 shows the relative file sizes for encoded media.

- Uncompressed – 270 Mbit/s
- MPEG-2, DTV – 4 Mbit/s
- MPEG-1 – 1.5 Mbit/s
- ADSL, cable modem – 500 kbit/s
- Analog modem – 56 kbit/s

Data compression

The raw data rate from a standard definition television camera is 270 Mbit/s. This has to be reduced to rates as low as 30 kbit/s for delivery to dial-up modems. How is a reduction in video data of almost 5,000:1 achieved, while still retaining a viewable picture?

This reduction takes place in several steps. The scaling usually takes place on the video capture card. The compression is performed by the codec software application running on the main processors.

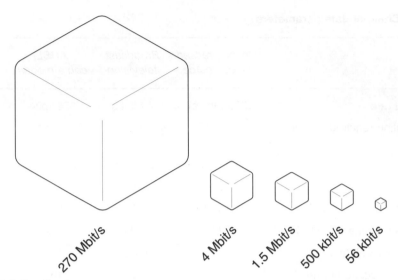

Figure 8.1 Relative file sizes.

The most popular way to encode is to first capture the video with a dedicated PCI card. This card is installed in the encoding workstation. The card converts the video signal into an intermediate format that can be handled as a computer file, usually one of the Audio-Video Interleaved (AVI) formats. AVI has become the de facto standard for computer audio and video files. From this point on, regular desktop computer technology can now be used for downstream processing.

The AVI files themselves cannot be delivered over the Internet for two reasons. The first is that AVI files are usually very large. Depending on the capture process, an AVI can be more than 1 Mbyte per second of video. The second is that AVI files can't be streamed in real-time over the Internet. You must download the entire file to a local drive before you can play it. Hence the need for compression and packetization.

Once captured, the AVI file is routed to the encoding software. The encoder uses a software codec to convert it from an AVI file to a streaming format (typically Windows Media, Real or Apple QuickTime). Finally, the streaming file is uploaded to a server for delivery over the Internet.

If you are making a live webcast, this process has to take place in real-time, so the computer will need a minimum level of processing power.

Codec

Codec is short for **co**mpression/**dec**ompression. Codecs are software programs that employ a mathematical algorithm to squeeze the media files into a more compact streaming format. Decompression then takes place in a compatible

Figure 8.2 Encoder system.

decoder, or media player, installed in the end-user's computer. The process can be likened to zipping and unzipping a file on a PC.

Codecs can be symmetrical or asymmetrical. A symmetric codec usually requires less processing and is more efficient. Streaming media codecs are usually asymmetrical; this means the encoding process requires much more processing than the decoder. Since only one encoder is required, but all the viewers need a decoder, it makes sense to put the complexity in the encoding end.

The players are usually downloaded over the Internet, so the executables must be kept to a reasonable size – very large downloads are not popular with the public.

Ingest station

The video capture can be carried out on a separate ingest station ahead of the compression process and the intermediate AVI file stored on a server. These files can be very large so you will need a generous-sized array of disk drives. Also beware of the 2 Gbyte limit for the file size for the original AVI format.

Most video content is edited into a finished program before conversion to a streaming format. The final cut can be dubbed onto videotape to transfer into the streaming encoder, but it is often simpler to transfer the program as a file directly from the editing system to the streaming media processor over a LAN.

Video capture

Most streaming media content is created in a conventional television format, either direct from a camera or as an edited program on videotape. Live streaming is a special case of encoding and places more exacting demands on the processing hardware.

The first step is to convert the television signal as a computer file format, often Audio-Video Interleaved (AVI). In the case of a live event the capture will take place at the venue. With videotape the capture will usually be at the encoding center. It is also possible to ingest files directly from non-linear editing systems.

The first problem you will encounter with video is that there are a large number of different formats that you might want to encode: analog or digital, component or composite.

The second is that videotape comes in many formats.

This list is by no means exhaustive; there are older analog composite formats (1-inch) and a number of other digital formats (D-1, D-3, D-5, D-9). The source material may even be supplied in a high-definition format.

I haven't mentioned audio-only sources. These again can be analog or digital, and delivered on tape, cassette and mini-disc or burnt onto a CD-ROM.

Table 8.3 Tape formats

Tape width	Name		Color encoding	Notes
3/4 inch	U-matic	Analog	Y/C	Archive material
1/2 inch	VHS	Analog	Y/C	Consumer format
	S-VHS	Analog	Y/C	
	Betacam (SP)	Analog	Y/C	
	Digital Betacam	Digital	YUV	
	Beta SX	Digital	YUV	
8 mm	DV	Digital	YUV	
	DVC-PRO	Digital	YUV	
	DVCAM	Digital	YUV	

live encoding

encoding from tape

file transfer from editing system

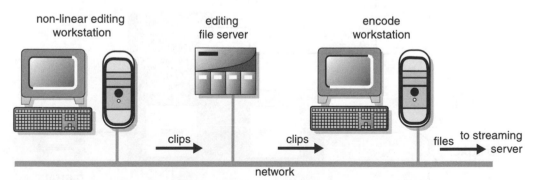

Figure 8.3 Video capture systems.

To add to all these formats there are the different interconnection formats for video:

- Analog composite (NTSC, PAL)
- Y/C or S-video (analog)
- Digital component (601, 4:2:2) – 270 Mbit/s
- DV (FireWire, IEEE-1394) – 25 Mbit/s, 5:1 compression

So you see that encoding is partly video format conversion.

Interconnections

Interconnection formats include analog composite and component, and digital component. All require processing to arrive at the final AVI file format. To this end the video capture card has several components: a composite decoder, analog-to-digital conversion, DV decompression and possibly hardware scaling.

If modern digital tape decks use component recording, why do most video cards have analog composite inputs? For historical reasons analog composite has become a standard for interconnections and is still in very common use.

Figure 8.4 Capture card blocks.

It is possible to find video cards with digital inputs (DV and 601) and these do offer the potential for higher quality encoding. The video cards also include a preview output so that the encoded files can be viewed on a conventional television monitor. Many video cards are designed as platforms to support non-linear editors, so will have many additional facilities that are not required for a straight encode.

In an ideal world the streaming format would be encoded directly from a 4:2:2 source (at 270 Mbit/s) – in fact this is the way that DVDs of motion pictures are encoded. In this way the studios can ensure the best possible picture quality for the DVD release.

To get the best possible encoding a digital source should be used, with a clean picture and a low level of noise. If a 601 source is not available DV can be used as an alternative. The mild DCT compression used by DV should not produce significant artifacts visible in the final stream.

The second best is an analog source; here Y/C is preferable to composite. Analog sources exhibit more noise, which can potentially use up bandwidth at the compression stage. Composite signals are first decoded, and there will be visible artifacts that will produce a slight impairment of the final encoded quality (called cross-color and cross-luminance).

There are different ways of compressing; the intermediate AVI may be at the same resolution as the original video, or it may be scaled to the target size. Each method has advantages and disadvantages. It is a trade-off between video quality and data rate. If many different output formats are required, an intermediate file may have to be stored for the duration of the encoding process. This file should be at least at the size of the largest encoded picture size, if not larger. So if you are encoding to 160×120 and 192×144, you may want the intermediate file at SIF resolution: 352×240. The AVI file may even be archived. But the higher the quality, the higher the storage costs.

The other consideration is the processing time, as a high-resolution file will take longer to process. The processing time can be important for two reasons. First, it could impact the throughput of work in a busy encoding center. Second, with live feeds the encoding has to take place in real-time, so the lower the resolution, the less CPU power required for the codecs.

VTR control

It is much simpler to encode a tape if the video capture application has a remote control facility for the VTR. This means that you do not have to start the capture on the fly, plus it allows batch encoding to a prepared schedule. Most professional tape decks can be controlled via an RS-422 port (DV decks can also be controlled through the IEEE-1394 interface). The port allows full transport control – Play, FF, REW and Stop – and gives status feedback plus a readout of the tape time code. Frame-accurate control allows the exact in and out points of the clip to be set in a record list. This avoids the need to trim the clip later in the encoding process.

Lowering the bit rate

A standard resolution television frame of 720 × 483 pixels (720 × 575 for 625/50), RGB sampled at 13.5 MHz, and an 8-bit resolution per sample. At a rate of 30 frames per second this is a total data rate of 248 Mbit/s, and that is without any synchronization or control data.

To stream video to a 56 kbit/s modem the bit rate has to be reduced by a factor of over 4,000. How is this achieved, yet still producing a recognizable picture?

There are two methods used to achieve this. The first is to scale down the video data. This can achieve a reduction of over 130:1, clearly a long way off the target ratio of 4,000:1. To reach this target a further reduction of 30:1 is required. This is achieved using sophisticated compression algorithms to remove redundant data, while still retaining a viewable picture.

Scaling

The simplest way to lower data rate is to scale down the original video size. Three techniques are used to scale down the signal; the first and most apparent is to use a smaller video frame size than a television picture. Since video is often shown as a window in a web page, it is perfectly acceptable to reduce the picture to one-quarter size (320 × 240 pixels) or even smaller.

This is called *spatial scaling*. It produces an instant reduction of data rate to one that is more easily processed by desktop workstations.

The second scaling is *temporal*. Broadcast television uses 25 (PAL, SECAM) or 30 (NTSC) frames per second to give good portrayal of motion. Film uses 24 frames per second. Video material that was originally shot on film is converted to one of the two television rates during the telecine process.

The third method of scaling down is to decrease the color resolution.

Dedicated hardware processors in the video card can be used for the scaling, or it can be a straight software process using the main CPU. For live encoding it is best to use the video card and relive the main processor load.

Spatial scaling

A smaller window can be used to display video; typical window sizes have resolutions of 320 × 240 or 176 × 144 pixels. This radically reduces the number of samples to one-quarter or one-eighth of a full size television resolution picture.

Table 8.4 Common image formats

Image format	Resolution	Frame rate	YUV	Application
CCIR-601 (NTSC)	720 × 480	30 interlaced	4:2:2	Broadcast television, DVD
CCIR-601 (PAL)	720 × 576	25 interlaced	4:2:2	
SIF (NTSC)	352 × 240	30 progressive	4:2:0	CD-ROM
SIF (PAL)	352 × 288	25 progressive	4:2:0	
CIF	352 × 288	30 progressive	4:2:0	Video-conference, Streaming video
QCIF	176 × 144	30 progressive	4:2:0	Videophone, Streaming video

Note: SIF, Standard Interface Format; CIF, Common Interface Format; QCIF, Quarter Common Interface Format.

Figure 8.5 shows these frame sizes in relation to an SVGA monitor display. Note also the recommended web page widths used when designing for 14- and 17-inch monitors, with 580 pixels being the traditional width for web page design. The QCIF frame is the ideal size to place a video window within a web page. There is still room left for the menus and textual content of interactive

Figure 8.5 Display resolutions.

applications. The larger frame sizes are more useful where video is the primary content and will occupy most or all of the display.

Temporal scaling

This is the process of dropping frames below the normal video rate of 30 frames per second (fps). For certain subject material the frame rate can be reduced to one-half or even more without serious degradation in picture quality. The deciding factor is the amount of motion in the picture. A talking head can be viewed at rates as low as one-fifth of television rates – of course a fast-moving subject like a sportscast would not be satisfactory at these low speeds.

This sounds like a big problem for streaming video, but much of the demand for low bit rate content is for applications like distance learning. Here the typical program uses a talking head, just the kind of material that can stand the highest temporal compression.

RealVideo will encode at a variable frame rate. The user sets the maximum rate, and then the codec automatically adjusts the frame rate based on the clip size, the target delivery bit rate and emphasis set for smoothness or visual clarity. One scene may be 7 fps, for example, while another is 10. A maximum set to 15 fps means the frame rate could vary anywhere between 15 and 0.25 fps.

Color resolution

The camera and CRT are both RGB devices. The usual coding is to take an 8-bit sample each of the red, green and blue values at each sample point or pixel. This gives a total of 24 bits, but it is often padded for ease of processing to give a 32-bit word. A 24-bit pixel can display 16 million colors. To reduce the bit rate of the streaming video, the bit depth of a sample can be reduced, albeit at a reduction in the number of colors displayed.

Table 8.5 AVI formats

AVI format	Bit depth			Padding	Bytes per pixel
	R	G	B		
RGB32	8	8	8	8	4
RGB24	8	8	8		3
RGB16	5	6	5		2
RGB15	5	5	5	1	2
RGB8	Indexed palette				1

This can be reduced to 16 bits (5:6:5, giving 65,536 colors), 15 bits (5:5:5 giving 32,786 colors) or to 8 bits (giving 256 colors). Note that the designation indicates the bit depths for R:G:B. Eight-bit coding uses a pre-defined palette of colors (indexed).

For very low bit rate channels, the reduction in color resolution can be acceptable, but continuous-tone objects will exhibit a posterization effect.

Sub-sampling

The alternative to reducing the bit depth is to use the perceptual redundancy of human visual perception. This allows the color resolution to be reduced relative to the luminance resolution, without apparent loss of picture resolution.

This is achieved by *sub-sampling* the color information.

YUV format

The red, green and blue signals from the camera are matrixed to give a luminance signal (Y) and two color-difference signals (Blue − Y) or U, and (Red − Y) or V. This is called YUV. It allows compatibility with legacy monochrome systems, and allows the color resolution to be reduced to save on channel bandwidth and reduce program storage requirements. YUV coding is the standard for interconnecting video equipment, whether as the 601 digital format, in IEEE-1394 compressed digital format or encoded as a composite analog signal (NTSC and PAL). Raw RGB is occasionally found in graphics equipment, and is the standard for display drivers (VGA).

Early composite digital video systems chose to sample analog video at four times the NTSC color sub-carrier. This rate of 13.5 MHz (4 × 3.375) was adopted for digital component sampling standards. Since the human visual system primarily uses the luminance information to resolve scene detail, the color information can be sampled at a lower rate with no apparent loss of detail. This is a form of perceptive compression. The luminance sampling rate is referred to as '4' after the multiplier used. The color sampling rate may be half ('2') or one-quarter ('1') depending on the performance required. So a YUV sample is referred to by the ratios of the sampling rates of the three different channels − 4:2:2 or 4:1:1.

YUV formats are divided into two groups: packed and planar. In the packed format, the Y, U and V components are stored in a single array. The 601 standard uses a single array. With the AVI formats two pixels are stored as a single unsigned integer value in one 'macro-pixel'.

The other format is the planar, where the Y, U and V pixels are encoded as three separate arrays.

Table 8.6 Sampling formats

Format		Nomenclature	Sampling
601	Packed		4:2:2
AVI	Planar	IYUV/I420	4:2:0 or 4:1:1
		YV12	4:2:0 or 4:1:1
		YVU9	16:1:1
	Packed	YUY2	4:2:2
		UYVY	4:2:2
		YVYU	4:2:2

It should be noted that 4:2:2 sampling represents a two-thirds reduction in bit rate over RGB 24, and 4:1:1 is a reduction of one-half. The number of bits per pixel averages to 24 bits for 4:4:4, 16 for 4:2:2, and 12 for 4:1:1 and 4:2:0.

More detail on these formats can be found in Chapter 4.

Result of scaling

The typical scaled video data rate at a size and frame rate used with analog modem is 1.15 Mbit/s. Compression to a rate suitable for delivery below 56 kbit/s will require a further 30:1 reduction. To reduce the rate even further some form of image compression has to be employed.

Compression

Compression removes information that is perceptually redundant, that is information which does not add to the perception of a scene. Compression is a trade-off between the level of artifacts that it causes and the saving in bandwidth. These trade-offs can sometimes be seen on satellite television. If too many channels are squeezed into one transponder, fast-moving objects within a scene can become blocky and soft.

Like scaling, compression of video splits into spatial compression (called intra-frame) and temporal or (inter-frame) compression.

Intra-frame compression

Single frames can be compressed with spatial, or intra-frame, compression. This can be a simple system like run-length encoding, or a lossy system where the original data cannot be wholly reconstructed. A typical example of a lossy system is JPEG, a popular codec for continuous-tone still images.

Inter-frame compression

The next method to compress video is to remove information that does not change from one frame to the next, and to only transmit information in the areas where the picture has changed. This is referred to as temporal or inter-frame compression. This technique is one of those used by the MPEG-1 and MPEG-2 standards.

Compression classes

The different algorithms are classified into families.

1. Lossless
2. Lossy
    - Naturally lossy
    - Unnaturally lossy

If all the original information is preserved the codec is called lossless. A typical example for basic file compression would be PKZIP. To achieve the high levels of compression demanded by streaming codecs, the luxury of the lossless codecs is not possible – the data reduction is insufficient.

The goal with compression is to avoid artifacts that are perceived as unnatural. The fine detail in an image can be gently degraded without losing understanding of the objects in a scene. As an example we can watch a 70 mm print of a movie or a VHS transfer, and in both cases still enjoy the experience.

If too much compression is applied, and the artifacts interfere with the image perception, the compression has become unnaturally lossy.

Packetization

This is usually implemented within the compression codec. There are two facets to the packetization. The compressed video file has to be formatted into IP packets to allow transmission over a standard IP circuit. The second is to wrap control data around the compressed video and audio data, so that the streaming server can control the real-time streaming of the media data.

Streaming wrapper

The packetization of the media is followed by a packet builder. This generates a Real-Time Protocol (RTP) hint track (metadata) that instructs the server how to stream the file. This is covered in more detail in Chapter 11. Note that there are proprietary streaming formats that do not use RTP.

Encoding hardware and software

Streaming media usually starts with a program recorded on videotape (I will consider the special case of live streaming in a different chapter).

The output of the VCR is connected to a video and audio capture board that is fitted to the encoding workstation. The board converts the video to a digital format, usually an Audio-Video Interleaved format (AVI). Apart from the video interfacing, the board has several functions that can ease the processing load on the workstation CPU.

Figure 8.6 Video card block diagram.

The functions of the card include the following:

- Decoding composite analog NTSC and PAL into a YUV format
- Demodulating the color component of S-video to YUV
- Analog-to-digital conversion
- Decoding DV (IEEE-1394) to YUV uncompressed
- Color pixel format conversion to an AVI format
- Interfacing to the PCI bus

The cards usually have a number of other facilities; these vary with different manufacturers and models.

- Spatial scaling
- De-interlace filter
- VCR control port
- Video preview output

The video preview facility may use Microsoft Direct Draw for DMA (direct memory access) to the workstation video driver. This saves loading the CPU, as a real-time preview at 30 fps would take considerable processor resources.

To achieve optimal system performance it may be necessary to use a computer with fast or multiple processors, especially for live events. The performance of the disk drives should not be forgotten. For archiving or file conversion, use a high-performance disk drive, for example a 10,000-rpm SCSI. This can help to offload performance requirements from the main CPU, freeing up more processing power for the encoder.

Encoding sessions

From the previous description of encoding and compression, it is clear that there are a huge number of possible parameter sets for encoding. It would not be productive to set up all these parameters anew for each encoding session. Instead, templates or profiles can be set up to suit typical content. Most codecs come with a number or profiles already prepared. For example, a template might be stored to encode a Beta SP tape to MPEG-4 for delivery over a corporate network at 500 kbit/s.

Encoding enhancements

Multiple bit rate encoding

Early deployments of streaming media often posted links to the media file at perhaps three different rates: 30, 100 and 300 kbit/s. So the onus was on the viewer to select the correct streaming file. First, this is an unnecessary complication for the viewer, and second it does not take any account of network congestion.

The leading codec suppliers developed multiple bit rate codecs to allow several streams of different bit rates to be bundled into one file. The streaming server then negotiates with the end-user's media player to determine the optimum rate to use for the stream delivery. No user interaction is necessary.

A typical example is SureStream from RealNetworks. With SureStream technology up to eight different bit rates can be encoded. The RealServer automatically selects the best bit rate to serve for the network conditions. The Microsoft Windows Media Intelligent Streaming is a similar feature.

All the viewer sees during network congestion is a gradual lowering of quality, rather than freezes typical of a fixed rate system.

Variable bit rate (VBR)

Streaming codecs by default use constant bit rate (CBR) encoding. DVDs and digital satellite television both use variable bit rate encoding. The DVD has a maximum file size; so, to give the maximum playing time, a low bit rate is indicated.

The MPEG-2 compression used differs from an analog recording, like VHS. The VHS tape has a fixed video quality, whereas at a fixed bit rate, the MPEG video will have a variable quality, dependent on the entropy of the original content. To avoid visible MPEG artifacts, the DVD encoding rate increases when there is rapid subject movement. During scenes with motion the bit rate increases from a typical value of 3 Mbit/s up to a maximum of 8 Mbit/s. The end result is a constant video quality for the viewer. The bit rate is a trade-off between artifacts and the file size. To achieve the optimum encode within the limit of the maximum file size of the DVD, two passes are used. The first analyzes the material, the second encodes using the parameters from the first. The process can be automatic, or for the best quality transfers the compressionist will manually adjust the encode rates on a scene-by-scene basis.

Similar variable bit rates can be used for multiplexed digital satellite television channels. The technique of statistical multiplexing allows channels to aggregate bit rates up to the total that a transponder can carry. If one channel needs more bits, it can borrow from the other channels. This technique is more successful the more channels there are in a multiplex. Statistical multiplexing can be used to add additional channels to a transponder, or to give better quality output when compared with an equal number of fixed bit rate channels.

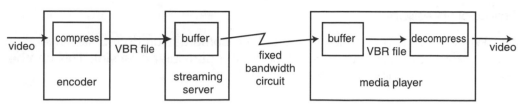

Figure 8.7 Variable bit buffering.

These techniques have been utilized by some proprietary streaming codecs, again to improve video quality within the constraints of the average channel bandwidth. The codecs use the server and player buffers to average the data, so that a continuous bandwidth is transmitted across the IP connection.

Figure 8.8 shows two streams, one constant and one variable, used across the same fixed bandwidth channel. Note that, during the action scenes, the VBR channel has an increased bit rate. The CBR channel will have a lower quality during these scenes.

Again, like DVD encoding, a two-pass encodes give better results with VBR. The first pass analyzes the entire video file to find the best encode rates. The second pass is the true encode and uses the data gathered from the first pass.

Obviously this technique can only be used when encoding a video file, rather than a live stream.

Figure 8.8 Variable and constant bit rates.

Time compression

The Windows Media encoder supports time compression during file encoding. This means that a clip can be adjusted to fit a particular time slot. This can be done without changing the pitch of the audio.

Batch encoding

Anybody who wants to encode more than two or three files will benefit from batch encoding. Most of the proprietary codecs offer some form of automation to process a large number of files. The alternative is to use a product like Anystream, designed for high throughput encoding.

Live encoding

Live encoding is often used for live events. The output of a camera or video switcher can be streamed directly to the Web. The main issue to watch for here is that the processing has to be in real-time. The software codecs have to keep pace with the incoming video signal, this usually means using a dedicated workstation – possibly multi-processor. To improve performance the workstation should not be running any other applications that may consume CPU resources. One typical application is a video preview; buy a video capture card that offers preview facilities without drawing on the main processor resource.

Import from video editing systems

Rather than using videotape as the medium for the final edited version of the program, video can be ingested directly by file transfer from a desktop video editing system. This can be as a DV, AVI or QuickTime file. A video capture card is not obligatory, but if the source file is in DV format it is decompressed to raw YUV before encoding. Hardware decompression on the card will increase the speed of the file encode as software decompression is processor intensive.

Encoding products

There are many products that you can buy for encoding. Both Microsoft and Real supply comprehensive encoding applications for their proprietary architectures. If you are going to be encoding into several different architectures and formats you may want to consider a third-party product. The first step is to decide what output formats you want. If you are coding for material for internal distribution on a company intranet, you may have the luxury of a single codec and a single data rate. If you are running the encoding shop of a web agency you may have to produce streaming files in Real and Windows media, both at six different bit rates (with smaller resolution for the lower rates), an MPEG-4 file for wireless applications, and 1 Mbit/s QuickTime and MPEG-1 files for distribution as progressive download over corporate networks. You may also have to encode in different versions of a codec, as older browsers may not support the latest version of a codec.

So you may well have to produce 20 versions of a video file. To keep down the cost of encoding it pays to use tools that can automate the encoding process. When you are choosing such a tool, you also need to consider what sort of pre-processing that you want. Even the most basic codecs offer simple clean-up facilities – cropping, normalization and levels.

Another consideration is integration with the rest of your workflow. If the streaming media is to be integrated with a rich media presentation, what architectures do you want to use? Do you want to use SMIL or Microsoft's HTML + TIME to synchronize the multimedia files? What platforms do you want to use: Windows, UNIX, Mac?

There are so many options, it may pay to get advice from a consultant. Alternatively you could outsource the encoding.

RealProducer 8.5

RealNetworks provide two versions of RealProducer 8.5. There is the basic version, a free download, and the Plus version with extra facilities. RealProducer Plus is a full set of tools for encoding Real audio and video files. Variable bit rate encoding with two-pass processing give the best encoding quality. The product includes de-interlacing and inverse telecine. For live encoding redundant paths can be set up to the streaming servers. Both versions can run on four platforms: Windows, Linux, Solaris and Mac.

Windows Media 8

Microsoft supplies a complete set of tools for encoding audio and video into Windows Media for streaming. The main tool for general purpose encoding, including live video, is the Windows Media Encoder 7.1. This can encode Windows Media Video 8 for streaming and Windows Media Audio 8 for both streaming and downloading.

More sophisticated encoding can be done with the command line Window Media 8 Encoding utility. This supports batch encoding, and variable bit rate encoding for the best quality encoding of pre-recorded files. You can set up two-pass encoding, which gives the best quality for download and play content.

Discreet Cleaner 5

This product, originally from Terran, has become one of the most popular encoding tools. It is a complete suite of applications to capture, pre-process, encode and publish rich media. It supports the three main architectures: Apple QuickTime, Microsoft Windows Media and RealNetworks RealVideo.

The product has comprehensive processing options for video and audio content. A preview window lets you see the effects of filters. The audio optimization includes dynamic range compression, noise reduction, and high- and low-pass filters. Video processing includes de-interlace and inverse telecine.

The EventStream facility allows you to synchronize other elements – HTML, Flash and GIF images – with the streaming files.

Anystream

The Anystream Agility Workgroup XE provides the solution for the busy encoding station. It can capture a video signal, either live, from tape or from a file, in a single pass. Files could be in AVI or Avid formats. This input signal can then be compressed to a number of different formats, each with a different set of parameters. Before encoding the signal can be pre-processed. The Anystream system includes cropping, de-interlace, reverse telecine and color correction for the video. The audio processing includes dynamic range compression, noise reduction and low-pass filtering. The big advantage of Anystream is that you can encode an MPEG-2 program stream for a DVD, a 320 × 240 QuickTime file, and 160 × 112 Real and Windows media for streaming, all in the same session. The encoding parameters are programmed into profiles, so jobs can be set up very quickly.

The output formats range from broadcast MPEG-2 down to PacketVideo MPEG-4 for wireless applications.

Once material is encoded, the Agility can be programmed to e-mail content producers to alert them that the content is ready for streaming.

Limits on file sizes

You need to watch files sizes when encoding. Some systems have limits that could easily be exceeded with high-resolution or long-duration files. Until recently, it was not possible to encode files that were larger than 2 gigabytes (Gbyte). This is a limitation of the original AVI format as the file could not be larger than a disk partition. The 16-bit file allocation table (FAT) used by DOS limits a partition to 2 Gbyte. FAT32 extends the partition size to 4 Gbyte, but is

Figure 8.9 Anystream Agility Workgroup.

not supported by some codec software. Partitions using other file systems such as the Windows NT File Systems (NTFS) are not subject to the 2 Gbyte limit (the NTFS file system is available on Windows NT® and Windows 2000 operating systems).

A new AVI format (called AVI 2.0, AVI Type II or extended AVI) supports larger file sizes, but not all capture software or hardware supports this, so beware.

Table 8.7 Streaming file sizes

Bit rate	Bytes per second	Gbytes per minute	Gbytes in 1 hour	Duration of 2 Gbyte file (hour:min)	Duration for 4 Gbyte file (hour:min)
30k	3,750	0.00	0.01	148:09	296:18
100k	12,500	0.00	0.05	44:27	88:53
500k	62,500	0.00	0.23	8:53	17:47
CIF, 352 × 240, YUV12, 30 fps	3,801,600	0.23	13.69	0:09	0:18
601 video (166 Mbit/s)	20,750,000	1.25	74.70	0:02	0:02

Table 8.7 gives files sizes for some typical streaming files. Note that a typical CIF resolution file reaches the 2 Gbyte limit in only 9 minutes.

As an example of a current format using 64-bit addressing, the Windows Media file container supports files up to 17 petabytes (10^{15}). This is equivalent to 200 million hours of uncompressed 601 video.

Summary

This chapter has described the processes of capture and compression. A straight encode can be a simple operation, but the need to encode in different formats and resolutions can complicate the processes. Much of this complexity can be hidden from you if you are using tools like Discreet Cleaner or Anystream Agility.

Choosing the parameters for an encoding session is a compromise between the acceptable level of artifacts and the data rate of the bit stream. The choice of codecs is determined by many factors: the architectures that you are using, the video quality required, the processing latency, the CPU resources required and, of course, the cost.

Closely allied to encoding is the pre-processing of the video material. This cleans up the video signal before the compression, removing artifacts like noise. Noise is the enemy of compression as it eats up valuable data bandwidth. So an encoding session is most likely combined with the pre-processing stage.

Video codecs saw much development in the 1990s with video-conferencing, MPEG-1 and -2 blazing the trail in techniques and algorithms. The result has been some very effective systems that can stand alongside legacy consumer distribution formats. Streaming media could never have happened without the compression codecs available today.

9 Audio encoding

Introduction

Audio can appear easy to encode if you compare it with video. It only takes a few seconds to set up a PC to rip your favorite CDs to an MP3 file. The MP3 industry has spawned a large number of encoding applications, many that can be used to process streaming audio.

There are a few pitfalls to avoid, but a modest investment in equipment can produce very good results. The problems encoding audio are most likely to arise if you want to set up live webcasts on location. You lose the control that you had ripping CDs back in the workshop. Also consider that music CDs are carefully crafted, with excellent mixes, controlled dynamics and superb sound quality. If you are recording direct from microphones via an audio console, realizing the optimum audibility is going to need several 'tweaks' to the sound.

Your local AM and FM radio stations use several techniques to ensure the maximum audibility and to increase the apparent loudness. If you want your webcast to sound as good, you will have to follow a similar path. It is easy to overlook or neglect audio sweetening for the Web. After spending hours editing the video until the pictures look great, the audio is processed with a simple preset template. But great pictures with unintelligible audio are not going to convey your message. Learn from the radio guys, they have been in business for a long time.

Much of the audio processing can be done with a PC workstation fitted with a sound card. The external equipment required depends on the job, but it could include an audio editing system, an audio mixing board and a variety of playback decks – CD or DAT. The audio source may well be a camcorder or VTR if it is an audio/video production.

This chapter has four parts: audio formats, capture and encoding, with the final part describing some of the more popular audio file formats. Audio encoding starts with a live audio stream from a microphone or mixing board. The stream is captured as a computer file then processed before encoding as a compressed file using a streaming codec. The result is another stream, but now it is in streaming media format.

The captured file may need some basic adjustments before compression, or it may need a comprehensive clean-up (see Chapter 10 for further details). Audio encoding may be for an audio-only stream, maybe 'Internet radio', or synchronized to a video signal for a multimedia presentation.

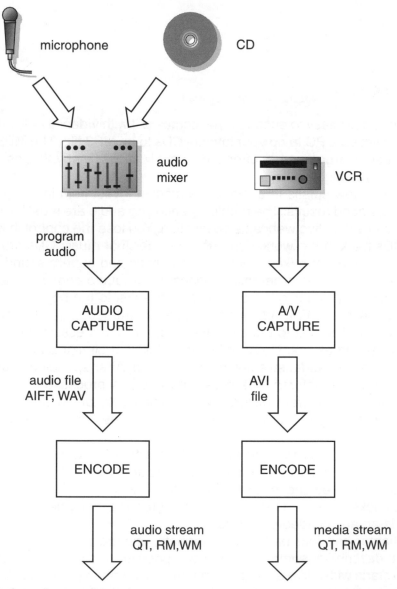

Figure 9.1 Basic audio encoding system.

Audio formats

Even in a digital world there is a vast legacy of analog audio equipment. Analog interconnections are often used between digital equipment. The most familiar audio connector is the RCA or phono connector. This is often used for audio and video interconnections of PCI cards. Although it can be used successfully for occasional use it is not suited to repeated mating and unmating. Many professional encoder cards have 'breakout boxes' with professional connectors.

Figure 9.2 Digi001 from Digidesign.

The Digi001 from Digidesign is a typical example of a professional audio interface for the PC. The 001 card unit fits a PCI slot in the workstation, and the 001 breakout box has all the interconnections plus the level controls.

If you want reliable connections that will not let you down during an important webcast, do not stint on connectors and cables. The best connector for audio is the very rugged XLR. You can drive a truck over one without damage, bar some surface scratches. Local interconnects between equipment can use unbalanced connections, but for the best performance use balanced connectors. These avoid grounding problems that can introduce hum, and also reject noise pickup in the cable.

Some equipment has poor immunity against RF interference. You would not want the chirping of a cell-phone breaking across an important corporate broadcast. The only way to establish the RF immunity is by tests, as manufacturers rarely give any information. Most professional equipment is very good in this respect, but beware if you use consumer equipment.

AES-3

This is the international standard digital audio interface. Its full title is 'Serial Transmission Format for Two-channel Linearly Represented Digital Audio Data'. That means it is stereo and uncompressed. It was a joint development by the Audio Engineering Society (AES) and the European Broadcasting Union. The standard is based on balanced, shielded twisted pair cable, and for transmission distances up to 100 meters. The usual connector is the three-pin XLR. The key parameters are shown in Table 9.1.

Table 9.1 AES parameters

Parameter	
Channels	Two: left and right or A and B
Bit depth	16–24
Coding	Linear 2's complement
Sampling rate	48, 44.1, 32 kHz
Pre-emphasis	On or off
Time reference	Time-of-day time code, hours:minutes:seconds:frames

The AES standard supports three sample rates: 32, 44.1 and 48 kHz. The usual rate that you will encounter is 48 kHz, the standard rate for professional equipment. If you want to incorporate material from CDs unfortunately a different sample rate is used. To mix the two, the CD signal has to be sample rate converted to 48 kHz. This can be done in software or in real-time by hardware. If you use software beware of the processing overhead.

The 48 kHz rate is well above the Nyquist criteria for sampling audio with a frequency response extending to 20 kHz, but allows for variable speed operation without losing the upper register. Most professional audio equipment uses this standard for interconnections. There is another standard that allows the signal

Table 9.2 AES data rates

Sample rate (kHz)	Data rate (MHz)	Upper frequency limit (kHz)	
48	3.072	15	Professional
44.1	2.822	20	Consumer (CD)
32	2.048	20	Broadcast

to be carried by unbalanced coaxial cable with BNC connectors. This means that you can use regular 75 Ω video cable and analog video distribution equipment to interconnect your digital audio system. Note that the AES format represents a continuous real-time stream, and is not a file format.

S/PDIF

Some consumer equipment is fitted with the Sony/Philips Digital Interface (S/PDIF). There are many converters between S/PDIF and AES, and vice versa.

Interconnecting equipment

Unlike analog audio, if you interconnect several pieces of digital audio equipment they must be synchronized to a common clock. This is standard practice with video equipment. To lock audio equipment together a word clock, AES signal or video signal can be used.

Figure 9.3 Digital audio synchronization.

Capture

Audio capture is the process of acquiring the live audio stream and converting it to a computer file format. This process is essentially very simple. The files are composed of a number of chunks. The header chunk describes the file format and the number of samples. The data chunk contains the audio samples as frames,

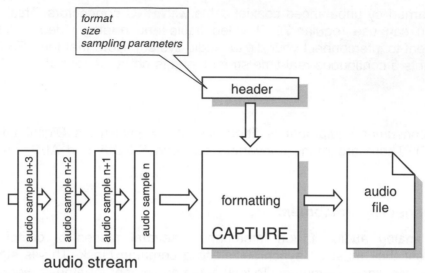

Figure 9.4 File formatting.

much like the AES standard. The file formatter adds a header chunk with all the necessary data to read the audio samples. To encode audio you do not really need to understand the file formats. Usually the configuration consists of just selecting the relevant format from a drop-down box on the user interface.

There are two common file formats: AIFF and WAVE. The AIFF (Audio Interchange File Format) is used by Apple Mac and UNIX platforms. The other, WAVE (Waveform Audio), is a proprietary Microsoft format and is the common format for PC applications. So the decision as to which file format to use is simple.

DC offset

A silent audio input should produce a code value of zero. DC offsets in analog processing can give a zero offset. There are two reasons to avoid an offset. The first is to allow equal positive and negative excursions to maximize the dynamic range. The second is that some codecs do not encode periods of silence to lower the audio data rate. The offset can be nulled out using the audio codec.

Ripping

Ripping is the conversion of audio CDs (recorded to the Red Book standard) into an audio file, usually MP3.

There are many programs that can be used to rip audio from a CD, ranging from freeware through to professional packages with full technical support. Most

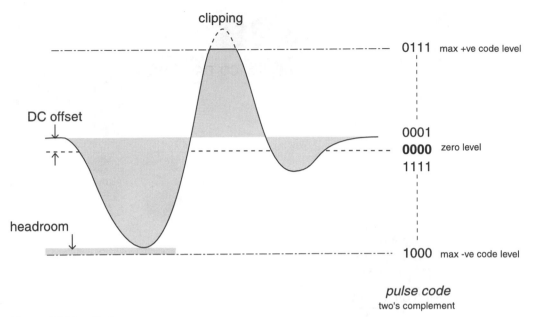

Figure 9.5 DC offset.

will read the CD at faster than real-time. This is a great bonus if you have a large number of CDs to encode.

Parameters to be adjusted when encoding:

- DC offset
- Equalization
- Dynamic range compression and limiting. Noise gates
- Normalization (gain)

Normalization

Once you have removed any offset, then set suitable compressor-limiter parameters; the signal should be normalized. This ensures the optimum code range is employed by the codecs by ensuring that the correct gain is set between the input and the codec. This can be adjusted manually, but most encoders will automatically normalize a file.

The goal of normalization is to ensure that the signal level is at a maximum without clipping. A small amount of headroom is set between the maximum excursions of the waveform and the high and low code levels. Typically the headroom will be set to 0.5 dB.

Normalization is always the last step to take with a file, so you should not hit the button until all the other adjustments have been made.

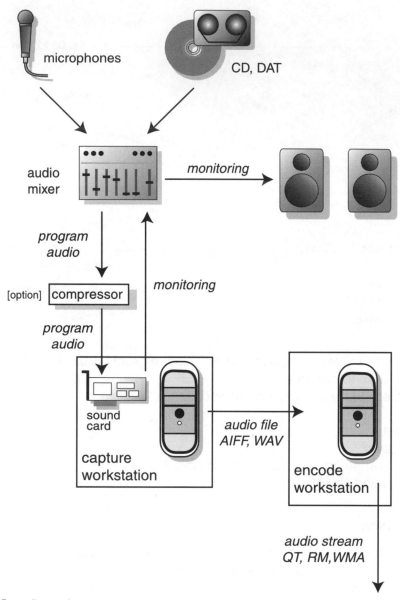

Figure 9.6 Encoding system.

Encoding

Once you have decided which codecs to use, it is straightforward to actually encode the audio files. The proprietary codecs have a simple menu system with a number of choices:

- Target audience, 28k modem, ISDN, DSL or T-1
- Speech or music
- Mono or stereo

Typically a codec template will exist for each combination of the above choices. You can usually change these templates, if the default settings are not to your liking.

QuickTime

Apple QuickTime supports a large number of different audio codecs, but only a few can be used for streaming. For speech the main choice is the Qualcomm PureVoice. This can encode intelligible speech at a data rate of around 7 kbit/s. There is a choice of two rates, full and half. The full rate gives about 9:1 compression ratio, the half rate is about 19:1.

To encode music you have a choice between the ubiquitous Fraunhofer MP3 and QDesign's music codec. The QDesign can encode stereo at rates of around 24 kbit/s but uses considerable processor resources for encoding. MP3 would need around 64 kbit/s for a mono channel.

RealAudio

The Real menu hides the encoder it selects. There is a choice of speech, music and stereo music, and then a selection for the bit rate that you want to use. Real have partnered with Sony to offer the ATRAC codec.

Windows Media

Microsoft has its own Windows Media codec for general audio compression and the Sipro Labs ACELP codec for low bit rate speech coding. Microsoft claims an equivalent audio quality to the MP3 codec at around one-third of the bit rate for Windows Media 8.

File formats

There used to be a large number of audio file formats before the drive to standardization. Sun, SGI, IRCAM, Soundblaster and Amiga all spawned different file formats. Most were developed to support computer-based music creation and editing systems, rather than for general audio sampling. The move now is to limit use to AIFF for Mac and WAV for PC. In professional circles an enhanced version of WAV is also found, the Broadcast WAVE Format or BWF.

Table 9.3 Some popular audio file formats

	Extension	WM player	Real player	QuickTime player
Audio streaming formats				
Moving Picture Experts Group standard 1, layers 1, 2, 3	.mpa	Y	Y	Y
	.mp2	Y	Y	
	.mp3	Y	Y	
	mpg		Y	Y
QDesign				
RealAudio	.ra		Y	
Windows Media Audio	.wma	Y		
Non-streaming (local playback) audio formats				
Audio Interchange File Format	.aif, .aiff	Y	Y	Y
Audio Interchange File Format, compressed	.aifc	Y	Y	Y
Sound File	.snd	Y		Y
UNIX Audio	.au	Y	Y	Y
Waveform Audio	.wav	Y	Y	Y

Most of the formats carry the device parameters and encoding in the header – these are called self-describing. Some older 'raw' formats use fixed parameters that define a single encoding; these are headerless formats. An example of a headerless format is the G.711 μ-law encoding.

The table on page 182 is by no means an exhaustive list of the formats that each player can process.

Audio Interchange File Format (AIFF)

This format was developed in the late 1980s by musical developers. It conforms to the Electronic Arts Standard for Interchange Format Files, EA-IFF 85. The file has a number of chunks. Three are obligatory: the header, common and sound data. A number of optional chunks can be added as required.

The format supports mono, stereo, three-channel, quad, four-channel and six-channel (5.1). The bit depth can range from 1 to 32 bits per sample.

Table 9.4 AIFF chunks

Chunk name	Chunk ID	
Header	FORM	Form type 'AIFF'
Common	COMM	Number of audio channels Number of samples in sound data chunk Bit depth Sample rate
Sound data	SSND	Audio sample frames
Marker	MARK	Pointers to positions in a file Example: start and end
Instrument	INST	Musical instrument/sampler control
Comment	COMT	
Name	NAME	
Author	AUTH	
Copyright	(c)	
Annotation	ANNO	(Use comments instead – COMT)
Audio recording	AESD	Channel status data (pre-emphasis flags)
MIDI	MIDI	MIDI data
Application specific	APPL	

Microsoft Waveform Audio (WAVE)

This Microsoft format is derived from the MS/IBM Resource Interchange File Format (RIFF). There are three data chunks:

- RIFF chunk (file format 'WAVE' and file size)
- Format chunk (mono/stereo, sample rate, bits/sample: 8 or 16)
- Data chunk (audio samples)

The format originally supported 8- and 16-bit mono or stereo. It has been extended to support many more formats, as the audio industry demands multiple channels, greater bit depth and higher sampling rates. These include MPEG-1, A-law, μ-law and Dolby AC3. Encrypted content found in Windows Media digital rights management is specifically supported.

EBU Broadcast Wave Format (BWF)

The European Broadcasting Union has developed a file format to meet the special needs of broadcasters. Their requirement was for seamless interchange of files between equipment from different manufacturers, and for program exchange between broadcasters. It is based on the Microsoft WAVE format. It adds a broadcast audio extension with essential metadata, plus a unique material identifier (UMID) to reference the audio content. The broadcast extension is analogous to the text chunks in the AIFF; the extension carries information about the audio program originator plus a date/time reference. Linear PCM and MPEG-1 formats are supported.

Summary

To many people audio encoding is MP3. It has been a phenomenally successful codec for the distribution of audio files, although it has been tainted by the Napster episode.

   Audio encoding is often thought of as an adjunct to the video encode. We are blasé about digital audio; the CD has been here for a long time. Ripping CDs to MP3 files is widely used and abused. The audio encoding should not be dismissed as trivial. The bandwidths available to Internet radio for streaming are much lower than an MP3 encode.

   The intelligibility of the soundtrack is a prime deciding factor in the acceptance of streaming media by the audience. It is important that live recordings are cleaned up before encoding to remove noise and compress the dynamic range. Music CDs should not require much pre-processing, as the recording will be very clean.

The three main architectures all offer alternative codecs to MP3 that offer higher compression, while still delivering a high quality. These codecs can even be used for audio-only streaming to 28 kbit/s modems. One easy way to almost halve the demands on the codec is to use mono encoding. Do you really need stereo for a talking-head presentation?

When you are encoding audio the requirements can differ widely. If it is for an Internet radio station, or to accompany video on middle to lower bandwidth circuits, you may want to use one codec. To encode music at a high bit rate for download to portable music players a different codec may be chosen. A third codec could be selected for speech.

The audio codecs available today are suited to a wide range of applications, from low bit rate speech for wireless applications up to high-quality surround sound with on-demand streaming movies for the broadband user.

10 Pre-processing

Introduction

The previous two chapters described video and audio encoding. The final quality of a media stream that is a server to the network can usually be improved by judicious pre-processing. Most compression algorithms provide the best results with a very clean source.

To optimize the picture quality for a given stream bandwidth, a number of steps can be taken to clean up the audio and video signals before compression. Perhaps the greatest distortion that impacts upon compression codecs is noise. In general, digital sources are better than analog in this respect. A signal from a DV camera is much quieter than a VHS tape. Unfortunately you will not always have control over the source. It might be archive material – or someone else may have shot it.

There are many other distortions that can impair codec performance; one example is the redundant fields present in material originated on film. To transfer film to video the telecine machine repeats fields to compensate for the different frame rates of film and television.

So, if you want to get the optimum results for your streams, the audio and video signals will benefit from some pre-processing before the encoding stage.

Video processing

Spatial compression can exploit regions of flat texture to reduce the data rate. Any noise in the area of even texture will stop this potential redundancy being removed. Temporal compression removes information that is repeated across many frames. This typically includes the background and other static elements in a shot. Information that changes between frames, for example a moving object, is transmitted as new data each frame.

If the original video material is of a poor quality, it may exhibit excessive noise and other distortions. The compression algorithm will interpret this as information that changes from frame to frame, so will encode as data. For a given bandwidth of streaming, a noisy picture will use up valuable data space that could be used for real picture information.

So to get the best quality encoding for your streaming media, it is important that you use a high-quality master free from visible noise. The lower the final bit rate, the more this holds true.

If the only available videotape of the program to be encoded carries visible artifacts and distortions, then the video signal should be pre-processed prior to compression. Several techniques can be used to clean up the video: these include noise reduction and color correction. Similarly the audio may require treatment, for example compression of dynamic range to suit limited audio playback facilities.

Video levels

Eight-bit television coding does not use the full 256 values for the range from black to white. The analog television waveform has negative excursion below black, used for synchronization. The composite waveform of NTSC and PAL has modulated color information above white level. As it was possible to exceed the black and white bounds, headroom was built in to digital coding. The BT 601 standard defines 220 levels from black to white. Computer video is much simpler, black having the value '0' and white '255'. To reproduce the full gamut of color values on the media player, the video range of 220 steps is re-scaled to 255 steps.

To give the optimum range, the black level may have to be adjusted; this is called lift (analogous to the brightness on a monitor). The gain control then sets the peak white level to the correct value (contrast on a monitor).

Gamma

Gamma adjusts the mid-tones of the image relative to the black and white. There are two default target gammas: Apple Macs use a value of 1.8 and Windows PCs use 2.2. This means that a given encode will appear darker on a Windows PC than a Mac. If you don't know what display the viewer is using, you will have to compromise, like 2.0. It also means that you should preview the resulting encoding on a browser on each operating system to check the settings.

De-interlacing

Television uses an interlaced scan, whereas the PC display uses a progressive scan. The streaming formats are all progressive, so the interlaced video source

Figure 10.1 Video levels.

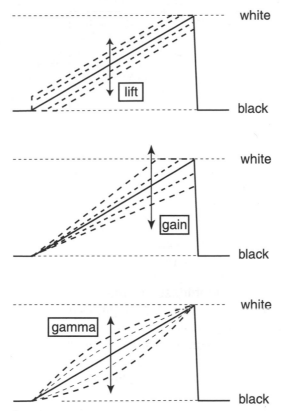

Figure 10.2 Lift, gain and gamma.

has to be converted to a progressive scan. An interlaced frame comprises two fields, one with the even numbered lines and one with the odd (in NTSC fields are captured every 16 ms). To generate the progressive frame the two fields are combined. Unfortunately if there are any moving objects in the scene, the result will be a horizontal streaking or feathering effect.

A de-interlace filter smoothes the two fields to give an average position for the object. Most codecs offer a de-interlace filter to improve rendition of fast-moving objects. The filter is only required for interlaced video.

Cropping

One easy way to cut down the amount of data is to crop the picture. Surely you want to encode the entire frame? Well the edges of the frame rarely contain useful picture information.

The original tube television receivers had non-existent voltage regulation for the EHT supply to the CRT. This meant that the picture size was inversely

Figure 10.3 Safe text area.

proportional to the picture brightness. To mask this change in size the picture was over-scanned, that is the raster was larger than the CRT display area. This also covered up poor scan geometry and drifts with age. So the viewer only saw the center 90 per cent of the picture. Aware of this, the cameraman would insure no important action took place at the edges of the picture. Any graphics are also designed to sit well within the actual display area. This is called the safe text area.

Media players display the entire picture, so the edge – usually lost on a television – is also displayed. This can usually be cropped before encoding with no loss of useful picture information.

Noise reduction

Noise comes in many different forms. It can be random, caused by electrical noise or film grain. Film-originated stock also has scratches and dirt. Tape is not without its problems – videotape suffers from tape dropouts. FM noise causes sparkles on satellite contribution links. If your material has already been compressed then decompressed, there may be visible block errors. Although they are artifacts rather than noise, cross-color and cross-luminance from composite video sources also eat into your bandwidth budget.

All these forms of noise require different treatment, although some noise is difficult to remove satisfactorily without introducing a different set of artifacts. For example, very heavy filtering can produce motion artifacts; this will cause smearing of fast-moving objects. There are three popular types of filters for cleaning up video: the two spatial filters, median and the brick wall, and the temporal recursive filter.

Median filter

These are used for the suppression of impulse noise. This could be tape dropouts or switching glitches. Impulse noise is usually black or white. A threshold detector separates the impulse noise from the picture information. A median filter then replaces the noise pixels with the median (not the mean) of a window of surrounding pixel values. It is also called a sliding window spatial filter. One of the advantages of the median filter is that it does not soften the edges of an object.

Brick-wall filter

A brick-wall filter allows both the horizontal and vertical spatial resolution to be filtered extremely sharply above a pre-set frequency point. This lets you reduce high-frequency detail out of band detail that cannot be resolved in scaled-down pictures at low bit rates. Typically film grain and electrical noise has a high-frequency spectrum, so this filter will remove both. To avoid the softening of edges, the brick-wall filters can apply a boost just inside the pass-band. Note that a brick-wall filter will smear out impulse noise, so the median filter should be applied first.

Recursive filter

Recursive filters are used to remove the random noise from film grain or electrical noise. For typical video material the main change from one frame to the next is noise. A recursive filter averages one frame with the next, reducing the noise but leaving repeated picture information unchanged.

   The only picture information that does not repeat should be moving objects within the scene. A motion detector can be used to separate real moving objects from noise. The recursive filtering can be made adaptive, and can be applied solely to the stationary areas of the picture. This avoids the smearing of moving objects if too much filtering is applied in an attempt to clean up a noisy picture.

Sharpening

Sometimes a picture needs sharpening. This is difficult without adding noise to the edges of objects. Once a picture has become soft, maybe through excessive dubbing, information has been lost forever. If you are careful a picture can be given a bit more snap, but beware of using too much sharpening.

Figure 10.4 Median versus brick-wall filter with impulse noise.

Unsharp masking

Many video processors offer a technique called unsharp masking or USM. This is a traditional technique to sharpen edges in an image that has been borrowed from film compositing. A thin, soft negative is sandwiched with the original positive. When a new exposure is made it sharpens the edges without increasing noise in flat areas. It produces a more pleasing effect than a straight sharpen.

Inverse telecine and 3:2 pull-down

When film is transferred to video (referred to as telecine), to maintain the correct television timebase the film shot at 24 frames per second has to be processed to 30 frames per second. Normally each frame is scanned twice, giving two interlaced fields. In the case of film this would give a field rate of 48, rather than the 60 of video.

To correct the field rate, alternate frames are scanned three times, that is the first and third fields are duplicated. This gives a 3:2:3:2 sequence to the scanning so that 24 frames become 60 fields, the normal rate for video.

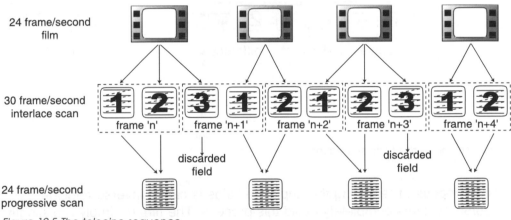

Figure 10.5 The telecine sequence.

Note that a video frame can be made up from fields from two different film frames.

If this video signal is to be efficiently encoded, the duplication of one field every five is redundant information that could be removed. This task is not as simple as it appears – the repeated field carries no label to indicate the duplication. The duplicate field has to be detected in the presence of analog noise (from the telecine image sensor). This noise makes the duplicated fields slightly different.

The second problem is that if video transfer of the film is edited, the 3:2:3:2 sequence can be disrupted. So that means that once a duplicate field is detected, the next duplicate cannot be assumed by simply counting fields.

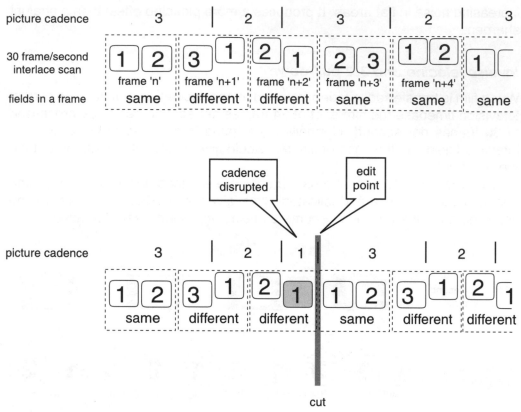

Figure 10.6 Editing the telecine cadence.

This process of removing the duplicate fields is called inverse telecine.

625/50 systems completely avoid this process. The film is simply run slightly fast, at 25 frames per second, and scanned directly to 50 fields in a normal interlace sequence. The 4 per cent increase in speed is ignored.

Audio

Most audio content will need some pre-processing before the streaming codec. This will include equalization, dynamic range compression, peak limiting and noise reduction.

Equalization

Often called EQ, equalization is seen everywhere from car audio to the recording studio. Equalization allows you to adjust the frequency response of the audio chain. The simplest equalizers are bass and treble controls.

Equalizers can be used to compensate for deficiencies in the original recording, and to allow for limited audio replay facilities of the average PC.

Bandpass filters

These give comprehensive control over frequency response with a number of bandpass filters, often called graphic EQ from the graphic layout of the controls.

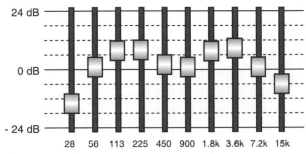

Figure 10.7 Graphic equalizer.

Parametric equalizers

The most flexible filters allow the bandwidth and center frequency of each filter to be adjusted. They are more used in the recording studio, where there is the luxury of more time than you are likely to have for a webcast. Always apply equalization with care; too much will not enhance the final result. For streaming typical adjustments could be as follows:

- Low-pass filter to remove high-frequency hiss
- High-pass filter to remove hum and air conditioning rumble
- Mid-frequency mild boost to give presence to speech

You may find problems with sibilance from some speakers. It can sometimes be reduced with a microphone shield; otherwise, a combination of EQ and multi-band compression can assist.

Dynamic range

Modern home audio systems can reproduce a very large dynamic range. DVD-A and SACD both offer 24-bit coding; home theater systems also offer a wide dynamic range. In contrast, streaming audio is often listened to with the limited facilities built into laptop PCs. A loudspeaker, maybe 1 inch in diameter, driven

Figure 10.8 Voice equalization.

with a modest power amplifier, cannot hope to reproduce a wide dynamic range. So, much like AM radio, intelligibility is improved if the dynamic range is compressed. Two processes are employed: compression and peak limiting. The compression ensures that the average loudness of the signal is relatively constant. This requires more sophisticated processing than a simple automatic gain control.

The more complex dynamics processors split the audio into bands, typically five. This band splitting was developed for the original AM radio processors, to give the most natural sound with high levels of dynamic range compression. By using phase-linear filters for the band splitters, the final mix will be free of non-linear group delay.

If you are going to host corporate webcasts, usually the executives will address an audience from a podium. As the speaker moves about the audio levels will change. During pauses in the presentation you do not want to amplify the background noise.

Peak limiting

Simple clipping generates unpleasant audible artifacts. For the best results you should use a look-ahead peak limiter. They reduce the gain fractionally before a peak, so gracefully reducing peak levels without the apparent distortion that you would get with straight waveform clipping. The amount of peak limiting you use depends upon the program content. If you want to retain musical transients to give punch to the audio the limiter should be used with caution.

Noise reduction

A noise gate reduces gain radically below a pre-set threshold. One application that can be very useful is to stop the dynamic range compressor from sucking up noise during pauses in a presentation. It should not be used if the background is contributing to the audio track; an example would be background music. If the noise gate were to cut the music in and out this would be irritating to the listener. The only way to set the threshold for the noise gate is to listen to the effect. The threshold can be gradually increased until the background noise cuts out. If there is unacceptable breathing of the background, it can be backed off until an acceptable result is achieved. The noise gate usually has temporal adjustments, so that there is a delay before it cuts in and out. If the gate is maladjusted, it can lead to clipping of the presenter's speech.

A noise gate offers a great advantage if your compression codec has silence detection. During periods of silence the compressor effectively shuts down. This means that the data rate can be reduced by a useful amount. Codecs that offer this feature include CELP and the Qualcomm PureVoice.

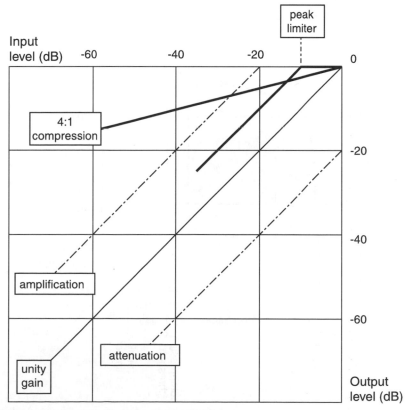

Figure 10.9 Compressor–limiter transfer characteristics.

The compression ratio alters the slope of the input/output transfer characteristic. The compressor will also have a gain control, as a compressed signal will sound louder than the uncompressed. The limiter prevents the output level exceeding a pre-set threshold.

Attack and release times

The dynamic range controls do not change gain instantaneously, that would just modulate the sound with its own level. Instead there is a delay before the control parameter is changed – the attack time – then another delay as the applied parameter is restored – the release time. The attack time is customarily very short, just a few milliseconds. It is long enough for brief transients; the limiter takes care of them. The release time is much longer, up to several seconds. This prevents the modulation effects that you would get with a very short release time.

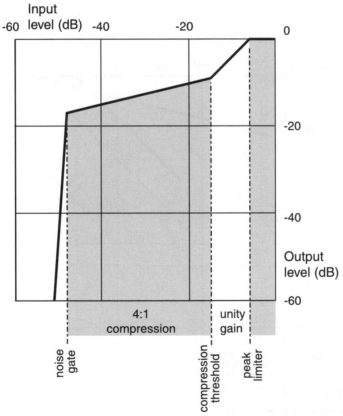

Figure 10.10 Compressor–limiter composite characteristics.

Usually all these controls are used together. The peak limiter is set to remove transients, then louder sounds are passed at unity gain. Below a set threshold, the quieter sounds are compressed to improve intelligibility. Everything below a lower threshold is treated as noise and gated out. This may seem like a lot of adjustment, but once you arrive at some good settings they can be stored for reuse with similar content.

Processing applications

Typical streaming media encoder applications include many facilities to pre-process audio. Some are implemented in software, some in hardware. The hardware products are best if you want real-time processing for live web-casts. A good example of a comprehensive encoding package is Discreet's Cleaner 5.1.

Cleaner 5

Cleaner 5 is not just a clean-up tool. It has all the facilities to take raw content and publish to the streaming servers. It processes both the video and audio. Cleaner 5 can perform the basic de-interlace and reverse telecine on the video. The signal levels and color can be adjusted and the noise cleaned up. The adaptive noise reducer uses spatio-temporal processing to clean up flat areas of color without degrading the edges of objects.

Cleaner 5 also has powerful audio processing capabilities. The product has a wide range of filters, including high- and low-pass filters with adjustable turnover frequencies. A useful filter is the deep notch filter that can be set to remove power line hum – which is often a problem at live events. This offers the facility to also notch out harmonics of the power frequency (120, 180 for 60 Hz power or 100, 150 for 50 Hz). A general noise removal filter removes unwanted background noise. If you want to change the sampling rate of the audio it can be used to re-sample an input file.

Once a file is processed it can then be encoded on the same platform.

Processing hardware

Pre-processing is not limited to software applications. Some manufacturers have hardware developed specifically to clean up video and audio. The dedicated hardware products process in real-time. Companies like Orban have been making high-performance compressors for the radio business for many years; more recently, Omnia has introduced similar product lines. If you want the best sound from a webcast you could consider a demo of the Optimod DAB6200 and the Omnia-3net. Both are units designed especially for the webcaster.

Pinnacle have a plug-in module (HiQ) for their StreamFactory encoder that gives a comprehensive set of pre-processing facilities. The module has hardware processing, leaving the main processor free for the compression codec.

Monitoring

It is vital that you monitor the results of any audio processing before the file is encoded. Although big monitor speakers will make the audio sound impressive, it is worth listening on some of the small speakers often used with desktop workstations – this is what your audience is probably using.

Summary

Noise is a killer for codecs. So before encoding, it makes sense to try and clean up as much of the noise as possible. That way you can ensure that you have the optimal encoding for a given stream bandwidth. This noise reduction applies equally to both video and audio.

The pre-processing products have a veritable toolbox of noise filters to deal with the different types of noise that you will encounter with different sources. The sparkle from a satellite link will need a different treatment from the tape noise from an analog VCR.

Video requires additional processing to remove some of the characteristics of the television system. This includes interlace scanning and the 3:2 cadence of content originally shot on film then transferred to video by a telecine. To cut down unnecessary data, the outside edge of a television picture can usually be cropped without losing relevant content. Television frame composition allows for over-scanning in the television receiver, not a problem with PCs. Some color correction may also be used; the rendering of color is different from the composite television systems.

The audio will usually benefit from dynamic range compression as well as noise reduction. The dynamics compression will make speech much easier to understand when it is played back on the small speaker in a PC. The processors work in three areas: peaks are limited to avoid clipping, the general audio is compressed by an AGC and then noise below a threshold is suppressed.

Last of all, do not forget to watch and listen to the stream after the selected treatments. It is the best way to judge the improvements that pre-processing can make to your streams.

11 Stream serving

Introduction

So you have successfully encoded your multimedia content. Now what? Much like a web page, the file is uploaded to the delivery server. That is where things diverge. A streaming server has to manage the delivery rate of the stream to give real-time playback. A conventional web server can only download the media file. Next a streaming server supports interactive VCR-like control of the media clip.

When a browser requests a web page, the files are delivered as fast as the network connection allows. TCP manages an error-free transmission by retransmitting lost packets, but the download time depends upon the intervening bandwidth available. TCP starts at a low rate then ramps up to the maximum that can be achieved. An accurate delivery is ensured, but timely delivery cannot be guaranteed. Streaming media has opposite requirements: the delivery must be in real-time, but reasonable levels of transmission errors can be accepted.

Streaming servers are proprietary to the architecture. The system architecture can vary from a single machine serving a small corporate training site, to large distributed server farms, capable of serving hundreds of thousands of streams for live events like breaking news footage, fashion shows and rock concerts.

Streaming can be used to stream live or pre-recorded content as a webcast – this is the television model. This can be used for web channels or live events. Alternatively it can be pre-recorded content that is streamed on-demand. This interactive experience is akin to using a CD-ROM or a web browser.

A webcast can be a mix of live and pre-recorded content. With live events the server is acting as a distribution point, just echoing the stream onto the viewers. For the pre-recorded content the server has two functions. The first is to recall the content from the local disk storage arrays and the second is to control the stream delivery rate.

In the case of interactive content the client or player is requesting the files from the server. With the simulated-live webcast, the server runs a playlist which streams files at the scheduled time to the player.

Table 11.1 Web server versus streaming server

	Web server	*Streaming server*
Advantages	Part of existing infrastructure No additional expertise or training for IT staff	Optimized media delivery Dynamic stream control Interactive media control Multicast support Improved server hardware utilization Supports live webcasting
Disadvantages	None of the streaming server advantages Only supports progressive download	Additional equipment required

Figure 11.1 Webcasting and on-demand.

Streaming

What is a streaming server? The usual server used for the delivery of multimedia content is the web server. Web servers use HTTP to deliver HTML pages and their associated image files.

TCP/IP is used as the transport layer over the Internet. The files are downloaded to the web browser cache as fast as the system allows. TCP incorporates flow control to manage the download rate. There is no pre-determined rate for delivery. TCP will increase the data rate until network packet loss indicates that the network is congested. At this point the rate backs off. Another constraint is the receive buffer. TCP uses a sliding window of data in transit. The receiver processes packets as they arrive. If data arrives too fast, the receive buffer will overflow. The receiver sends messages to the transmitter to slow down, to stop the buffer from filling.

Suppose that you want to stream a stream encoded at 40 kbit/s. The TCP transmissions could start at 10 kbit/s. The transmitter then ramps up to 100 kbit/s, where network congestion sets the upper limit. Other users come on to the network, and the transmission throttles back to 30 kbit/s. At no time has the data rate matched the data rate at which the stream was encoded.

Now consider if this clip lasts for 30 seconds, the complete file size is 150 Kbytes. This is downloaded to the browser cache. Now suppose we move up to a 20-minute presentation encoded at 300 kbit/s. Now the file size is 45 Mbytes, very large for the cache.

When you stream content in real-time, the media packets are processed by the player as they arrive. There is no local caching, so the local storage issues are solved. That still leaves the rate control problem. If the stream is encoded at 40 kbit/s it has to be delivered at that rate. One of the functions of transport layer protocol is to regulate the stream rate. But what happens in the example where the network is congested and the best rate is 30 kbit/s? The player runs out of data and stops, one of the main complaints about streaming.

There are ways around this, but the first is to encode at a rate below that which will suit the worst-case network conditions. That may be hard to predict, so there are more sophisticated ways; the usual is to encode at several rates, then automatically select the optimum rate for the propagation conditions. This switching between different rate files is another task for the server.

One of the great attractions of streaming is the interactivity. The user can navigate the clip with VCR controls. The server has to locate and serve the correct portions of the clip.

From these examples it can be seen that the streaming server has several additional functions over a standard web server:

- Real-time flow control
- Intelligent stream switching
- Interactive clip navigation

HTTP does not support any of this new functionality, so new protocols were developed for streaming media. Under the auspices of the IETF several new protocols were developed for multimedia real-time file exchange: RTSP, RTP and RTCP. There are also a number of proprietary protocols using similar principles. Windows Media uses Microsoft Media Server (MMS) for the delivery framework; the stream is in Advanced Streaming Format (ASF).

Real-Time Streaming Protocol (RTSP) is the framework that can be used for the interactive VCR-like control of the playback (Play, Pause, etc.). It is also used to retrieve the relevant media file from the disk storage array. RTSP can also be used to announce the availability of additional media streams in, for example, a live webcast. Real-Time Protocol (RTP) is used for the media data packets. The Real-Time Control Protocol (RTCP) provides feedback from the player to indicate the quality of the stream. It can report packet loss and out-of-order packets. The server can then react to congested network conditions by lowering the video frame rate or gear-shifting to a file encoded at lower bit rate. Ideally the real-time media stream is delivered by UDP over IP. The control protocols use TCP/IP for the bidirectional client–server connection.

Figure 11.2 The streaming protocol stack.

Streaming file formats

To stream media files in real-time, they must be encoded into one of the streaming formats. These formats have timing control information that can be used by the server to manage the flow rate. If the client is using interactive control, the file index aids the navigation.

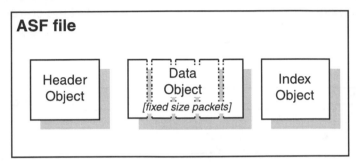

Figure 11.3 Typical streaming file format.

The main formats are the Microsoft advanced streaming format (.wmv and .wma extensions), RealNetworks (.rm and .ra) and QuickTime hinted movies (.mov extension).

Web server and streaming server

If you already have a web site with web server capacity, and you only stream occasionally, it is possible to use that web server to deliver streaming files. There will be no control of the stream delivery rate. It may arrive in large bursts if the network bandwidth is available. The client PC will have to cache the large media files until the material is played out. The web server will use HTTP over TCP/IP.

Hint tracks

The MPEG-4 team has adopted the QuickTime concept of hints tracks for control of the stream delivery. A streaming file is called a movie. The movie file container contains tracks. A track could be video or audio or other clip data. The track consists of control information that references the media data (or objects) that constitute the track. This means that several different movie files could reference the same video media object. This can be very useful for rich media presentations. One video file can be re-purposed into several different presentations – maybe multiple languages or a number of levels of detail (introduction, overview and in-depth). A movie is not the video and audio media files; it is the metadata or instructions for a specific presentation of the media data.

A streamable movie has a hint track in addition to the video and audio (MPEG-4 files are not necessarily streaming media). The hint track gives the server software application pointers to the RTP information to serve the relevant media chunks. This information allows the server to deliver the correct video material in the sequence stipulated in the track file, and at the correct rate for the player display.

Figure 11.4 Typical streaming file format.

Adapting to network congestion

Both RealNetworks and Windows Media offer a way of changing the bit rate of a stream as network congestion varies. To get the best viewing experience we want to stream at the highest rate possible. But if the network slows down, rather than attempting to continue with a high bit rate it makes sense to throttle back the bit rate. If the congestion eases then the bit rate can revert to a higher level. That way the viewer is not subject to stalling streams, just a graceful degradation in quality. These technologies only work with unicasting.

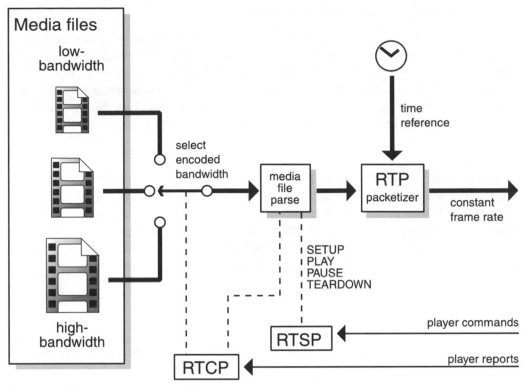

Figure 11.5 Streaming control.

The Real-Time Protocol maintains the correct delivery rate over UDP/IP. The RTSP framework supports the client interaction with the stream, the VCR-like controls: Play, Pause, etc. The streaming server application can use RTCP reports from the player to measure network congestion and switch stream rates for multiple bit rate media files. The player can report lost and delayed packets, and the reception of out-of-sequence packets.

RealNetworks SureStream

SureStream allows different encoding rates to be combined into a single media file. The streaming server will choose the appropriate data rate for the prevailing conditions by negotiating with the player. The lowest rate, called a duress stream, is a backstop, and will be streamed if congestion is very bad. When you are calculating the server disk space, a SureStream file takes the space of the sum of all the components. As only the RealServer can extract the correct component, a web server will serve the file in its entirety, including all the different rates.

Windows Media multiple bit rate video

This is a similar feature, allowing several different bit rate encodes to be associated in a single file. The streaming server will then stream the best rate for the current network conditions. Windows Media Encoder comes with predefined multiple bit rate profile, but the profiles can also be customized to suit your special requirements. If you want to multicast a file that has been coded at multiple bit rates, only the highest rate will be transmitted.

Drawbacks

If you want to serve at different rates then better results can be obtained by encoding a small picture, at low frame rates for low bit rate streams, and a larger picture for stream at higher rates. So you may want a 480 × 360 pixel frame at 30 fps for a 1 Mbits/s stream and 160 × 120 at 6 fps for an ISDN link. So these automatic rate-shifters have their uses, but are not a complete answer. The big advantage is that the process of changing bit rate is invisible to the user.

QuickTime and alternate movies

This is a less sophisticated method of offering different bit rates. You can encode a movie as several separate movies encoded at different bit rates, and maybe with different language audio tracks. The player follows a pointer to the master movie. This then references the alternate movies. The correct file for the bandwidth available is served to the player.

MPEG-4 and scalable streams

The MPEG team has proposed a different way to cope with variable network bandwidth. A basic low-resolution stream is transmitted. Additional helper streams can carry more detail. If the bandwidth is available then these extra streams allow a better quality picture to be assembled by the player.

Loading content

Whether you are using a managed service or doing your own serving, the first step is to deliver your content to the streaming servers. The encoding probably takes place near to the video editing facility or at the venue for a live webcast. The servers have to be located close to an Internet backbone, unless you are only streaming over a local area. So in all probability the encoder and server are geographically separated. The simplest way to deliver the content is via a file transfer, using FTP. Some encoding systems have the ability to automatically transfer a file immediately after the encoding has finished.

Figure 11.6 Encoder connections.

Live streaming

The file can, of course, be sent on a CD-ROM. If the content is a live broadcast, then neither of these methods is suitable – it has to be streamed. The methods of doing this are covered in the chapter on live webcasts.

The media encoder typically connects to the server using TCP for a bidirectional control link and a unidirectional media stream, using UDP. It is very important that the circuit used for this connection has plenty of capacity. Any packet loss will be visible by all receivers of the webcast.

Announcing the content

The player usually locates streaming media by a hyperlink embedded in a web page. This link contains not only the URL for the content, but also the instruction to start the media player.

Web links

The usual way to announce streaming media files is by a hyperlink in a web page. The link points to a small file on the web server. Windows Media calls this the stream redirector or ASX. Real use the RealAudio Metafile or Ram file. Once the browser receives this file, using the MIME type, the metafile is passed to a streaming plug-in. The metafile has the full address and filename for the streaming content. The media player than transmits a request to the specified streaming server for the media file. This may use MMS or RTSP for communication rather than the HTTP used with the web server. If all goes well the correct clip is streamed to the player – success.

The metafiles can list several files to be played in sequence.

SMIL

If you are streaming rich media, then a number of different clips and images have to be synchronized for correct playback at the client. One way to do this is

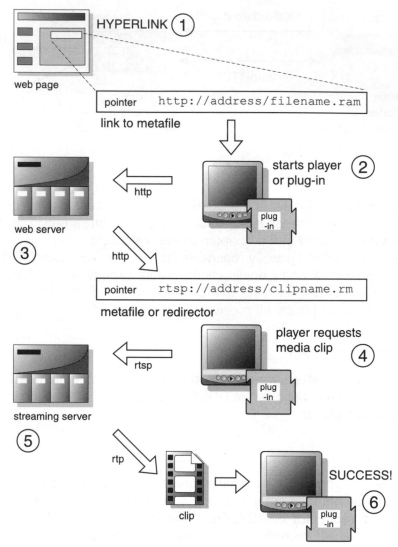

Figure 11.7 Linking to streaming media.

to use the Synchronized Multimedia Integration Language (SMIL) to write a control file.

SMIL is supported by the Real and QuickTime architectures.

HTML and TIME

This is the Microsoft alternative to SMIL. Timed Interactive Multimedia Extensions (TIME) allow you to add media synchronization information to HTML pages. It uses elements from the XML-based markup language to allow streaming video to be synchronized to images and text. Using HTML and TIME together, you can create rich media presentations within a web page. The TIME support was introduced with Internet Explorer 5.

Webcasting

Webcasting can be live, pre-recorded or a mix of both. A webcast at its simplest can be just a single clip. If you want to play out a sequence of clips you can set

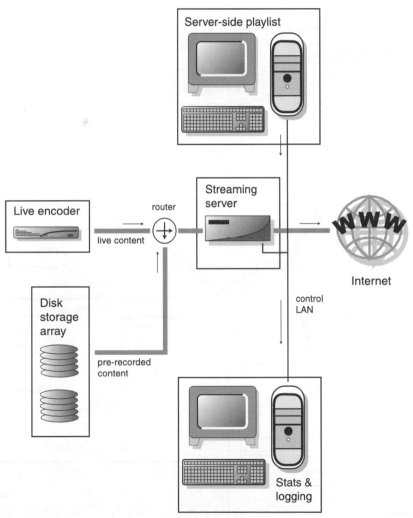

Figure 11.8 Live and simulated live webcasting.

up a playlist. Even if you are streaming a presentation, you may want an introductory promotional film, and possibly some follow-up material after the main presentation. The playlist controls the server to play the relevant clips at the specified time. A playlist can be scripted but there are products designed to run schedules of streaming clips. A typical example is the Lariat StationManager.

Splitting and relays

A streaming server can handle several hundred simultaneous clients. The only real way to establish how many clients, would be by conducting load tests.

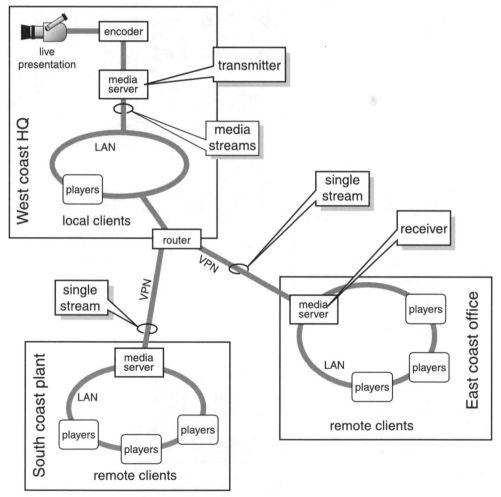

Figure 11.9 Splitting a live stream at remote sites.

To serve to a large number of clients, extra servers have to be used. For on-demand serving, they can be added in parallel, but for live streams a different architecture is used to save network resources. A relay server splits the live streams downstream, so what starts as a single live stream from the encoder fans out like the branches of a tree. Take the example of a CEO's webcast from the headquarters on the west coast to two other remote sites on the south and east coasts.

If only a few clients were watching at the remote sites, the streams could be delivered directly from the server at headquarters. But each client will be using bandwidth on the trunk networks, all carrying the same data. If a large number of clients at each site are watching the webcast, the server will be unable to handle the load. The alternative is to use local servers at the remote sites to receive a single stream, and then locally distribute it. This saves bandwidth on the long-distance circuits and reduces the load on the originating server.

You may be thinking that this is a really important broadcast, what happens if the link goes down? Companies like RealNetworks have come up with a number of solutions.

RealServer 8 includes the facility to set up backup links. You set up redundant transmitters, usually two servers in parallel. If the link from the designated transmitter breaks, the receiving server will automatically fall back to the next available transmitting server. The clients will see the webcast has stopped; if they refresh the link, the stream will continue using the backup path.

Multicasting

If you are webcasting live to a large audience, a regular unicast establishes a separate network connection to each client. This uses considerable network resources, even though each client is watching exactly the same material. Multicasting offers a solution by serving a single stream. This is then routed to all the clients. So the network routers are doing the distribution rather than the streaming servers.

The drawback with multicasting is that you need to have control over the routers. First they have to be multicast enabled, which is not necessarily the case. There are different algorithms for setting up multicast routes: dense and sparse. If you are streaming over a corporate network within a single domain, multicasting has much to offer. It is when you want to multicast to the public Internet that problems can arise. The network of peer-to-peer connections that link a server to a client may not be multicast enabled, or the routers may not be set up to multicast across domains. In 2001 much work was being undertaken to try and overcome some of the obstacles to multicast over the Internet.

If you are multicasting you cannot use automatic rate changing. The server transmits a single stream, and is not aware of the clients, so cannot negotiate to serve at a certain rate. To get around this you may have to transmit three or four different rate streams from different server ports. The player connects to an appropriate port for the bandwidth available at their local end.

Multicast network

If you are setting up a multicast to several sites, and want to use Virtual Private Networks (VPN) for the intermediate connections across the corporate WAN, note that IPSec does not support multicasting. The way around this is to unicast to a splitter server at the remote site, then multicast locally. You will need to make sure that clients can only see one multicast server. Since the same IP address is used for the multicast, the client could potentially receive several duplicate packets. The player will not decode the stream correctly in these circumstances.

Announcing a multicast is different from retrieving on-demand content. With on-demand, the browser requests the media file. When the file is retrieved the header carries information necessary for the player configuration. Once you join a multicast, there is no header. Instead, a small message file gives the browser/ player the necessary information (like the port number to use). This message can use Session Description Protocol (SDP – RFC.2327) or Microsoft uses the media station NSC file. The media station is analogous to a television station, so the station represents the channel, and not the media streamed (programs transmitted) over the channel. The NSC configuration file will set up the player correctly to receive a multicast. The ASX file that announces a multicast, points the player to the NSC file.

RealNetworks support a form of multicasting with a control back-channel. This allows full statistics to be gathered from the clients, but has the advantage of multicasting the media data. It is best suited to small audiences; a very large multicast would have problems with the server capacity required to handle the unicast control traffic.

On-demand serving

On-demand serving is more like running a web server. The viewers choose their own content, and then a fast disk storage array delivers the content, as required, to the streaming servers. Each client has a unicast connection with the server, so the more viewers, the higher will be the server loading. A popular site will use many servers in parallel. The Internet traffic loading can be balanced across all the servers.

The server hardware does not need many facilities: a fast CPU, plenty of RAM and at least two network-interface cards (NICs). If the server has very high loadings, or there are network problems, you will need access by a separate

Figure 11.10 On-demand server farm.

network port for control messages, so always install at least two NICs. The system will be more reliable if the load is spread over several small servers, rather than one large multiple processor server. This also gives redundancy against hardware failure.

Inserting advertisements

If you a running a commercial site you will want to add advertisements to the content. They can be the same banner ads used on web pages. The alternative is to insert clips into the stream just like a regular television spot. This is called interstitial advertising.

Standard web banners are 468 × 60 pixels. For insertion in streaming video, a smaller size may be required. If you are streaming QCIF or CIF the banner may have to be one-quarter the size to fit in the video window.

The simplest way to place video advertising around an on-demand clip is to top-and-tail the content with pre-roll (gateway) and post-roll ads (bumper) using an SMIL file (Synchronized Multimedia Integration Language) to play the clips serially. The sequence command is used to place ads before and after clips. With the Real player, if the parallel command is also used, the viewer cannot manually step through the playlist to jump over the ads. The parallel command also ensures that the second clip is pre-rolled to avoid any glitches when

Figure 11.11 RealServer ad serving.

changing clips. RealServer can use a proprietary ad tag in the SMIL file (<RealAdInsert/>) to automatically insert the URL to the advertisement clip. Since the advertisements may be changing hour to hour, this avoids the necessity to keep updating the SMIL file.

Windows Media use active server pages to generate dynamic playlists to the same end of dynamically assigned URLs to advertisements.

In both cases the ad servers are linked to the streaming servers to generate the correct URLs. The ad servers often use solicited cookies to track users and ensure that targeted advertisements are used where possible. This means that a webcast, although streamed to a wide geographic area, can carry advertising that is local or relevant to the viewer.

Playlists

If you are streaming regular webcasts you will need a means of playing out clips to a prepared schedule. Just like a television station, clips can be put in playlists

Figure 11.12 Lariat StationManager channel schedule. © Lariat Software.

and streamed on cue. This means that corporate presentations and distance learning can be scheduled at fixed times. The viewer tunes in at the appropriate time to catch the required stream.

You may want to publicize the schedule just like a TV guide. You can hand code playlist for the streaming server, but it is much easier to use an application designed for streaming publishing.

Lariat StationManager

This application makes it easy to schedule program clips into webcast. The StationManager can run a number of separate channels, each channel representing a single stream. A channel can be continuous, running 24 hours a day, or just for set periods of an hour or so. The clips can be live webcasts or played out from pre-encoded files. So, for example, a live corporate presentation could be preceded by a pre-recorded introduction. After the live slot, you could schedule to repeat an archived recording of the live presentation.

The software looks much like an appointments diary. You simply select a time slot, and then drop in the relevant file.

The StationManager keeps a database of the available program clips on the content servers. Each entry gives program details like the running time and file formats. A clip can then be selected and dropped into the schedule. Upcoming schedules of your webcasts can be placed into a page on the company web site if you want to publicize the schedules in advance.

Logging and statistics

So you have set up a stream-serving infrastructure. But what is the return on the investment? With any system it is vital to monitor the traffic to the clients. This is partly to see who is watching what, and partly to find out the utilization of the servers and network elements. You will want to know what the audience is for clips, and perhaps more important how many are watching the entire clips and how many watch only the first 10 seconds.

The monitoring can be performed at the client or at the server. The television model is to monitor activity at the receiver – as with the Nielson reporting. With streaming media, there is a back-channel from the player so server-side reporting can also be used.

Several companies have products that can collect server logs, and then process the data into reports. These include Lariat, Accrue Software and WebTrends. MeasureCast have specialized in audience measurement. They use a combination of comprehensive server logging, and complement this with client side statistics gathered from selected streaming media users. The client side statistics can give more demographic information than the raw server data. The two are combined to provide comprehensive statistics for the webcasters.

Figure 11.13 Lariat StationManager.

The basic information that the servers log can include information about the client. This can be client IP address, connection protocol (RTSP, HTTP), player version, operating system and version, language setting, and the CPU speed.

The logs also collect session information. This includes the time the request was logged and how long the stream was watched. You can see from the reports if viewers watched all of a clip, or dropped out in the middle. It is also possible to see when user interactions were taken. So if an interactive presentation is being viewed, you can log if the viewer has selected a hotspot link. It is possible to turn off this reporting on the players for users concerned about privacy.

More detailed information can also be collected about the transmission quality packet loss, number of resends and how many packets arrived out of order, early or late.

This information for a single client is collated with other client access logs into viewing statistics for content producers and service quality for network administrators. These are some of the statistics that can be collected:

- Number of concurrent streams
- Number of hits
- Time spent viewing content
- Amount of content delivered
- Number of unique viewers

Logging software will collect information from unicasts, but if you are multicasting the server will not be aware of the clients (unless you are using RealNetworks back-channel multicasting). The only way you can identify clients is when they first log in to request the stream redirector (ASX or RAM file) from a web server.

Figure 11.14 Lariat MediaReports.

One very useful statistic is the type of player being used and the stream bit rates. This information can be used to justify (or otherwise) the number of formats to encode. You may be able to drop one of the architectures because it has a very small audience. That is going to save you the costs of both the encoding and serving.

A typical example of a reporting package is Lariat MediaReports 2.5. Logs from all the different servers are collected and collated at a central point. The results are stored in a database, from where any number of reports can be generated for the interested parties.

Proprietary server architectures

Windows Media Services 4.1

Microsoft's streaming server is bundled with Windows 2000 server as Windows Media Services. Windows Media Server supports several different delivery mechanisms. This is so that the streams can be delivered through corporate firewalls.

MMS and UDP

This is the streaming mode of choice. This gives full support for real-time delivery and client interactivity. Some network administrators set up the firewall to block UDP traffic, so this protocol cannot always be used.

MMS and TCP

This is the next choice. This is where the streams have to pass through a TCP port.

HTTP and TCP

This is an alternative for firewalls that will allow regular HTTP web traffic. The Windows Media Services still provides controls like fast forward, reverse, etc. The stream will suffer from the TCP retransmissions and rate adaptation.

The server will attempt to connect by each protocol in turn until a satisfactory dialog is established. Windows Media Services also support multicasting over IP.

RealServer

RealNetworks streaming server can be deployed on Windows and UNIX platforms. The server uses similar delivery mechanisms as Windows Media, to enable delivery through firewalls.

RTSP and TCP

This is used for the control connection. It gives full client–server interactivity.

RTP and UDP

This is the optimum choice for streaming the media content.

RTP and TCP

This is second choice for streaming the media content if the firewall blocks UDP data.

HTTP and TCP

This can be used for progressive downloads if no other delivery is possible. The media file is wrapped with the HTTP format, a process called 'HTTP cloaking'.

RealServer supports SMIL for rich media presentations.

Apple QuickTime

QuickTime started as a CD-ROM format, and was developed for progressive downloads. QuickTime 4 supports true real-time streaming. Apple adopted the RTP for streaming over UDP. If this is blocked by corporate firewalls the alternative is progressive download over HTTP.

Server deployment

Video server hardware

The streaming server has to read the media files from disk, packetize it and deliver at the correct rate to give real-time playback. These tasks then have to be performed for multiple concurrent streams. The real-time requirement contrasts with the asynchronous operation in a regular office server application. In the latter case, at times of peak resource demand, file delivery is delayed. With a video stream this would result in stalling playback.

As the performance of server components improves with time, it is becoming easier to meet the demands of streaming.

The areas to focus upon include:

- Disk drive performance
- Network card performance. It can be advantageous to use multiple cards for streaming and control
- The system and I/O bus bandwidths
- Symmetrical multi-processor CPUs

- Strip out unnecessary software services, leaving the resources for uninterrupted stream delivery
- System memory should be large enough to manage multiple high-speed streaming buffers

The basic configuration can be calculated from the bandwidths, but test and measurement will be required to determine the true capacity of a server configuration. To aid testing, Microsoft supply a Load Simulator that can provide dummy loads during the server tests.

One way to get good performance is to scale wide, with many small servers, rather than one big multi-processor server. This also makes the system more tolerant to faults; you can lose a single server from a cluster, without losing the whole site.

Once you have determined your available bandwidth, and how many users will connect to the system, you can then decide on a server design. You may want a separate staging server to test content before it is placed on the public server; alternatively this could be a different directory.

Streaming server

A different approach to using a generic Windows or UNIX server platform is to use a server with an operating system designed from the ground up for streaming. The Vividon Content Accelerator product line can serve up to eight times the stream rate of conventional server (for a given rack footprint). For example, the SDA-5000 can serve up to 9,500 streams with a total throughput of 650 Mbit/s from a box only five rack units high. The servers can handle the popular architectures using the HTTP, MMS and RTSP/RTP protocols. A network of content accelerators can be controlled, monitored and managed from the Vividon Service Manager.

Hosting

If you want high-performance streaming to large numbers of public clients you are going to need a fat pipe to the Internet backbone. If you do not want to install a T-3 line, the easiest way is to use a hosting facility or a content delivery network. The hosting providers are usually located at hubs of the Internet with intimate and very wide band connectivity to the backbone.

If you are running a web site, you will have already looked at the pros and cons of outsourcing the servers. Outsourcing has advantages from the point of view of physical security. The service providers are usually located in secure buildings, with standby power facilities, halon fire extinguisher systems and multiple paths to the Internet backbone. If all the servers are remote from your corporate network, there are no issues with unauthorized access and firewall configurations. On the other hand, if your files contain confidential information you may want the servers on your own premises, managed by local staff. If you are using DRM with pre-encryption, this may not be so much of an issue.

The companies will offer a number of different services:

● Turnkey hosting
● Shared hosting
● Co-located hosting

Turnkey hosting is the simplest to implement; you upload your media files using FTP. Everything else is done for you.

Co-location gives you more control; you rent secure cages and install your own server plant. You get reliable power and connectivity. Your servers can be monitored by telnet from your own location.

Take care to study the service level agreement (SLA). Think carefully about the service you really need. Will your business suffer because of site outages? Can you work with more relaxed service reliability?

High availability

If you want to set up a system with high availability the system should be secure, reliable and easy to maintain.

It may not be unusual for video servers to be called upon to serve up video content at any time day or night to anywhere on the globe. To achieve a higher level of system availability will require a fault-tolerant design. This may come in the form of redundant hardware such as power supplies, fans or NICs, or in the form of redundant multiple server architectures. To minimize downtime, 'hot-pluggable' components such as disk drives, power supplies and fans are also desirable.

Security

Don't forget security when planning your systems. If you are streaming around the clock, and it becomes a core business service, then server outages could impact upon your business.

The security of your streaming provision is determined by many factors. There are the physical threats, like fire and theft. Redundant, mirrored server sites are a good way to deal with these issues. Then there are power outages – do you need uninterruptible power supplies?

If you are using a reputable hosting service, then most of these issues will be covered, but check the service level agreements.

The other threats come from hackers. If they can gain access to your servers they can wreak havoc. There is also the denial of service attacks. The best route is to call in a network security consultant to advise and audit your systems.

Authentication and authorization

Access to the origin server has to be restricted to authorized users. There are three types of users, the system administrators, the content creators uploading content and the viewers of the content.

Authentication is used to verify the identity of a client. You may not want to know, in which case anonymous authentication can be used where no user name or password is required. Authorization then allows authenticated clients access to confidential information. A database can store lists of authorized users in the three categories. The users gain access by password.

If your media is of commercial value, or confidential, then some form of digital rights management provides much greater protection against unauthorized access to your content.

Summary

The streaming server is a type of content server that uses a special software application to deliver streaming media in real-time to the players. It differs from a normal web server in having constant flow control, rather than the rate-adaptive transmissions of TCP.

There are two types of transmission: live and on-demand. The on-demand gives the interactivity that sets rich media applications apart from traditional video delivery systems. The user interaction is via an out-of-band bidirectional control channel.

The control channel can also control the streaming delivery rate to react to network congestion. By encoding material at several different rates, the server can select the appropriate stream for the prevalent conditions.

Streaming is usually over a one-to-one connection between the server and the client, called a unicast. The alternative option for a webcast is the multicast. The server transmits just one stream, and any number of clients can connect to the stream. This potentially saves network utilization, but has yet to be deployed universally across the Internet.

One of the most important aspects of managing a streaming system is the server logging. This is where you can measure the audience, and establish the return on your investment. It also provides vital information for the network administrators to tune the systems and identify possible bottlenecks.

The streaming server is an effective replacement for other delivery media for multimedia content that can offer lower costs, immediacy and interactivity.

12 Live webcasting

Introduction

In some ways webcasting is no different from encoding back at the shop. The main issue is that you usually only get one shot at it, so everything must be carefully thought out in advance. There are some golden rules for webcasting:

- Capture clear audio
- Minimize the camera movement
- Check the encoder CPUs are up to the task
- Make sure the backhaul is secure
- Make an archive copy

And always take at least two of everything – just to make sure.

Most of the issues for live events relate to the streaming in multiple formats and at multiple bit rates. The codecs available in 2001 have limits, typically four streams from one box. As the clock speeds of workstation central processors head past multi-gigahertz rates, the capabilities will increase.

Planning a webcast

Perhaps the first thing to consider is: what is the requirement? Is it a single-resolution, single-format stream, or will you need to produce several streams? Once that is clear you can start planning the backhaul from the venue to the streaming servers.

The backhaul

If you are really lucky it is a corporate presentation, and everything is on a local network, right down to an Ethernet jack in the meeting room. If it is at a remote venue that is when a site survey helps. Is there a T-1 line to the venue? Some convention centers and stadiums have very good telecommunications links, and their staff are well versed with hosting television crews.

If you are webcasting from the middle of a field you may have to fall back on a satellite backhaul. It is getting easier all the time to arrange this. Local television stations use them all the time for live news insets. You have the advantage that you do not need full broadcast video bandwidth. There are services available now from companies like DirecWay (Hughes Network Systems) for two-way IP connectivity. They use a VSAT (very small aperture terminal) dish to link up to the satellite. These antennae can be less than half a meter in diameter, so you do not have to call on a big uplink truck with a 4.5-meter C-band dish. The equipment is easy to use; the terminal equipment hooks up with a USB connector to the encoding PC.

If the webcast is very important it is best to have a backup, maybe a dual-ISDN line. A 56 kbit/s modem could suffice if it is an audio-only webcast.

If you have the opportunity to use a cable modem, they do have drawbacks. The cable companies do not in general offer the same reliability as the telephone companies. Plus bandwidth is not guaranteed, and there could be

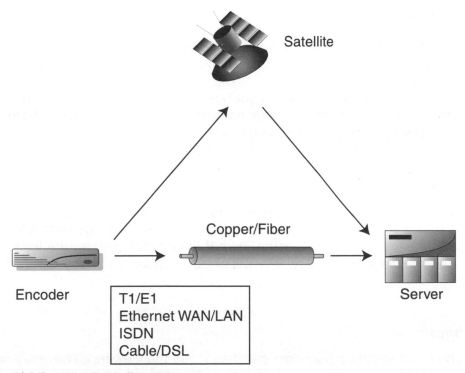

Figure 12.1 IP connection to the server.

contention at the node, if there are a large number of other users on the same fiber.

Whatever you use it is best to have a direct circuit to the server. If you use the Internet, you could get packet losses. That would distort the signal before it has even reached the distribution server.

You do not have to encode at the venue, you can backhaul the video and audio, and encode back at base. It just needs more bandwidth to do it that way. If your event is being used for television, it would make sense to encode at base; the facilities are better and there is less to go wrong.

The rig

So you have planned what streams you want, and how you are going to get them from the venue. The next step is planning the capture. For video you will need cameras and a video switcher. For audio, microphones and a mixing board. Plus there is ancillary equipment: video lighting, camera support (tripods), microphone stands, and lots of cable for power and for signals. Out in that field you will even need a generator.

Distribution and serving

Once the IP connection is established to the server, all you have to do is enter the IP address of the server, plus the port number, and probably a log-in name and password.

If you are multicasting, have you got one of the special multicast addresses allocated? Did you check that the network supports multicasting? Do the expected clients support multicasting?

Publicity

Last of all, have you announced the webcast? Does the potential audience know where to link to the stream? If you sent out e-mails, were the data and time correct? Make sure the webmaster has got the correct URL for the links, and then double-check on the day. You will not be popular if nobody can find the webcast.

Logistics

Will you need to set up help-desk facilities to aid the viewers? They may have browser problems or connection difficulties. The networks have to be up to the

video
cameras

pre-recorded
inserts

Switcher mixes
cameras and any
local tape inserts

microphones

video
switcher

video
mix

Audio
mix-down

audio mix

encoder

Audio/video
capture &
encode

audio mixer

VCR for
backup
recording

streaming
media to
network

Figure 12.2 The live encode.

task. If you are making corporate webcasts the network may not have the capacity for multimedia traffic. If a wide-area network includes long-haul links, they may be running close to capacity. It may be necessary to use additional circuits to link directly to additional servers at remote sites.

If the webcast includes e-mail feedback, you will need to set up the facilities to connect the encoding site into the net meeting.

Audio/video crew

Most of the set-up for a live webcast is all in a day's work for a technician from an audio/video facilities company. To employ such a company is probably the best way to undertake a big webcast. The only thing that is different from a normal live event or conference is managing the signal after the streaming encoder.

Video capture

If you are shooting for the Web, the production should reflect the final viewing experience. Just as the movie has panoramic shots and big sets, television is designed for a smaller screen, with close-ups and more domestic size sets. Webcasting has another set of rules. The images have to be simple and uncluttered. Keep close in to the subject and avoid wide shots. The less motion there is, the better the encoding will be. Subject movement is difficult to avoid, but you can keep the camera still – very still. It is essential that the camera should sit on a tripod wherever possible. If the camera has to move, use a dolly or a SteadiCam to keep the motion smooth. You should try to avoid too many panning shots; the background smears into a blur at low bit rates. The more subject movement, the less spatial detail that can be transmitted.

The amount of movement is going to be dictated by the final bit rate. If the encoding is only for distribution over broadband circuits, then the camera work can use more movement – it is, as always, a trade-off.

The camera

You may not be making a program for one of the networks, but a good camera will help with a clean signal. A three-chip CCD camera can be purchased at very low price now, so there is no need to borrow the family's holiday camcorder. Two good camcorders to consider are the Canon XL1 and the Sony DSR-PD150. Many camcorders have zoom lenses with built-in image stabilizers; these will take out the shakes from a hand-held shot. This can be very useful if you cannot use the camera on a tripod.

To connect the camera to the encoder there are several options. If the encoder is very close you can use an IEEE 1394 connection, but the cable length is limited to 4.5 meters. For longer distance you will have to use analog connections, ideally S-video, but as a last resort composite NTSC or PAL. If you are using professional cameras, you can opt for a digital hookup using the 270 Mbit/s SDI connection. This will not introduce any artifacts to the camera signal, and is the best choice if available.

Lighting

A camera will give a much better picture if the set is properly lit. I know that modern cameras can produce reasonable pictures by ambient domestic lighting, but you want the subject to stand out with some punch to the picture. The lighting should isolate the main subject from the background. A high light level will also avoid any camera noise intruding into the video picture.

So you should expect to use some video lighting equipment. Follow the usual rules of a key light to model the subject, a fill to limit the contrast, and background lighting for the rest of the scene.

Chroma key

If you are shooting a presenter against a blue screen, so that they can later be composited over a different background, use the best tools. It is a very useful production technique, especially for a talking head. The Ultimatte products have long been the choice of videographers for this sort of work. You will need to take care with the lighting to get good results; it is best to use a crew who are used to the equipment.

Introductory splash

If viewers log in early to a webcast, maybe to check everything is operating correctly, you will need some sort of splash screen so they can confirm all is well. This can be a holding slide, or a short video clip. The encoder can be set up to stream this before switching on cue to the live webcast.

Graphics

If you want to add graphics to a streamed presentation they can conventionally be keyed into the video signal. After they have been through the streaming codec they will be rather soft; at low bit rates they may be unreadable. An alternative is to deliver them as a separate synchronized stream. RealNetworks streams can carry synchronized text and Flash files. Windows Media can have a PowerPoint presentation synchronized to the video stream. These technologies will produce sharp, easily readable text to the viewer.

If you are going to use separate graphics files delivered from a web server, make sure it has the capacity if you are making the webcast to a large audience. Because the graphics are synchronized, all the players will request the file at the same instant.

Audio capture

You can watch poor quality video if the audio quality is good, but high-quality video with poor-quality audio is not acceptable. This is especially true for the talking head.

Mixing audio for the Web is a little different from mixing for music production or for television. For the Web simple, clear sound is best. Background music might set the mood for a feature film, but for the Web it just gives the encoder more data to compress. We are used to listening to stereo audio, but for webcasting it is not usually important – it just uses bandwidth. It also eases the mixing if you only have to produce a mono signal.

If you are mixing a group of people you will have to ride the faders, shutting down the microphones for everyone except the current speaker. This will maximize the ratio of the speaker to background noise.

Microphone placement

The secret of a successful webcast is to aim for clear, intelligible sound throughout the presentation. The correct placement of microphones is critical in obtaining the optimum sound quality. No amount of equalization and dynamics processing is going to rescue a poor signal. The goal of microphone placement is to achieve the highest possible ratio of the level of speech to the ambient sound (background). Other factors may impede this goal – aesthetics may dictate microphone placement. How do they look from the camera?

The golden rule is – get as close as possible.

It is worthwhile buying expensive microphones. They are more rugged and have a much flatter frequency response. It is difficult to get a clean encode from the peaky response of a cheap microphone.

Microphones are categorized by their directional characteristics, some pick up sound equally, called omnidirectional, and others are biased to sound from one direction, unidirectional or cardioid. You can also get microphones with a figure-of-eight or bidirectional pattern. The unidirectional are good for speakers, as they do not pick up the background noise from the audience.

Microphones come in many different styles:

Hand-held. Some speakers like to hold the microphone, but it is more suited to the variety performer on television than the general presenter. You cannot use your hands for expression, to turn a script, to point at a slide.

Lavalier and clip-on. These are good for standup speakers. They keep the microphone close to the mouth, yet are unobtrusive to the camera. They can pick up rustle from clothing if the speaker is moving around. The microphones

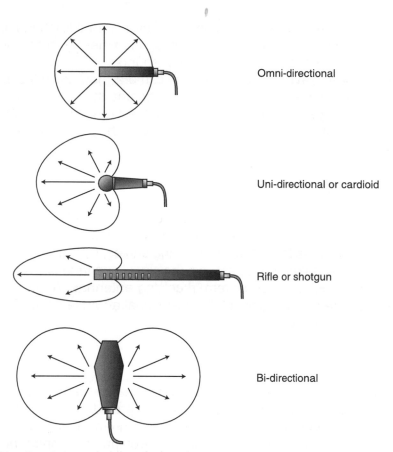

Omni-directional

Uni-directional or cardioid

Rifle or shotgun

Bi-directional

Figure 12.3 Directional characteristics of microphones.

have a special frequency response to compensate for the position on the chest; this can give an unnatural boom to the voice if not equalized.

Stand microphone. These are good for speakers on a stage. Beware of the speaker who walks about, his/her voice will fade if he/she gets too far from the microphone.

Sportscasters' headsets. They are unsightly in shot and not really suitable for most webcasts. They are a strictly practical choice for the sportscaster, so that they can hear the producer's talkbalk over the roar of the crowd.

Rifle or shotgun. These look impressive, but they are a last resort, when you cannot get close in. That's why they are used at ball games, to pick up the players.

There is no reason why you cannot use more than one microphone; in fact this can usually give the best results. For example, use a tie-clip microphone and a stand mike, then mix the two to get the best sound.

One microphone to avoid at all costs is the camera-mounted mike. If you want to pick up the zoom lens motor, the tape transport and the cameraman coughing they are just fine. They are meant for news-gatherers working in tight spots.

A windshield is often useful. If you are outdoors, they are obligatory to avoid wind noise.

Radio microphones

One problem with microphones is always the cables; they get in the way and they can get in view of the camera. The way around this is to use a radio microphone. This saves the issues with trailing cables, but introduces a new set of problems. As a speaker moves around, the signal can fade or even disappear. The way around this is to use several receiving antennae. A special receiver, called a *diversity* receiver, picks out the best signal and uses that. This will give excellent results – at a price.

Backup

Microphones and their cables get a lot of physical abuse, and as a result are prone to unexpected failure. So it makes sense to provide redundant equipment. For important webcasts, for example a company's quarterly call, the show is not going to wait while the sound crew fixes the equipment. Important speakers should have two microphones, and spares should always be on hand. A company president's time costs far more than a microphone.

Encoding

Live encoding is different from encoding back at the shop. It has to be real-time. Often if you want to encode to many different formats, the encoder can sit rendering the video until the streaming files emerge some time later. With a live webcast, you have to have the horsepower in the CPUs to process the streams as they come out of the camera. If you are streaming multiple formats make sure the equipment is up to it: do thorough testing before you get to the venue. Some low bit rate encoding can use more CPU resource than higher bit rates, so the processing power required is not directly related to the bandwidth. If the CPU utilization exceeds 75 per cent you have no safety margin for the live encode. If you are encoding several streams, split the load between multiple encoders.

In the late 1990s, if you wanted to webcast you had to build your own encoder, with a desktop PC and video card. For road use at live venues what you need is a rugged rack mount box. Today there are several such products. A typical example is the Pinnacle StreamFactory.

Pinnacle StreamFactory X2 Pro

This is a complete encoder in a box, designed especially for the demands of live encoding. It has dual CPUs that give it enough processing power to simultaneously encode Real and Windows Media streams. It can also run Sorenson Broadcaster for encoding in the QuickTime architecture. The input module can handle IEEE 1394 DV signals, as well as regular SDI digital video, and analog composite and S-video.

One feature that makes it really handy for webcasting is the built-in pre-processing module. This offers a wide range of audio clean-ups, including a dynamic range processor, noise gate and comprehensive equalization. The controller lets you set up pre-set configurations for rapid set-up on the road. It includes a de-interlace filter for the video. By pre-processing on this separate card, the main CPUs are free to devote resources to the main encoding.

The rack mount case is only 1.75 inches high, making it easy to fit into flight cases for road use. One useful feature is a 48 V DC power input; this is the standard battery voltage used in telecommunications plants.

On-site file archive

A live stream can be archived to a local disk, for on-demand playback at a later date. A local copy of the streaming file also provides security against failure of the outgoing telecommunications circuit.

Summary

Streaming offers a new way to distribute a live presentation to remote viewers. The previous alternative was to rent a satellite transponder for a live television hookup. Only the larger enterprise had the budget for this technology. Now any business with an IP network can distribute live audio and video for a modest outlay.

With a live webcast you only get one shot, so good planning is essential. Make sure that the network is up to it. If you are using a corporate network, check in advance for potential for bottlenecks. If you want to multicast, check that the network routers and the clients support multicasting. And do not forget, it only takes one vital cable to be missing, and the show does not go to air (or the Web).

Just because an event is live does not mean production standards should be relaxed. To get the best quality webcast you need to capture stable pictures and clear audio.

Much of what I have said in this chapter will come as second nature to the experienced event organizer. It is no different from providing video and sound reinforcement facilities for a rock concert or a product launch.

13 Media players

Introduction

For most of us, the player is the first component of a streaming media architecture that we encounter. Many computer users will have three or more players installed. Apart from the odd software update to get the latest version we are unaware of the mechanics of the players.

For the content creator the player is the simplest part of the end-to-end system. The designers of the architectures have made the players robust, and foolproof to deploy. You will rarely have to be concerned about the set-up of a player, except perhaps setting configurations to receive streams through firewalls.

To make sure that you have the largest possible audiences for your streams, it must be easy for viewers to install the player. By its very nature the player should not intrude between the content and the viewer. The ideal player should have the following characteristics:

- Free of charge
- Automatic installation
- Small size executable
- No configuration
- Invisible software upgrades
- Modest use of processor resources

As a viewer, the player you choose will be guided by the formats of the content that you want to watch. The content provider has made the key decision. You can choose not to download that plug-in, and not to watch this content.

The requirement to have a proprietary player has limited the number of streaming formats, weeding out all but the few. Nobody wants his or her PC cluttered with 10 different players; ideally we would only want to install one.

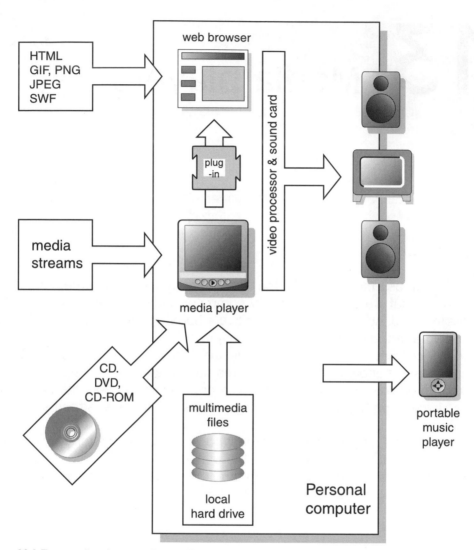

Figure 13.1 The media player as the multimedia core of the PC.

The leaders have been Real, as pioneers, and Microsoft with a huge installed OS base. It has been tough for other players to compete against the brutal realities of the marketplace. QuickTime has a wide base, partly due to its popularity for CD-ROMs, but Apple were slow to the streaming market, choosing to focus on the progressive download.

Most players are available in different versions for different operating systems, so if you are running Linux, for example, you should still be able to view streams in the proprietary architectures. The popular operating systems come with players already installed.

Portals, players and plug-ins

Players can be used in three different ways, as a portal, a player or as a browser plug-in. Apple, Real and Windows Media players can all be used as portals to streaming media content. The player can be used as a basic player, just open the file and play. The third way is to use the player as a plug-in to a web browser. The streaming is then treated as an integral part of a synchronized rich media experience.

The plug-in is the method of choice for rich media. Text and graphics can be seamlessly combined with the video stream into a unified presentation.

The open standard of MPEG-4 has changed the status quo. Rather than developing proprietary codecs, a potential player supplier can license the technology.

Figure 13.2 Player and plug-in to web browser.

Figure 13.3 Windows Media player as a media portal, with the integrated media guide. Screen shot reprinted by permission from Microsoft Corporation.

Typical player

Players share a number of features, although the exact details vary from vendor to vendor. First there is a video display area. This can be resized, using interpolation to scale up pictures if a large screen size is set. The VCR style controls enable the viewer interactivity. Hot spots on the display area can also be used – much like a web page – to link to alternative content.

Most players have additional controls for the audio (graphic equalizer) and video (brightness, contrast, color). A status display shows time code and data stream rate.

Figure 13.4 Typical media player.

Players and plug-ins

A player can be used standalone or as a plug-in for a browser. Each has its merits. The browser-based approach is suited to rich media application. Just as a browser renders images and text into a unified display, the media player plug-in makes video just another component in the display.

The player is called with an HTML <embed> command or as an ActiveX object. The control line launches the plug-in. Parameters can control the size and appearance; you want just the video display, or you may want to embed the full player in the page. If you are using the straight rectangular video display, as an option the transport controls (Play, Pause) can also be embedded.

Against this approach is the checkered history of browsers. Authoring content that has the same layout and functionality on all the different browsers and different operating systems has proved quite a challenge.

This has been a consequence of the development of HTML. The standard was the language. The MPEG-4 standard has taken the opposite approach, specifying the player. That way guarantees a consistent look for content, however it is authored.

The standalone player treats a stream more like a CD-ROM or a DVD. The player is dedicated solely to the playback of streams. Rich media is still possible; the Real player can render Flash, text and pictures.

MPEG-4 players

The MPEG-4 player can potentially offer the content creator much greater flexibility in the formats it can handle. Whereas a conventional media player is limited to HTML text, images, Flash and streaming audio/video, the MPEG-4 player can render a wide variety of two- and three-dimensional objects. The object can be natural (like rectangular video objects) or synthetic (like avatars).

Figure 13.5 MPEG-4 media objects.

The incoming media files are decompressed as audio-visual objects. The objects are layered in the correct order as specified in the scene descriptor. The MPEG-4 player then processes the video objects into two-dimensional representations appropriate to the player's point of view. This representation is then rendered to the video display. A similar process applies to the audio objects, the only difference being that the objects are mixed rather than layered. The viewer has the ability to change the viewpoint of three-dimensional objects. A joystick or similar input device can be used to change the scene coordinates.

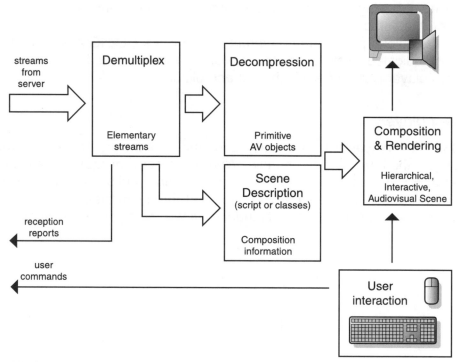

Figure 13.6 Basic MPEG-4 player system.

Proprietary players

The majority of players in use today are part of a proprietary architecture. The players are multi-purpose in that they can function as a media portal, a standalone player or a plug-in to a web browser. The players can all play files from the local storage, hard drive or CD-ROM, or from a stream. Most vendors sell a version of the player with extended facilities; the basic version is a free download. Typical extras include an audio graphic equalizer and controls for the video display, like contrast and brightness.

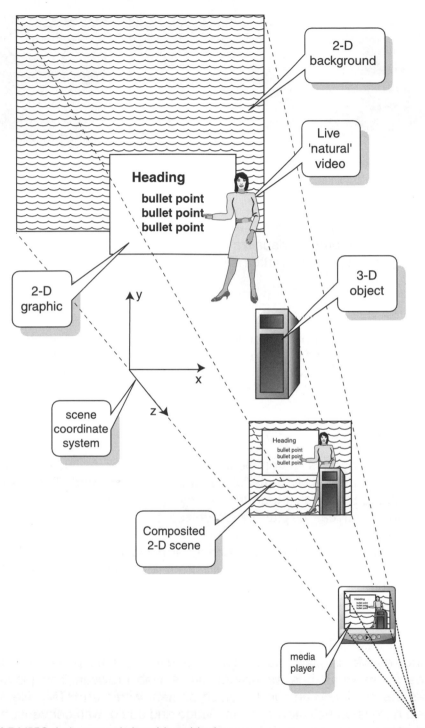

Figure 13.7 MPEG-4 player rendering video objects.

Figure 13.8 Popular media players – QuickTime 5, RealPlayer 8 and Windows Media 7.

The players also provide visualizations to accompany music files. These are moving, fractal-like, colored patterns.

QuickTime

Apple QuickTime player has been enhanced beyond its original functionality for playing CD-ROMs. It now has full support for streaming media. The player installs with a Picture Viewer that can display still images. The QuickTime Pro version can save movies, create slide shows and add soundtracks.

RealPlayer

The RealOne player is a complete media portal for exclusive multimedia content, and for audio-only material using the 'Radio Tuner'. The RealPlayer can use SMIL to render an integrated rich media presentation. As well as video streams the player can display synchronized text (RealText) and images (in RealPix format).

So, for instance, while you are watching a music video, you could read the lyrics (RealText) and browse through stills from the concert all presented to you at the same time.

Windows Media player

The Windows Media player is available as a standalone player, but its true strengths come when it is integrated into a web browser. The player then becomes the rendering engine for video content within an HTML file. So the emphasis here is on rich media, linking video and audio, with conventional web text and images, and also with PowerPoint presentations.

On2

On2 Technologies have focused on high-end streaming. Rather than follow the rich media vein of the three main architectures, On2 have developed codecs aimed at the broadband VOD market. On2 offers plug-ins for the Windows Media, Real and QuickTime players for its On2 VP3 codec.

The superior performance VP4 codec is offered as a player, both for PCs and, through their custom services team, for set-top boxes. 640 × 480 video at 24 or 30 fps can be delivered at quality claimed as 'near-DVD' at a bit rate of 450 kbit/s. This opens the VOD market to DSL and cable modems. By using set-top boxes for playback, the movies are displayed on the television rather than the PC. This brings streaming to the shared experience of television viewing, as opposed to the lone and interactive PC user.

Java players

A number of companies, including IBM (HotMedia), have developed players based on lightweight java applets, rather than the conventional players. Clipstream Technologies offer the VideoClipstream 2.0. This video and audio player is a 42 KByte download. It is small enough to be stored in the browser cache, as it can easily be reloaded. It has the advantage of streaming via HTTP over TCP/IP, so there are no issues with corporate firewalls.

Television set-top boxes

Streaming is not just for PCs. Many set-top boxes can display an IP stream on a regular television receiver. The main issue to watch with television is the use of graphics. If you are using text alongside streaming video in an SMIL presentation, regular web text is usually too small for a standard definition television. HTML text usually displays by default at about 12 points; on an interlaced 525-line receiver this will most likely be unreadable.

Wireless and portable devices

Now we have become familiar with streaming to PCs, we want the same access to information on the road. At the turn of the century we finally caught up with Star Trek with our personal communicators. The new generation of radio devices offer wider bandwidths than the early cellular phones, but still not enough to beam us up to the mother ship.

The MPEG-4 standard has many features that make it particularly suited to wireless delivery. The scalable streaming is very useful in the wireless environment, where channel fading can cause considerable packet loss.

Figure 13.9 Wireless video players. © PacketVideo.

Companies like PacketVideo and Emblaze have end-to-end solutions for encoding and serving streaming media to hand-held devices. The connection could be to a third generation smart phone or by wireless networking to a PDA. The streaming client is usually embedded to give the small footprint demanded by these devices. The wireless operating system like Symbian can support media players. The Pocket PC and Windows CE from Microsoft are lightweight operating system alternatives. Pocket PCs now have display sizes of 320 × 240, big enough for a video window or full screen display.

Audio players

Audio-only players were the first to become popular, spurred on by the huge demand from music lovers to download tracks over the Internet. Many do not support true streaming, but can download-and-play MP3 files. They act as a jukebox inside the PC, with the ability to rip CDs, store MP3 files on the hard drive and download to portable flash players like the Rio. Some form of library management is included to find tracks and set up playlists. Typical examples include WinAmp and MusicMaster. The major operating systems offer similar products with iTunes from Apple and integral music facilities in Windows Media.

The lack of video has led many of the players to offer a number of visual features. One that is popular is the ability to change the look or chrome of the player by re-skinning with any number of different designs. Another is the visualization, where random colored patterns change in time to the music.

Digital Rights Management

Several players have integrated Digital Rights Management (DRM) clients. Determined thieves can extract the media data when it is in the clear between the DRM client and the media player. Most of the clients have means to detect tampering, and to report this back to the rights server and shut down the streams. Microsoft have taken this a step further by integrating the decryption into the operating system kernel. By these means a secure audio path to the sound card can be ensured. You could still extract the video data, but what use is a movie without a soundtrack?

MPEG-4 Intellectual Property Management and Protection

MPEG-4 has accepted the principle that one-size-fits-all is not wholly appropriate for DRM. Instead, the level of complexity and the security offered is left to the application developer. In other words, the complexity can scale with the cost. This reflects the different demands for DRM: it may be to protect confidential information, or it could be to encrypt pay-per-view movies.

So the MPEG-4 Intellectual Property Management and Protection (IPMP) framework leaves the details open to different DRM system vendors.

Summary

This has been a brief chapter, but players have to be simple to gain general acceptance by users. Many proprietary players have come and gone. The installed base is dominated by the three main streaming architectures, Microsoft, Real and Apple. These players can be used as media portals, as players or as plug-ins to a web browser, and all have similar feature sets. New players were emerging in 2001 to view MPEG-4 compliant streams.

The choice of player is largely personal; they all produce an equivalent video and audio quality. New codecs are released at regular intervals, so the quality improves year on year. Many users are happy to install all; some may only want the pre-installed codec that comes with the operating system.

The main architectures all offer fully featured portals, but for many applications the chrome is a distraction from the content. Compare with digital interactive television, with simple navigation and discrete packaging. The portal is useful for locating content, but can be replaced by a browser plug-in for display of the wanted content. Perhaps the audio player is the exception, where the portal provides visual stimulation and information to accompany the music.

A core component of the player is protection of intellectual content, or digital rights management. This enables content vendors to successfully monetize their content by protection of their intellectual property.

The player is reaching an exciting stage in its development. It is breaking free of the reins of the PC, and finding its way into everything from hand-held wireless devices through to the television set-top box.

Section 3

Associated Technologies and Applications

14 Rights management

Introduction

The Internet is a public network and open to all. Owners of content who want to distribute over the Internet may want to restrict access to their intellectual property. It may be confidential corporate information, or it could be entertainment media sold through an e-commerce site. Rights management offers systems that can control access and aid the successful monetization of content. Like many other issues related to streaming, there are numerous choices to consider when installing a rights management system.

Some very determined pirates and hackers lie out there, waiting to steal your intellectual property, either for gain or as a personal challenge. In choosing a system you will have to judge the level of threat; the more secure a system, the more it will cost. With increased security, authorized users will find it more difficult to access the required content. So there is a trade-off between cost, security and ease of use.

There are two main facets to rights management. The first is the maintenance of artists and producers' contracts and royalty payments. The second is the secure delivery. The latter is commonly referred to as Digital Rights Management (DRM). It is the technology that allows owners, distributors and providers of content to deliver content securely to consumers. The rights management can also control who has access to content, for example restrictions to geographical areas. DRM can also be used standalone, to protect confidential information.

There is a certain amount of controversy around digital rights systems. Perhaps the medium with the longest history of rights is the printed book. It is recognized that the intellectual property of the author is protected against unauthorized imprints. But there is also the concept of fair use, without which the public library would not exist. To make a copy of a book using a photocopier is expensive and the result usually lacks an adequate binding. So it is easier to buy a new book. As we migrate to the electronic medium, a digital clone can be made simply at no cost (ignoring the disk space). So fair use – with the attendant risks of illegal copying – becomes difficult to police.

E-commerce systems already exist to protect the integrity of financial transactions when ordering goods. Traditionally these goods are physical, and the online transaction merely replaces mail order or telephone order. The goods are then delivered by mail or parcel service. When the goods are streamed media, not only does the transaction have to be secure, but the goods also have to be protected against unauthorized access.

Authentication and trust

Consider a person going to the local store to make a purchase. The storeowner will recognize that person by their gait as they walked in, their physical appearance, and by their voice. They have already authenticated the customer as a trusted customer. The customer pays by check; the storeowner hands over the goods. The key words here are authentication and trust.

The same customer now travels to an out-of-town store. The checkout clerk does not know the customer, so refuses the check. The customer has the option of paying by charge or credit card. The card is authenticated then the transaction authorized by the terminal. The store trusts the credit card company to pay them for the goods. The customer walks out of the store with the goods – everyone is happy.

As retail transactions become globalized, the opportunities for fraud escalate. The mail order/telephone order sector has procedures in place to authenticate customers. Most will only ship goods to the address where the payment card is registered. Card suppliers have added extra digits to the card number that are not printed as part of the embossed number, or carried in the magnetic strip. This can be used during a phone transaction to confirm that the purchaser has the actual card in their possession, not an impression.

The usage contract

Digital commerce is based on the usage contract. The content provider and the user agree a contract, possibly involving the payment of fees. Then the user receives the right to use the content.

As the user views the content, usage reports are returned to the content provider.

Conditional access – the television model

Television is funded by advertising, subscription or, in the case of state-controlled networks, from government taxation (in some countries independence of the state networks from government interference is provided by the use

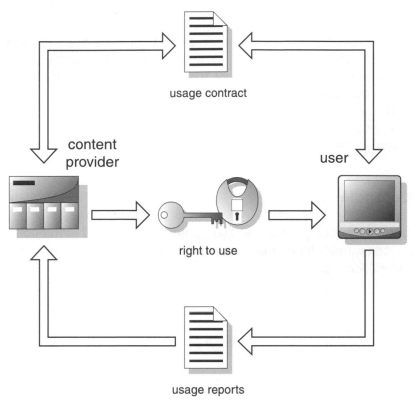

Figure 14.1 Usage contract.

of a license rather than an income from taxation). A limited number of channels also offer pay-per-view, primarily for movies and for major sporting events. Channels funded by advertising, sponsorship or taxation can be broadcast free-to-air or 'open'. Subscription-based channels and pay-per-view use encryption to protect content against unauthorized viewing – conditional access.

Advertising and sponsorship

When corporations first started to use the Internet, funding for the web site came from either the marketing budget or from advertising. The subscription model is starting to become popular, especially for sites providing information. This is partly as consumer resistance to banner advertising is increasing, and also as a result of the often-limited revenues generated from advertising. The page-based Internet media (HTML) has mainly used the banner, with pop-ups also popular. Streaming media offers the possibility of following the television model, with interstitial spots or breaks as well as banners.

Conditional access

The television broadcasters have chosen closed systems of conditional access to protect subscription and pay-per-view channels. The receivers or set-top boxes use smart cards and possibly a phone back-channel as part of the authorization procedures.

Streamed media is usually viewed on PCs. These users have great resistance to add-ons, software dongles and other additional hardware, so other methods have to be used to authenticate consumers.

The value chain

Content and payment form a cycle. The content is delivered to the consumer for use. The consumer then pays the intellectual property owner (through intermediaries) for the content.

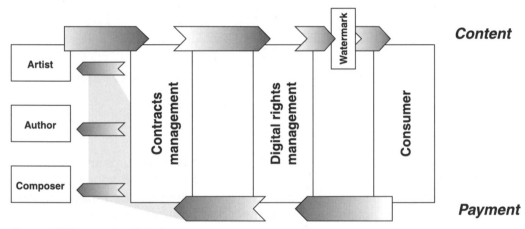

Figure 14.2 The payment cycle.

The Digital Rights Management system ensures secure delivery of the content in accordance with business rules defined by the contracts. The monies collected are then apportioned by the contracts management payment to the relevant parties.

Content distribution

Although an artist may want to sell work directly to the consumer, most content is sold though a conventional distribution chain. A DRM system should support the classic supply chain: content creator; publisher; aggregator or portal; distributor; retailer; and finally the consumer.

The DRM should also support traditional product marketing tools like promotional offers and viral marketing. Finally, the methods of payment have to be flexible, all the way from subscriptions through to micro-payments and electronic purses.

Digital Rights Management

Digital Rights Management is the use of computer technology to regulate the authorized use of digital media content, and to manage the consequences of such use, for example a payment.

A Digital Rights Management (DRM) system encrypts the content so that distribution can be controlled in accordance with the agreed rights and their terms and conditions. To this end it wraps prices and business rules around the content to enable the payment transaction.

Figure 14.3 Exchanging the license.

For the transaction the DRM is tightly integrated with the chosen e-commerce systems. Streaming media is representative of the many formats that an Internet content provider may want to manage, deliver and sell. The digital information could also be electronic books, research reports or graphic images like still photographs. Most DRM systems are designed to protect some or all of these different media formats. The initial developments in DRM were for text files. Not all these systems can handle streaming media. Encryption tends to be at file level. For a streamed file the encryption has to be implemented at packet level, otherwise the media playback cannot start immediately.

This, plus the intimate connection required to the player, has led naturally to many DRM solutions being proprietary to the codec format. The MPEG-4 format has a more open interface.

Why do we need DRM?

Digital content is subject to many forms of piracy:

- Illegal copying
- Loss of data integrity – tampering with content
- Peer-to-peer distribution

Perhaps the best example of peer-to-peer distribution was the case of Napster. If there is a secure DRM, then e-commerce can be used for online content. This electronic distribution removes the manufacturing costs of physical media and can simplify distribution. Within the corporate networks it can protect valuable and confidential information. For a distance-learning project it ensures protection of intellectual property.

Piracy protection

Two methods are used to fight piracy: one is *encryption* and the other is *watermarking*. Encryption gives the primary protection. Should the encryption be compromised, watermarking enables the tracing of the possible sources of the piracy.

Business models

The DRM has to be very flexible to accommodate the many different ways a consumer can purchase the content. There are many business models for monetizing online content.

Usage

There are several ways to sell content. There is rental or outright sale. The rental may have qualifiers applied; it could be for a fixed period or for a certain number of plays. Then there is the video-on-demand model, where a payment is for each viewing of the clip.

Delivery

The delivery of content can be as a download or stream. The download might be for music files to be used by a portable player or a PDA. Streaming could be for ephemeral content that is only watched once. A third possibility is to archive the file, while it is streaming, for repeat viewing. If it is possible to download content to portable players, security is potentially compromised. Microsoft has developed an interface that allows content to be downloaded securely from the Windows Media Player to portable audio devices that support the SDMI (Secure Digital Music Initiative) standard.

Promotion

DRM enables many forms of product promotion. The first is to let the viewer see a preview. This may be the edited highlights or the first few minutes of the clip. The preview may be at a lower resolution than the main clip. Other forms of promotion may be special offers – 'pass this on to five friends and get a free play'.

Payment

The traditional method for mail order payment is by credit or charge card. This is not a good method for very small transactions; it may only cost 10 cents to listen to a single music track. So other methods have to be used that have a lower cost overhead for such low-value transactions.

Subscriptions, long popular with print media, are another method of collecting payments. They are more suited to a service rather than pay-per-view. Subscriptions are usually prepaid. An alternative for business-to-business transactions would be to bill in retrospect. Account payments can support a fixed rate service or pay-per-view.

For the business selling content to the consumer, the prepaid purse or micro-payments are the alternative. With the purse, the customer buys credit from the clearing house. This credit is stored securely in the DRM client. The value is decremented as content is viewed. Micro-payments are aggregated by the clearing house into larger transactions, perhaps made at monthly intervals.

Business rules

The business model will dictate a set of business rules. The DRM client uses the rules to gain access to the content. The terms and conditions can change with time so the license issuer must be able to change the rules or revoke a license. This may be necessary for legal or business reasons, or the content may become outdated or inappropriate. A good DRM system should allow the revocation of content even after it has been downloaded.

Wrapping

This is the process of securing the content and associating with the content the business rules to enable unwrapping by the media player. The processes are not necessarily concurrent. Encrypting may be performed at the same time as the media is encoded, and the business rules added later.

Figure 14.4 Wrapping the content.

There are two different points where content files can be encrypted. The first is before media is placed on the content server. The second is to encrypt on-the-fly, as the content is streamed to the media player. The latter is the model that has been used by conditional access systems for pay-per-view television.

Pre-encryption and on-the-fly

Pre-encryption systems usually package the clip file as a whole, rather than packet by packet. For live use this is not an option; for webcasts the encryption has to be on-the-fly. To meet this need, a different form of encryption has been

Table 14.1 Pros and cons of the pre-encryption and on-the-fly methods

	Pros	Cons
Pre-encryption	Content is secure on the server No serving overheads	Not suited to live streaming Single key per file
On-the-fly	Can be used for live webcasts New key per stream	Additional server-side processing Content can be compromised on the streaming server

developed, where the processing takes place at the point of delivery. This on-the-fly encryption has a second advantage that a new key is generated for each stream. Pre-encryption generates a single key for the file at the time of wrapping. So if the key should be compromised, all copies of the file can be opened.

On-the-fly encryption can be an additional application running on the streaming server, but this will lower the number of streams a given server can deliver, typically by 30 per cent. The alternative is to use a bridge or router at the output port of the streaming server that can perform the encryption. This allows the use of a standard media server.

Unwrapping

The final user or the consumer wants to view and listen to the content. To decrypt the content, first the user has to obtain authorization. This authorization, suitably modified by the business rules, then initiates the decryption of the content.

This is a typical sequence that is followed by the DRM client:

1. The first step is to send a request for the content and, if necessary, undertake a financial transaction.
2. If the client has credit, the commerce server transmits the authorization key.
3. The DRM client requests the business rules from the rights server and the media file from the content server.
4. The rights server forwards the business rules.
5. The content server streams the media.
6. The DRM client allows access to the media according to the business rules.

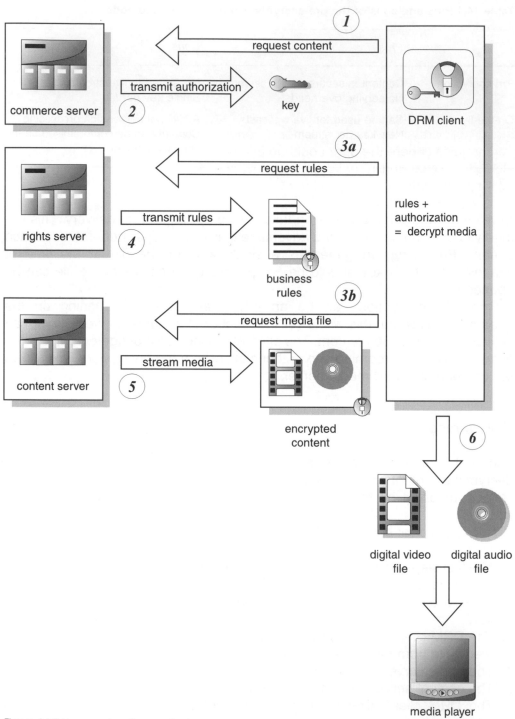

Figure 14.5 Unwrapping the content.

The exact sequence varies from product to product. Note that the business rules can be downloaded each time and are separate from the content. This allows the content owner to change the rules at any time without the necessity to re-encrypt the media file. A movie might be initially available on a pay-per-view basis, then at a later date released for outright sale. The publisher may want to add or withdraw special offers.

This division between the product and the promotional wrapper gives the retailer of virtual products greater freedom than the vendor of physical merchandise (where the offer could be printed on the packaging). It also allows pricing to be changed in real-time, much like the street vendor or an airline trying to fill empty seats at the last minute.

The authorization can be issued in several ways. It could be from a subscriber management system (long used by pay TV) or it could be an e-commerce system.

The rights management parties

There are several parties in any content transaction. Each is looking for a different set of features in a DRM system. The final choice has to satisfy all parties if the commercial model is to be successful.

Content creators/publishers

Content can take many forms. The first focus was on music distribution, a consequence of the Napster debacle. The distribution of video content is very much tied in to satisfactory security, much like the delayed release of the DVD. Live events are an area where pay-per-view could be applied. A technology close to streaming media is the interactive video game; DRM would enable the online sale of games.

The target devices for streaming are not just PCs; they could be wireless PDAs or portable music players. Content will have to be re-purposed for the requirements of each device. Content for the PDA requires careful design to be compelling within the limits of a small display area.

Compatibility with media players

Which player do you choose? Corporate users can choose a single system. B2B and B2C suppliers may want to offer the user a choice. Two of the popular streaming architectures already include DRM systems (Real and Windows Media). If you want to support several architectures you may end up having to interface with three different DRM systems.

Commerce

When you are selecting a DRM system, you need to look at the features on offer. Does it support cross-selling? An important factor is the transaction costs for micro-payments. Can you make retrospective changes to the business rules? This allows price changes for downloaded content that already resides on the customer's PC. Is it possible to revoke access to content?

Reseller

The reseller could be a retail web store or a content portal, aggregating content from several suppliers. The content could be sold on through several stages, before the final purchase by the end-consumer. A distributor may buy content from many creators and sell on to the consumer. Distributors will want to set up the business rules for the trading of content, and may want to add further rules, add their own margin and then add special offers.

So the DRM systems should support modification and additions to the business rules by trusted partners in the value chain.

Consumer/user

The end-user first gains authorization from the clearing house or data center. Then he or she is free to open and view the encrypted content. Now a consumer may want to preview content before making the decision to buy. This purchase may be outright, or could be for a fixed period rental. Consumers are often encouraged to forward media to friends – a process known as viral marketing. The DRM system has to support secure super-distribution for this personal recommendation to operate.

Payment and usage information is passed back to the clearing house. An electronic purse can store a small cache of credit within the media player. This avoids the need to clear every transaction. DRM systems should have means to silently report tampering back to the data center.

Super-distribution

Super-distribution is commonly used in viral marketing. This is where customers pass content to friends, perhaps in the belief that it is a shared secret. Content that is passed from user to user has to have persistent protection after copying. So each user will have to make an individual transaction to gain authorization to use the content.

Issues for the user

So far I have considered the providers' issues. The choice of DRM is also an issue for the consumer. If the system is too complex, there are thousands of other web sites out there, only a click away. Another major issue is payment security. Customers have to trust the supplier with their credit card details. The consequence of this fear is that reputable traders can lose potential business. There are steps being taken to counteract these fears where trusted third parties act as brokers for online transactions.

A good DRM system should be transparent to the end-users. The acquisition of the software executables should be automatic and not require manual intervention from the user. Browsers now include rights management pre-installed. The second is that the financial transactions must be simple and secure.

Most DRM systems allocate the license to a node and not the user. Some attributes of the PC are used as part of the key, for example the file may be locked to an IP address. If you want to move protected media between a desktop PC and a laptop this may require a nodeless DRM. Note that this is not copying; the content is moved to the portable machine and then moved back to the desktop.

Clearing houses

Subscriptions could be managed by a web site database. All that is required is secure authorization and usage statistics. If the consumer pays for content the clearing houses will process the micro-payments from consumers and pass payments to the content providers. An electronic purse may hold a small local cache of credit.

Financial clearing house. A facility that receives financial transaction records, resolves the transactions, and makes the required payments to the value chain participants and value chain delegates.

Usage clearing house. This is a facility that gathers reports and statistics of how DRM protected media is used by consumers and by other participants in the value chain. It resolves the requirements for usage reporting and provides reports to specified recipients.

Third-party revenues. The DRM supplier has two possible sources of revenue, a fee for each transaction or by a license for a fixed period (typically annual). The clearing houses usually charge per transaction.

System integration

A large system is going to require many disparate software systems to be integrated. Is middleware required to ease the integration of DRM with back-office systems? These include e-commerce systems, contracts management, digital asset management and the clearing house.

Contracts management

Most DRM systems produce comprehensive statistics and reports of consumer usage. To apportion payments to the relevant parties the DRM operator may well need other software products, specifically a contracts management package. These products are outside the scope of this book. Good examples can be found in *System 7* from Jaguar Consulting and *iRights* from Ness. These products have modules for the following functions:

- To manage contracts with artists
- To acquire content from production companies
- To track the usage of content
- To distribute royalties to artists

The contracts management application often sits at the hub of the business. Gateways link to the DRM, and to the digital asset management system that may be used as the content library or vault.

Encryption

Cryptography has two uses within DRM. The first is to encrypt content for confidentiality or protection of the owner's rights. The second is for the protection of the certificates that are used for authentication and for access control (authorization).

There are two families of cryptography: shared secret and public/private key. A shared secret key (also called a symmetric) uses the same key to encrypt the content and then to decrypt it at the receiving end. In cryptography the clear file is called *plaintext* and the encrypted version is called *ciphertext*. The scrambled ciphertext can only feasibly be decoded with the key. One way to crack the encryption is to try many different keys until the correct one is chanced upon. The more characters in the key, the longer it will take on average to find the key. This cracking can be made more difficult by changing the key at certain intervals. Shared key encryption is efficient and suited to large files – just like media files. An example of a shared secret is a personal identification number

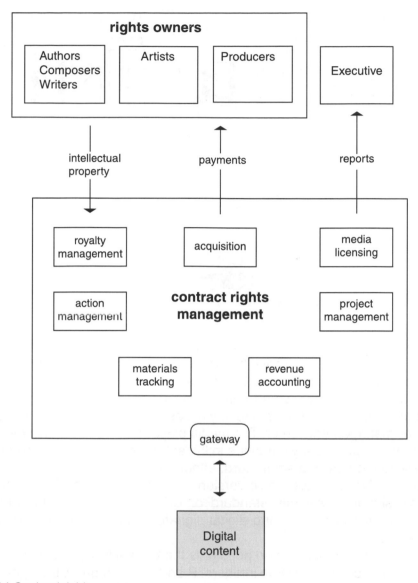

Figure 14.6 Contract rights.

or PIN used to withdraw cash with an automated teller machine. The PIN is used to verify the physical credit card. The PIN is a secret shared by the bank computer and the authorized holder of the card.

The problem with a secret key is the secure distribution from one party to the other. Different methods can be used to deliver the key. One is the secure courier. Another is the telephone callback. One party phones the other, and says 'call me

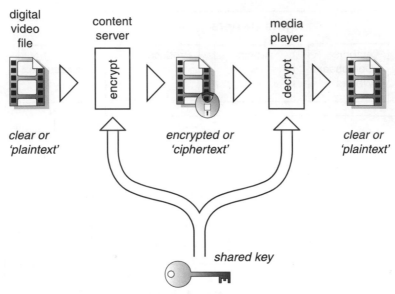

Figure 14.7 The secret, shared encryption key.

back'. The other party calls back to an unlisted phone number, now the original party has authenticated they have the wanted party and can divulge the key.

The courier is not a viable option for e-commerce systems. Pay-per-view conditional access uses a smart-card in the set-top box, plus a phone link to connect to the box. Each box is uniquely accessible, so can be shut down by the subscriber management center. The media player in a PC is a much more open system than the proprietary hardware in the set-top box. There is also consumer resistance to the use of a smart-card, although such systems exist.

The alternative is an electronic version of the telephone callback. This uses the digital signature security standard or DSS. Once the rights server has authenticated the client from the digital signature, then the secret key can be exchanged.

One algorithm that has proved popular is the Diffie–Hellman key exchange. It starts with two publicly available integers, P and G. Each party, the rights server and the client, generate private keys, X and Y. The Diffie–Hellman algorithm is then used to generate public keys, E and F, which the two parties exchange. Each party then uses the other's public key, their own private key and the public number P to generate a common number. This common number K is now a secret shared by both parties. Note that at no time has this shared secret key been exchanged over the Internet.

This description is somewhat simplified; the full description can be found in the IETF RFC 2631: Diffie–Hellman Key Agreement Method. This shared key can then be used to encrypt the media file.

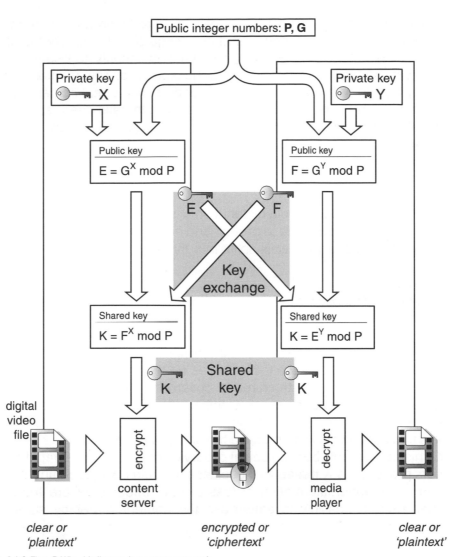

Figure 14.8 The Diffie–Hellman key agreement.

Note that the Diffie–Hellman key agreement can be intercepted by a man-in-the-middle attack, as there is no authentication between the two parties. Such authentication could involve the prior exchange of digital signatures.

Watermarking

For a content provider to trace the sources of piracy, two clues are necessary. The first is the source of the stolen content and the second is the client that compromised the security. These clues can be introduced as a watermark to identify the source of stolen content and as a fingerprint to identify the client.

Watermarking embeds a persistent signature to identify the source of the content. It can be highly visible, like an embossed logo. This is often used for preview copies. Something more subtle is needed for the real content, just like the watermark on a piece of paper or bill. Automatic web spiders can continuously search the Web looking for open (unencrypted) content that carries watermarks.

Security

Before setting up a secure media distribution system, it is a good idea to look at your goals. What are you trying to protect and how much do you want to spend on security? The security analysis splits into three areas:

1. The content
2. The monetary transaction
3. The server infrastructure

DRM gives protection of the content and often includes the monetary transaction. The transaction can use mature technologies from the e-commerce arena. The third area, the server infrastructure, is covered by normal enterprise level computer security (outside the scope of this book). The infrastructure should be protected for several reasons. One is the value of the content asset library; another is that attack could compromise the brand of the publisher, aggregator or retailer. This attack could be from denial of service or loss of data integrity.

Hackers present many threats to a business. It could be through unauthorized access to confidential information or loss of data integrity, where the hacker alters the content, possibly to embarrass the content owner by substituting inappropriate material.

The threats

Network

- Identity spoofing (man-in-the-middle)

Client

- Cracking encryption algorithms
- Plug-ins
- Clock roll back (to fool license)
- Direct connection, VGA and speaker outputs

There is nothing that can be done about the last threat, just as somebody can sit in a movie theater with a camcorder.

Third-party audit

Before investing a considerable sum in a DRM product, find out how secure it really is. Ask to see third-party audits, or instigate your own. A DRM supplier told me once that 'our system is secure – we don't need a security audit'!

Caveats

No encryption is proof against determined efforts to crack.

- DRM makes piracy difficult, but does not prevent it
- Other methods of defense of property rights will be necessary
- Watermarking aids tracing of stolen content
- Some level of theft is inevitable and should be included in the cost of sales

Examples of DRM products

This section gives a number of typical examples of DRM products. The first, InterTrust, has products for the protection of a wide range of different file types, not just streaming media. Real and Microsoft have products specific to their own architectures. Finally, WideVine is a format agnostic system designed to encrypt on-the-fly.

InterTrust

InterTrust has pioneered the development of DRM systems. They support a wide range of formats including video, audio, software and text that support DRM (PDF and MPEG-4). The initial applications have been for documents and audio files rather than video streams. InterTrust has been active in the development of intellectual property management and protection for MPEG standards. They have partnered with Envivio to develop MPEG-4 streaming products.

The InterTrust product line is called the Rights System. The Packager family of products enables content owners, distributors and service providers to create digital products from content and package them for distribution. This is accomplished by first encrypting the content. The next step is to create a Rights Pack that contains the usage rules for that content. The Rights Packagers support distribution of media files by download and streaming.

The Stream Packager encrypts streaming content without compromising efficiency or system security. The packager encrypts separate chunks of the streaming media. At the player the encrypted chunks are then consolidated back into a complete stream for an authorized user.

The Rights System includes a number of server products: the Authorization Generator, the Content Rights Server and the Membership Rights Server. When a user pays for or acquires the rights to a particular piece of content, the Authorization Generator creates an authorization (proof of purchase). The Authorization Generator is designed to integrate easily into existing e-commerce environments.

The Content Rights Server verifies user requests for content rights. It processes the authorizations from the Authorization Generator. The Content Rights Server then delivers the content rights as a Rights Pack file. The Rights Client software at the user's player processes the Rights Pack. This lets the player access the content according to the usage rules. The alternative method of enabling content access is the Membership Rights Server. This product is designed for content supplied by subscription or membership of a club. The system verifies that the user has valid membership before delivering the Rights Pack.

Figure 14.9 InterTrust product matrix.

The Rights System Client family consists of four products. The DRM system is not limited just to PC platforms, but also supports cellular phones, portable music players and PDAs. The footprint of each client is optimized for the platform. The initial deployments have been in music distribution.

RealNetworks Media Commerce Suite

RealNetworks have developed a fully integrated DRM system for the Real architecture. The RealSystem Media Commerce Suite comprises four components:

RealSystem Packager. A set of tools for content providers to securely package streaming media files.

RealSystem License Server. This is an HTTP server that generates licenses for access to secured media. They are issued in response to a request from the player client.

RealServer secure plug-in. This plug-in enables the RealSystem Server to stream the encrypted content files.

The Real player client also requires an upgrade, the **Media Commerce Upgrade**. This allows the RealPlayer to decrypt protected content (with the extension .rms) in a trusted and tamper-resistant environment.

These components interact with existing content delivery mechanisms, a retail web server and a back-end database.

Encrypted RealMedia files can be delivered by virtually any mechanism: traditional File Transfer Protocol (FTP) downloads, peer-to-peer networks, multicasting or even on traditional media like CDs or DVDs.

The content server stores identifying information for each content file: the secured content key and a globally unique identifier (GUID). The GUID is supplied by RealSystem Packager and makes it available to the retail portal server during content licensing.

A retail portal server sends client requests to RealSystem License Server then returns the license generated by RealSystem License Server to the consumer's player.

Windows Media Rights Manager 7

Microsoft's Windows Media Rights Manager provides a secure end-to-digital media e-commerce solution for Windows Media. This solution enables both

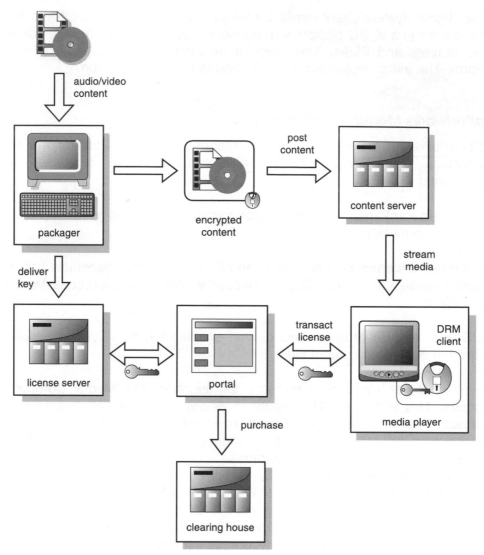

Figure 14.10 RealNetworks Media Commerce Suite.

application service providers and Internet content providers to manage, deliver and sell streaming media. It supports download-and-play and conventional streaming.

   The Windows Media Rights Manager system is designed to work with third-party credit card software that is compatible with MS Site Server 3.0. The Windows Media Rights Manager allows the publisher to set up the rules for the transaction. The player then uses these rules to open the encrypted content.

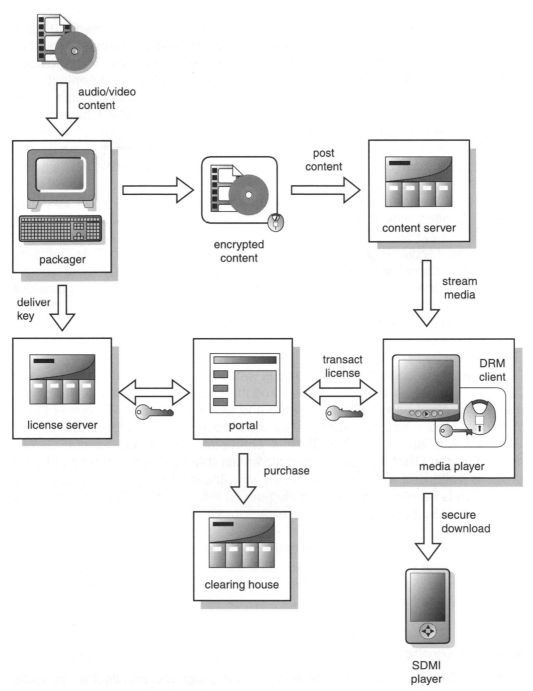

Figure 14.11 Window Media Rights Manager.

Flexible business models

New licensing rights have been introduced with Windows Media Rights Manager 7 to help enhance the creation of new, innovative business models.

Licenses are issued independently of the actual media files. This provides flexibility for the business model and allows wider distribution of content. The Rights Manager checks for the consumer's license every time a media clip is played. If users do not have a valid license they are directed back to the registration web page.

Because licenses and media files are stored separately from the media, the licensing terms can be changed without the need to encrypt the media file again and then redistribute to the client.

Windows Media Rights Manager supports rental or subscription business models. Limited play previews allow potential purchasers to look before they buy.

Windows Media Rights Manager can pre-deliver licenses. This helps to remove the consumers' resistance to the acquisition and playing of secure media files. One feature is silent licensing, which means that a content provider may 'silently' deliver the license to the consumer, without the need for the consumer to intervene.

Secure Audio Path

One area where content can be stolen is within the user's PC. If the clear audio data passing between the DRM client and the sound card driver is intercepting, then the content can easily be diverted and saved to the disk. To prevent this, Windows Media has a feature called the Secure Audio Path (supported by Windows ME and XP). The DRM is embedded in the OS kernel. Before decryption the DRM kernel component verifies that the path to the sound card driver is valid and authenticated. If any unauthorized plug-ins exist, then the decryption is barred. This prevents plug-ins on the sound card from copying the audio data. Microsoft certifies valid drivers for security.

Controlled transfer to SDMI portable devices

Windows Media Device Manager permits the secure transfer of protected media files to Secure Digital Music Initiative (SDMI) portable devices or the removable media for those devices.

Widevine Cypher

Widevine Cypher is an 'on-the-fly' encryption product. It is architecture agnostic and supports Windows Media, RealVideo and QuickTime. A normal streaming media server is deployed for the appropriate architecture. The output streams

Figure 14.12 Widevine Cypher.

are then passed through the Cypher network bridge. The bridge negotiates the keys then performs the real-time encryption.

A shim decrypts the stream at the client. The shim also monitors the media player for tampering and reports any such actions back to the rights server. The normal interactive play controls pass back through the shim and bridge to the streaming server.

As the Cypher encrypts streaming media on-the-fly, it can be used to protect live webcasts.

Summary

If you want to monetize content, that content has to be protected against theft. You may have confidential corporate information to protect. Digital Rights Management can provide you with solutions. Digital Rights Management can be expensive to license and operate. You need to define your goals for content protection. Identify possible threats. A cost-benefit analysis would be very sensible.

The level of security that you use is very much a compromise. Strong security does not come cheap. You need to balance the potential loss of revenue against the cost of the DRM solution.

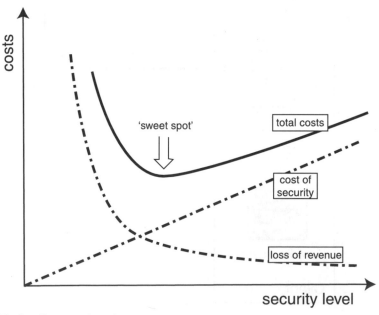

Figure 14.13 Finding the sweet spot.

Traditional text file DRM packages the entire file into a secure container. To stream, the encryption has to be in chunks, so that the player can render the file immediately. Securing the client is quite a challenge, so most DRM systems have means of identifying tampering that could compromise the security.

Live webcasting requires an on-the-fly encryption system, rather than the pre-encryption employed in the majority of systems.

A successful system is probably going to be more difficult to set up than a media encoding system. You will also have to be constantly vigilant against efforts to compromise the system.

15 Content distribution

Introduction

Efficient content distribution is vital to the publisher of streaming media. As early as 1997, the codecs then available offered a remarkable video quality at bit rates as low as 100 kbit/s, but the viewing experience did not live up to that potential.

Watching a stream as it stalled and hiccupped led many web content creators to stick with animated vector graphics. Even by 2001, streams often passed over 20 router hops before the last mile to the viewer. The routes switch as traffic varies, leading to varying latencies. The streaming infrastructure is shared with the general Internet, which only offers best-effort delivery.

Contrast this with television. The signal leaves the master control suite at the television station and then travels over a dedicated microwave link (the studio–transmitter link or STL) to the tower. The viewer sees the picture a fraction of a second after it leaves master control. Alternatively, the signal passes through the cable-operator's head-end then fans out through dedicated fibers to the set-top box. Both delivery channels have a fixed (and very short) propagation delay. They also have bandwidth dedicated exclusively to the channel. It is not surprising that they both exhibit a high quality of service. The cable operator owns and operates his entire infrastructure right through to the set-top box in the home. This gives complete control over service quality.

For streaming video to be universally accepted as a means of delivering media, the service quality has to closely match television. Without that, the business of monetizing entertainment content delivered over the Web is going to be tough.

There are many facets to distribution: improving the utilization of the Internet, delivering to the edge and alternative carriers to the switched Internet. Much of the technology focus outside codec development has been to address these distribution issues. There are a number of pinch-points that can make streaming a less than satisfying experience. The first is the network-to-network peering

Figure 15.1 Improving the delivery quality.

points. The next is the backbone of a network and the third is the last mile to the consumer. For live events the encoder-to-origin server link can also present problems. More and more fiber is being laid to augment the backbone bandwidth, but as ever, demand exceeds capacity. Just look at web sites. An index page used to be under 50 Kbytes. Now many have well over 200 Kbytes of Flash graphics. As the public use more broadband for the last mile, although it removes a bottleneck, it also creates demand for higher bit rate streams.

One family of solutions is the Content Delivery Networks (CDNs). The CDN attempts to improve the streaming experience, while giving more efficient utilization of the intervening network. So the viewer should see less of the stalled streams that mark the long-haul delivery of content. The service provider also benefits, as less bandwidth is required to connect to the Internet backbone.

Several groups of content creators and providers have formed to research and implement improvements to the distribution of content. The public demand simple ways to access content. If you watch cable television, all the programming is accessed through a simple user interface and a single monthly payment is made to the cable company. Finding and paying for content over the Internet can be difficult, and often there are doubts about the safety and security of payment methods. Peer-to-peer file-sharing systems have pointed the way to simple methods to locate content, but they did not have to bother about systems for collecting and distributing payments.

One industry-wide group investigating the issues related to efficient content distribution is the Kendra Initiative in the UK. They are researching an open architecture and non-commercial, format agnostic transport system for content distribution over the Internet. The work started in 1996 at the City University in London. Kendra has a number of aims beyond improving the viewing experience through efficient content distribution, including rights management systems.

One challenge is to improve accessibility, performance and reliability while minimizing the storage space required for caching and the network utilization. The hope is to build and investigate a model for the delivery of broadband content.

Kendra is also cooperating with the International Webcasters Association (IWA) to solve some of the factors that are hindering the wide deployment of multicasting. Initial use has been limited to corporate intranets, and the public Internet has not experienced the potential advantages of multicasting.

Content Delivery Networks

The basic premise of the CDN is to serve content closer to the user rather than across the Internet. This is called edge serving. If you are not using a CDN to view streaming media, a request for content traverses the Internet from network

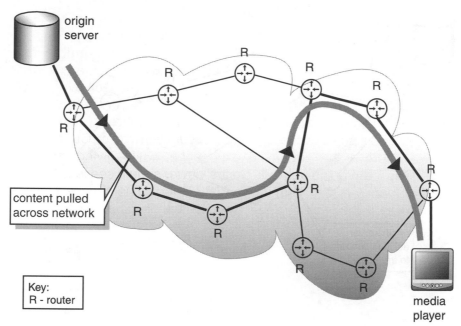

origin
server

content pulled
across network

Key:
R - router

media
player

Figure 15.2 Serving from the origin.

to network; it typically passes through 20 routers. The content data then returns, possibly along a different path through another 20 routers. At each stage packets can be lost or delayed, but streaming requires a regular data delivery rate to the player. Any congestion is going to result in the often-seen picture freezes and loss of the soundtrack.

The CDN avoids the effects of this transit congestion by serving the content from the user's point-of-presence – at the edge of the Internet. The CDN places special edge servers in the ISP providing your local point-of-presence. The CDN then uses a control network overlaid on the Internet to respond to requests for clips and to manage the delivery of clips from the content origin server to the edge servers.

The CDN has four main components to help provide high-quality streams local to the user:

- Smart routing
- Edge caching of content
- Proxy serving
- Splitting of live webcasts

Smart routing is an overlay above the regular Internet routing. Requests to the origin server for media clips are intercepted and redirected to the nearest

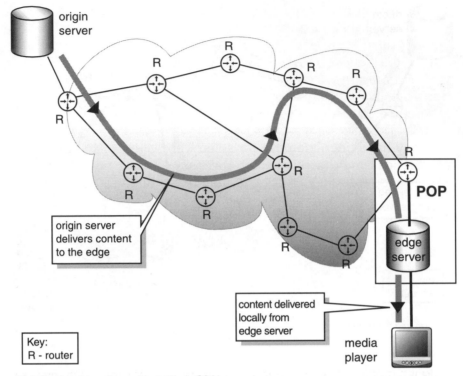

Figure 15.3 Serving from the edge with a CDN.

available edge server. The smart routing also delivers content from the origin server to the edge server by the best route, bypassing congested links.

The downside is the cost of the provision of the edge servers. So the ROI for the deployment of the CDN depends partly on the saving in bandwidth costs that can be achieved.

Another problem stems from the open structure of the Internet. It is not a network, but a federation of interconnected networks linked through peering agreements. In the year 2000 there were over 7,000 networks in North America alone. No one network handled more than 5 per cent of the overall traffic, with most carrying less than 1 per cent. So it is unlikely that one network alone will handle a request. In all likelihood a connection will pass through several peering points between different networks. Typically an ISP will offer a service level agreement (SLA). This complex network of connections makes it difficult to guarantee an end-to-end service once the data leaves the service provider's own network.

If you are setting up media streaming over a corporate wide-area intranet, the situation is simpler. You are most likely using a single network provider, so a closed CDN system can be installed over the network.

If you are serving content to the public, you will have less control over the quality of delivery. This is the enigma. The end-user's ISP receives their revenue from that end-user. If the user has opted for a low-cost service, there is little incentive for the service provider to invest in edge servers. So, although a content provider may have partnered with a high-performance CDN, there is no guarantee that this performance extends all the way to the final end-user. Clearly there is a case for the content providers to educate the users – there is no free lunch. The user of rich media will have chosen an ISP with much more care than may have been the case for static web pages.

These realities limit the number of successful CDNs operating within the public Web. If you want high-quality delivery to the public the simplest route is to approach the large CDNs like Akamai and Cable & Wireless's Digital Island. In 2001 Akamai had over 13,000 servers deployed around the Internet, and Digital Island had over 2,600. These global networks have the resources to handle very large numbers of media streams, as well as conventional HTML files. An ISP is very unlikely to install a range of different proprietary edge servers. The ISP is already having to provide servers to deliver the three main architectures: QuickTime, RealNetworks and Windows Media. To provide three of each for many different CDN architectures is not a satisfactory business proposition. For the corporate user, serving content over corporate networks, there is the freedom to choose any single system for in-house use.

The answer is standards and cooperation – like the Kendra Initiative. Cisco's Content Alliance is another organization that is attempting to forge the technologies for peering agreements between content distribution networks. Many companies including AOL and Digital Island support Content Bridge, yet another cooperative organization promoting efficient distribution.

Overlay network

To provide high-quality delivery some intelligence is needed to control the transmission of multimedia streams. The Content Delivery Networks use a control layer overlaid on the Internet. This layer can capture requests for files, and then manage the delivery by the most efficient way to give a high quality of service at the media player.

The CDNs aim to improve the streaming experience by three main processes: splitting, caching and proxy serving.

Local proxy

This is the basic edge server. The delivery from origin to user is split into two hops. The first is from the origin to the edge. The second is from the edge to the client. If streams are delivered locally to the client the RTSP and RTCP control messages

Figure 15.4 *The overlay control network.*

are exchanged locally rather than across the network. This cuts down control latencies and the network traffic to provide a better streaming experience. It also makes interactive applications much more responsive to the user. The CDN feeds the content to the edge server through content accelerators.

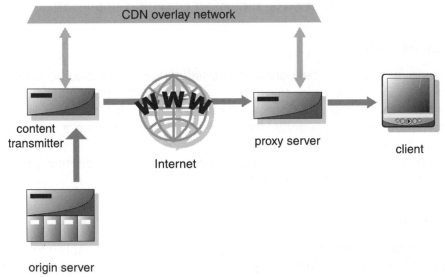

Figure 15.5 *Proxy edge server.*

Edge splitting

The local proxy offers another opportunity to make more efficient use of the network. If more than one client logs in to a live webcast at the same point-of-presence, a single stream is hauled to the POP. Cache servers then split the content and serve directly to the multiple clients. This has two advantages. The first is the reduction in network traffic; only one stream crosses the backbone. The second is that the clients are receiving the stream from a local server, rather than a long-distance negotiation through 20 or so routers.

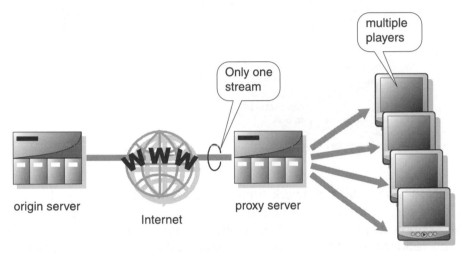

Figure 15.6 Edge splitting server.

Local caching

If a client requests content on-demand, that content is cached at the POP as it is streamed. If a second user requests the same file, then it is served from the cache, not the origin server. Caching has long been used for static web content. It greatly improves performance for popular pages, and also saves capacity on the main Internet backbone, by serving content locally to the user. One potential issue with a cache is stale material. Some content is very dynamic, for example news sites, and changes from hour to hour. So it is important that the CDN keeps the cache synchronized with the origin server. Another issue with the cache is reliability. If content is being sold to the users, it is vital that a disk failure does not stop the stream. You would not want to get into disputes about the satisfactory delivery of a paid-for clip. So RAID storage should be used in the cache server.

The CDN is providing a smart buffer close to the user. The client will now get a similar quality of service as if it were connected directly to the origin server.

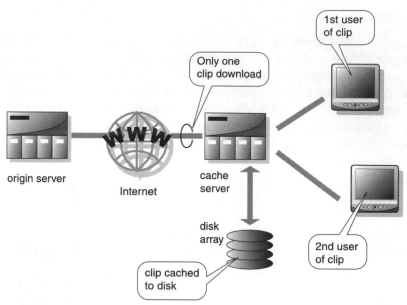

Figure 15.7 Edge cache server.

The CDN is also saving network traffic because the clip is only downloaded once, then served from a local cache.

It all sounds a good idea, but in reality a massive amount of disk storage would be required to cache all the streaming media clips that are downloaded daily. Cache servers were originally developed for the speedy serving of graphic content for web sites. But the file sizes are usually under 1 Mbyte. Consider a 30-minute video clip encoded at 300 kbit/s. That is a file size of around 70 Mbytes. Now you want to put your top 100 programs available on-demand. Now that is 7 Gbytes. Place that on thousands of cache servers, and the business proposition is beginning to look untenable.

The alternative is to provide a quick response to a request for streaming content. The wait for the first frame of video is the crucial period; that is when you can lose the impatient browser. If the first 30 seconds of a clip could be cached, the remainder can be streamed on-demand from the origin server to the edge server. To the viewer this process can be made transparent by assembling the two halves in a playlist.

Reporting

The cache server provides full reporting data back to the origin server. This means that the origin server can collect the same usage statistics as if the content were being served directly to the client, and not via a proxy server.

Network controller

The core of the CDN is the network controller. This can intercept requests for streams and redirect the player to the nearest cache server. So the DNS server, rather than using single IP address for a URL, will return the IP address of the correct edge server for the current conditions. This redirection can take into account network congestion and server utilization.

Figure 15.8 Redirecting the player to the edge server.

When the media player receives the metafile from the web server (4 in Figure 15.8) the URL addresses the CDN controller (5). The controller then redirects the request to the optimum edge server (6) and the content is streamed to the player (7). The redirection can load-balance requests across a number of server clusters.

Figure 15.9 Content network.

Content network

As a clip travels from the origin server to the edge it may be cached at several points across the Internet.

Akamai

Akamai have the most extensive CDN with their FreeFlow streaming network. If you have your content 'akamized', the reference tag uses an ARL or Akamai Resource Locator instead of a URL. The Akamai CDN uses this ARL to divert the browser request for a streaming file to the optimum edge server to retrieve the content.

Digital Island Footprint streaming network

This CDN overlays Cable & Wireless's extensive fiber and satellite network. When you select a media file link on a web page the URL in the content metafile is replaced with a 'super URL' that redirects the user to the Footprint network. The media player is then redirected to the appropriate edge server. Digital Island uses a Best Distributor Selection, or BDS, to redirect requests to a new rendezvous point with a content distributor (edge server). The BDS algorithm takes into account the network distance from client to server, the network conditions and the loading on the servers.

Corporate intranets

The corporate network has a different set of requirements from the public media viewer. An enterprise may want to use streaming for corporate communications, sales presentations and distance learning.

Planning

Within an enterprise there will be conflicting demands. The different user departments – training, marketing – will want the flexibility to schedule webcasts at times to suit themselves. They will want a high QoS whatever the network loading.

   Conversely the IT department will want to maximize utilization of the network by the proper scheduling of high network demands. IT will have to keep important services like transaction processing and mail running reliably, whatever the streaming load. The solution here is for the network to be content aware, so that the service provision can be controlled for the different applications.

Return of investment

You must have a top-down strategy to properly fund the network resources to provide for the agreed levels of use for streaming media. When scoping the ROI for the additional network cabling, router and switches, remember the legacy costs. These include duplication costs for VHS tapes and CD-ROMs, plus their distribution costs. Another cost is travel time and expenses for meetings with regional and branch offices.

The corporation probably wants restrictions on the content that can be accessed. This is partly to stop the viewing of inappropriate content in working time; the other reason is to manage the bandwidth requirements for the wide-area circuits (to lower costs). Many companies rely on streaming for financial news and other corporate information. So controlled access to the Internet is becoming a necessity.

Firewall

The corporate network will already have a firewall to protect the internal networks from unauthorized access. The firewall listens to network traffic passing between the corporate network and the external Internet. Most firewalls are set up to block all incoming traffic and to restrict outgoing traffic. The outgoing traffic allowed is most likely TCP and HTTP. All UDP traffic is blocked, but that is the optimum network transport layer for streaming video. Streaming can pass though if it is cloaked as HTTP traffic or streamed over TCP. Neither provides the best streaming experience, especially if you want interactivity and the best control over the streaming delivery rate.

The firewall has two ports: one on the corporate side, the other in a so-called demilitarized zone (DMZ). The DMZ is where equipment that has to be accessed from the Internet is located. This will include Internet and extranet web servers.

If you want to provide staff with access to streaming media from the Internet, rather than passing the files through the firewall, a separate proxy streaming server can be used. The proxy allows your network administrators to set up access control rules, but does not allow external access to the internal network.

There is a potential issue with cached content – it may be that you need authorization to view a file. If the file is sitting on a cache it could easily be copied. RealServer Proxy gets around this by encrypting the file and the file name. The only way to access the file is to stream it. Material is retrieved from the cache and decrypted for streaming after an accounting connection is established to the origin server. This way, full usage reporting is maintained.

The Real player can be configured to point at the proxy server rather than trying to connect directly to the origin server. This would be the normal set-up in a corporate application.

Figure 15.10 Corporate intranet with proxy server.

The CDN and managing bandwidth

The proxy server can be used as a cache to sensibly manage the delivery of large files over external links. Suppose that you have a remote office connected by a T-1 line (1.5 Mbit/s). The link was originally leased for transaction data to the company databases and/or e-mail traffic. Both applications use relatively small files, so a T-1 has the capacity for a mid-sized office.

Now you want to start streaming internal presentations across the link. A high-quality encoding (at say 1 Mbit/s) is going to use the entire capacity of the link, clearly not a viable option. One way around this is to place a proxy server at the remote site. This can be preloaded with the presentation overnight, and then viewed from the cache during office hours. So during the day the T-1 line is left free for the regular data traffic.

A second solution would be to segregate traffic. Existing transaction processing, e-mail and other data traffic can use the T-1 line, and media traffic can utilize a VPN over the Internet.

The solution with the proxy server is *pushing* content. Most CDNs rely on a request from a player before content is delivered. This is called *pull* delivery. It has advantages in that the cache does not waste disk space by storing unwanted material. The disadvantage is that the first user to request a clip has to wait for delivery. Later users of the same clip will get a prompt response to their request.

The advantage of pushing is that the administrators have more control over wide-area network utilization, but this is to be balanced against the above-mentioned storage costs.

Running a reliable webcast

Computer equipment and software is not renowned for 100 per cent reliability. Fiber cables can get severed. So if you are planning to host important webcasts, it is worth considering what would happen if the webcast went down. Even if you have taken great care in selection of equipment with a long mean time before failure ratings, the unexpected can always happen. So for a highly available system, it is best to assume that things will go wrong, and accordingly plan systems that are fault tolerant.

As an enterprise uses streaming more and more, then the requirements for high availability increase. Once streaming is core to corporate communications, the expectations of the systems approach those of the phone system. Conventional splitters are single points-of-failure in the delivery network. Real's iQ network lets you design in redundancy to improve the QoS of the corporate network.

RealSystem Neuralcast

RealNetworks have developed an architecture called Neuralcast Technology. It is part of the RealSystem iQ product line. Neuralcast allows a network of servers to be linked in a flexible manner to support highly reliable distribution of live webcasts.

One of the features of the system is support for redundant paths from the encoder or origin server through to the media player. This means that if any part of the network is no longer available, the content delivery will fail-over to another path, thus ensuring the continuous delivery of the stream. Where the redundant streams reconverge at a RealSystem receiving server, the server accepts the first packet and ignores any other packets that duplicate the same media data.

A peer-to-peer network can be set up, so that servers can act as transmitters or receivers. This means that live content can be injected anywhere in the network.

push initiation

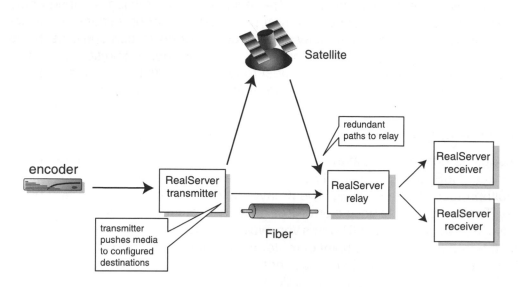

Satellite

redundant
paths to relay

encoder

RealServer
transmitter

RealServer
relay

RealServer
receiver

RealServer
receiver

transmitter
pushes media
to configured
destinations

Fiber

pull initiation

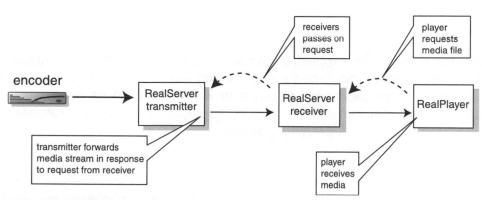

receivers
passes on
request

player
requests
media file

encoder

RealServer
transmitter

RealServer
receiver

RealPlayer

transmitter forwards
media stream in response
to request from receiver

player
receives
media

Figure 15.11 RealSystem iQ.

The distribution can be push or pull. The push system transmits content to all the receivers that it has been configured to feed. Pull awaits a request from the player for content. The receiver feeding the player then requests content from the origin server. The push distribution can use forward error correction to correct for packet loss. This allows a unidirectional stream to be transmitted to edge servers, with no requirement for a back-channel. This can be very useful for satellite distribution by multicast. The level of error correction is configurable to suit the network conditions. Different paths can be set up separately, so for example a satellite link which may already use error correction could be set to a low value, and a high value set for a congested Internet connection. If a back-channel exists, the receiver can request resends of corrupted packets; this can be used in combination with or instead of forward error correction.

Improving the QoS

Alongside edge serving many strides are being taken to improve the quality of service (QoS) of the Internet. Two of the initiatives are resource reservation and multi-protocol label switching. The IP layer of the Internet uses best-effort delivery. The complexity to ensure error-free delivery is located at the server and client using a protocol like TCP. IP works very well; it uses a simple network system. But as the traffic grows to the point of router congestion, then packets are dropped. This causes delays and jitter. This is not a problem for general data traffic, but is an issue with real-time applications like multimedia and voice-over IP.

Even if you opt for a CDN, improving the intermediate network can only help. The challenge to improve the quality of service is to implement improvements without increasing complexity at the core of the network. Some technologies can be employed on closed systems like intranets, but rolling out developments to the public Internet is not as easy.

RSVP

Resource Reservation Protocol allows a client (the media player) to request a guaranteed network resource for unicast and multicast data flows. Resource Reservation is complex, and too much of an overhead to be generally used across the Internet, but can be usefully deployed at the edge. Potentially it delivers the best QoS delivery for packets.

MPLS

Multi-Protocol Label Switching (MPLS) has emerged as a step on the road to photonic networks. It is used not just for IP (hence the qualifier multi-), but also other packet-switching protocols like frame relay. The label contains layer 3 routing information to indicate the next router hop. This means that the routers can simply switch the packet, using the data in the label. The data takes the label-switched path rather than using the usual router paths. This means that the labels can be assigned to allow control over the network traffic, hence providing potential routes around congestion.

Diffserv

Differentiated services or Diffserv allows coarse information about the service requirements of a packet to be coded in the IP header. It replaces the type-of-service or traffic class field in the header and determines the priority within the router. Diffserv marks traffic at the input to a network and is unmarked when the packet leaves that network. To operate, Diffserv requires a service level agreement at network peering points.

There is no holy grail for improving the quality of service for media streams crossing the Internet. There are a number of solutions that deployed together can improve the streaming experience, without requiring a complete swap-out of the network infrastructure. Diffserv can assign packet priorities, MPLS allows control over traffic and RSVP can reserve resources at the edge. None of these protocols can make bandwidth available if the network is overloaded, so they are not a substitute for proper traffic engineering.

Satellite delivery

Some people are looking up to the sky for the answer to Internet congestion. Satellite communication can be used in two ways. One is to supplement the Internet backbone; the other is for direct connection to the user. Satellites are particularly useful for handling peak demands for popular webcasts. The satellite hops can completely bypass the backbone, by streaming multicasts to the edge of the Web. The Internet can be used for the back-channel to gather usage statistics and manage authorizations. The main bandwidth-hungry content data travels via the satellite circuit.

Cidera and mediaXtranet from Vyvx Broadband Media both offer satellite-augmented delivery.

Multicast

Satellites are an efficient way to distribute multicasts to widely dispersed audiences. Any POP within the footprint of the downlink can potentially receive a multicast feed, without all the intermediate routers that a fiber connection would entail.

Satellite to the user

So what about the person who has had enough of the city and headed for a cabin in the hills? Technologies like ADSL to connect to a telco are limited to a range of about 5,000 meters from the central office. One solution for remote sites is to use satellite delivery of broadband content. Satellites are also a good way to multicast a single stream to large audiences. They do not have the capacity for on-demand streaming to the very large numbers that the terrestrial circuit can offer, but are more suited to the burst transmissions of general web page downloads, where many users can share the same bandwidth.

Satellite can be one-way or two-way. One-way uses a regular telco back-channel through, for example, a dial-up circuit. This is an asymmetric configuration, but for the average user, the much lower bandwidth of the back-channel would be no more of an issue than that experienced by the ADSL user. Note that in some countries the regulatory authorities do not allow private uplinks, stemming from paranoia about security and state control.

VSAT

The use of very small aperture terminals has revolutionized satellite commu-nications. The 4–5 meter diameter dishes common with C-band have been supplanted with compact Ku-band antennae, less than 1 meter in diameter. Typical capacities of a geo-stationary satellite (in the year 2000) were in the region of 108 Mbit/s of bandwidth per cell. A cell is about 640 km in diameter.

Hughes Network Systems have a system called DirecWay. This satellite distribution offers several advantages for the multicasting of live events. Only one stream is sent up to the satellite, and then any authorized user within the antenna footprint can participate in the webcast.

The Ka-band is now being used in the search for more free space in the RF spectrum. This band uses a compact dish with small beam width, but does suffer attenuation if there is rain in the path of the beam.

Summary

A compelling viewing experience demands a media stream that does not stall, that does not lose the audio. To achieve this goal, the bottlenecks that slow down the data packets have to be eliminated. As a clip is transferred from a live encoder or an origin server, the first impediment may be the link to the backbone. This is often a problem for live webcasts. The capacity of the available existing circuits may not be sufficient. Satellite back-haul may be an option.

The next step is to cross the backbone. Improvement in capacity has been assisted by the ever-increasing bandwidth of the fiber backbones, but the capacity of the last mile has not kept pace. Many incumbent utilities are burdened with a historic infrastructure designed for the plain old telephone service. The investment required to bring fiber to the curb is staggering, with a long payback time. This is an area where the television broadcaster wins hands down. They have a fixed cost for transmission. It makes no difference if there are a hundred or a million receivers within range of the tower.

Even if the end-to-end connection could be established satisfactorily, it is unlikely that all the remaining components are going to have excess capacity. Traffic always expands to fill the excess. So how can the traffic cross the Internet without suffering delays?

Content Delivery Networks (CDNs) mean that files no longer have to be served right across the Internet. Instead, content is delivered from servers placed at the edge of the Internet in your local point-of-presence. This edge serving makes for a much better viewing experience, without all the problems that packet loss and delays can cause as clips transit the Internet routers.

Edge serving by CDNs has been very successfully applied to static web content. To extend this to streaming is not trivial; the demands for disk space at the caches are potentially enormous. The method can be applied successfully within a closed system, where a sensible booking system can be used for space. This could be a corporate network or a campus-wide system.

On the public Internet it is possible for special events with very large audiences to use caching effectively. The alternative is a hybrid approach – a prefix of the media clip could be cached to give a rapid start to the stream. The remainder of the stream is then pulled from the origin to the edge. The CDNs are content-aware and can apply smart routing algorithms to avoid traffic bottle-necks in the Internet, potentially lowering packet loss and delay. A big advantage with the CDN is that a live webcast can be split at the POP. This replaces a stream per client with a single stream from the origin server. The final goal would be the ability to multicast across disparate networks; this offers the best potential to reduce network congestion for live webcasts. The on-demand user is a more difficult customer to satisfy with high-quality delivery. If content is little used there is no advantage in caching; there are going to be different standards for popular content, which could possibly be dispersed to the edge, and content that is used very occasionally. To expect otherwise would need a CDN with a capacity that would not make economic sense.

As the bottlenecks are removed and the performance of streaming improves, more companies will want to use rich media – so the traffic will grow and congestion will increase. So the improvements will have to continue at a pace to keep up with ever-increasing demand; it is just like building a highway network – traffic expands to meet the capacity and is regulated only by congestion.

16 Applications for streaming media

Introduction

In the short time span of 5 years, streaming has evolved from the initial development into a major communication medium. Although streaming can be used standalone to deliver audio and video content, it is more often deployed as a component in a wider system – often called rich media. This chapter explores some of these applications.

The advent of SMIL (Synchronized Multimedia Integration Language), along with Microsoft's TIME, has given content producers the tools to seamlessly assemble video, audio, animated vector graphics and stills into a compelling and interactive experience that is rich media. At a simple level one of the most-used styles is a combination of PowerPoint slides with audio and video. Such multimedia presentations can be used for sales promotions, distance learning and product launches. It adds another component to the marketing mix, one that has the immediacy of video with the interactivity of the CD-ROM.

The early applications have been:

- Training
- Entertainment (Internet radio)
- Corporate communications
- Marketing

Some applications use streaming as the primary focus, others use streaming as a tool. A typical example of the latter is the use of streaming media as a proxy for broadcast quality content in digital asset management systems. Another use is for the rapid approval of clips, often needed when making commercials. The video production industry needs to exchange preview dailies (rushes) of clips to interested parties who could be in another continent; streaming media is an ideal vehicle.

Rich media

Rich media used to be the preserve of the CD-ROM. Tools like QuickTime allowed a combination of text, graphics and video to be combined into an interactive presentation. In contrast, web content was limited to text and still images. The later development of Flash allowed content creators to enliven their static web pages with compelling vector graphics. Streaming media now allows regular video to be added to web pages, so the same mix of formats, that was once restricted to the CD-ROM, can now be delivered in real-time as a stream.

Before embarking on a rich media project, it's best to sit back and think 'what and how am I trying to communicate?' If you want to webcast, you should aim to use it because of its strengths – if you are using it as a substitute for a different medium your results may be less than optimum. Above all it must hold the attention of the audience. That dictates the maintenance of high production values.

Whatever the codec designers may claim for video quality, once the stream has been carried over the Internet the results can be less than satisfying. If you want the viewer to enjoy the experience you should always plan for worst-case delivery quality, possibly offering alternative streams for narrow- and broadband users.

Many examples of rich media have indicated a complete lack of appreciation of the experience gained by the producers from other media formats. Some of the results of best communicators can be seen in regular linear television programs. They use a combination of video and graphics that has been developed over a

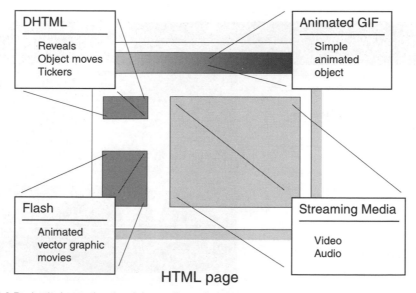

Figure 16.1 Typical elements of a rich media web page.

period of 50 years to produce content that is compelling to follow and easy to understand.

You will notice that there is a strict limit on the amount of information presented. A television program will rarely convey more than six key facts in 30 minutes. The graphics are kept simple. As web developers have discovered, people will not read vast amounts of text on a screen. Often they 'graze' the text, linking rapidly from one page to another.

The next point is to deliver a good quality image – that means restricting the aggregate data rate to sensible levels. The well-known saying is that the viewer will not wait. After a few seconds waiting for a download most viewers will click away to another site.

Another rule gained from the CD-ROM is to make it interesting by involving the viewer. Interactivity is the answer here. To reinforce the experience, make it immersive.

The news site

One of the most successful applications for streaming has been the financial news site. The traders have an insatiable demand for content, and they also have broadband access to the Internet. Rich media allows interviews to be combined with general text stories from agency feeds. Unlike television there is more freedom in the use of text. The screen resolution of the typical computer display is higher than a standard-definition interlaced television receiver, so more background information can be given in text form.

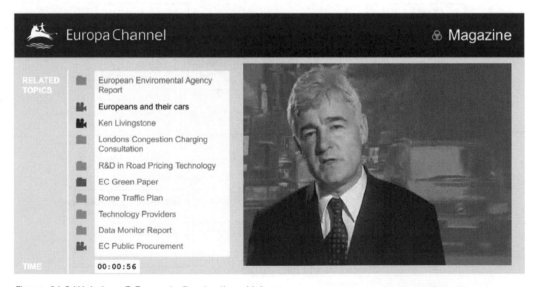

Figure 16.2 Webzine. © Tornado Productions Ltd.

The Europa Channel illustrated in Figure 16.2 is a concept for an Internet news channel. Alongside the anchor there is a choice of links to streaming clips or web pages for a 'drilldown' into the background of a story. Note the clean graphic style. There is nothing superfluous to detract from the message and the essential requirements for navigation.

Corporate communications

The corporate webcast has become an integral part of the quarterly earnings call, but streaming is not just for investors. Most departments can use streaming, either to replace meetings or to convey information – product training, conveying HR policies and general corporate messages – the possibilities are immense. Streaming becomes vital for corporations with many remote sites, or to communicate to distributors, agents and resellers.

Staff training

Staff training is a prime user of multimedia technology. In 2001 Microsoft released Producer as a tool to use alongside PowerPoint for the creation of rich media presentations. In a typical presentation, the speaker can be shown in a streaming video and audio clip. You can link a PowerPoint slide presentation to the video clip so that the slides change at the correct point in the script during the video clip. The synchronization can be extended to HTML pages, so, for example, one page could have a Windows Media window embedded to show a video clip. Another part of the presentation may have audio only. At this point a different page layout without the video player could be used.

A presentation is prepared offline with MS Producer. What about the live presentation? Companies like Virage and Sonic Foundry have products to help you publish live rich media presentations. The presentation is encoded as a video and audio file, and the slides are captured as they change. The live stream is also archived so viewers can watch on-demand at a time that may be more convenient than viewing the live stream.

Product launches

The Eloquent Corporation have adopted streaming media as a key component of their product line. Their LaunchForce application is designed to provide a complete rich media solution for online product launches. Rather than the city-by-city roadshows that are typical for the launch of new products, LaunchForce uses Windows Media video and audio streaming, along with synchronized PowerPoint slides, to give a live audience the run-down on a new product.

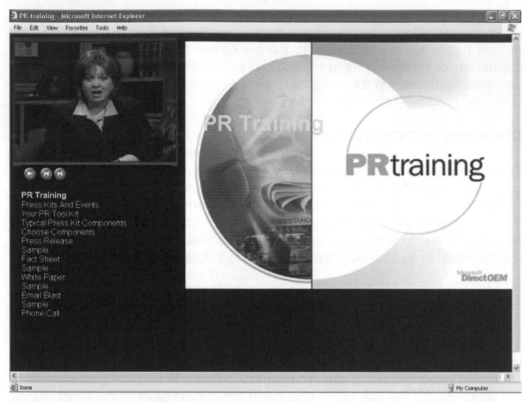

Figure 16.3 Microsoft Producer output on a web browser. Screen shot reprinted by permission from Microsoft Corporation.

Eloquent recognizes that not every corporation has the in-house skills to put together a compelling presentation; it has set up a professional services division that can help you to publish the launch. Although you could launch a product by mailing out a CD-ROM, the advantage of streaming is the immediacy of a live presentation. The audience can interact with the presenters, asking questions by phone or e-mail, or respond by online polling. This feedback is key to involving the audience in the launch – a CD-ROM mailout can so easily end up in the trash.

Music promotion

The Web has a long association with music, stemming from the use of the Internet to download MP3 audio files. So it is natural to use the Web to promote and retail music. This site was designed for a broadband service provider. It has clips of the band performing, backstage interviews and other content of special interest to fans of the band. Two versions were created, one broadband for delivery at 250 kbit/s and a simpler version for delivery at 28 kbit/s. Many younger people – the potential audience – may not have broadband access, so it is important not to exclude them. By offering alternative low bit rate content, perhaps audio-only, they can use low-cost dial-up modems to access similar content to broadband connection.

The style is very different from the average web page; it is more akin to television or the CD-ROM. Note that the small size of the video playback area does not detract from the overall design. Relevant graphics merge with the video into a seamless tableau.

Figure 16.4 Broadband version of a music promotion site. © BTopenworld, produced by Tornado Productions Ltd.

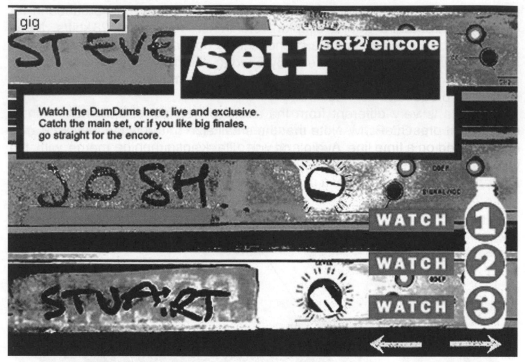

Figure 16.5 Narrowband version of a music promotion site. © BTopenworld, produced by Tornado Productions Ltd.

The media player has been embedded into the background image, so the player surround does not impinge upon the overall graphic design. Some of the usual web design conventions are used for familiarity; note the drop-down menu to select other pages on the site. The site is designed to display full-screen.

An alternative site for narrowband users offers the same experience, with similar graphics and navigation. The page was designed to fit in a 475 × 325 window in the main portal, so did not need branding. The video content plays in a separate media player, launched by the user, and so does not need space within the main window.

The graphics are a scaled down version of the broadband. As the display window is less than one-quarter the size of the broadband, corresponding savings in download time are realized. Even though the window is smaller, the same amount of textual content has been retained.

Producing rich media

A skilled multimedia developer will have no problems adding interactive video and audio into existing rich media web pages, but a certain amount of hand scripting is bound to be needed. For the less skilled there are a number of tools to ease the creation of presentations.

Microsoft Producer

Released in 2001, this tool is aimed at the internal communications staff of a corporation. It is a plug-in to PowerPoint. The production process starts with a PowerPoint presentation. As the presentation is run through, the slide changes are recorded on a time line. Audio and video tracks can then be synchronized to the same time line. At its simplest you can make a voice-over to accompany a PowerPoint presentation. For a more compelling presentation, a video clip of the presenter speaking can be added.

Other elements can be incorporated – like still photographs and links – and the whole placed into an HTML page for delivery. Microsoft supplies a number of templates for the page layout, much like a word processor. As the final integrated presentation is a web page, the Internet Explorer browser can be used to play the final presentation.

The advantage of Producer is that it is simple to use; any PowerPoint user could soon learn to use the extra facilities. Note that the output does not have to be streamed; it can also be distributed via FTP or CD-ROM.

Discreet Cleaner 5.1

Cleaner has a facility for programming synchronized events called Event-Stream. This lets you create interactive rich media applications. All of the main streaming architectures offer some level of interactive features. Cleaner lets you add stream navigation, synchronize HTML to streaming media, embed links and add interactive hotspots. Cleaner is agnostic towards the streaming architecture. So you can author once and then encode many times to all three streaming architectures.

Digital asset management

Many businesses have libraries of video material, and not just broadcasters. Advertising agencies and large corporations can both have extensive archives of commercials and training material. As you build up a library of video clips, gradually a problem becomes evident. How do you find the clip you want? With text documents you can search for a string of characters to locate relevant material. With video and audio you do not have this luxury. Traditional libraries, of tapes on shelves, often have either simple card indices or a computer database.

The initial use of asset management was for television news archives, to give journalists and program researchers full access to the vault. Asset management is not limited to internal use; it can also be used as an aid to the marketing of video content to the consumer or for sales to other program makers.

A typical example would be a health information provider that wants to sell videos. The use of a powerful video search engine helps potential customers to find the right product for their needs – a useful adjunct to the selling process. The potential purchaser can preview material, find the right video, then order a VHS tape or DVD or, alternatively, watch a stream. Video libraries can also be used in higher education. A university can record lectures as streams and make the files available on-demand to students. Again the asset management makes the lecture archive searchable.

There are several issues to be overcome with an asset library.

- How do you access the library from remote or dispersed sites?
- How do you find material that you want?
- How do you preview the material?
- How do you distribute the material?

The obvious way to offer access is through a web browser. That way the user can use a conventional search GUI, and the media can be viewed with a player plug-in. The drawback is that the library material may be on analog tape – Betacam – or for more recent material, Digital Betacam or DV. Clearly you cannot stream the video over the corporate network; that would require 25–50 Mbit of bandwidth.

The solution is to use a hierarchy of lower resolution proxies. That way you start with lightweight downloads, and as you narrow the search larger resolution

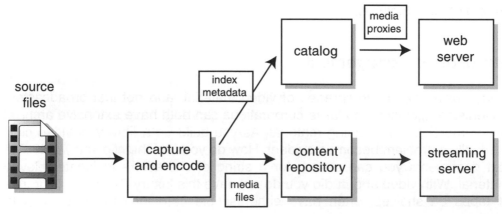

Figure 16.6 Video catalog.

media files can be viewed. That way the speed of search and the network utilization are optimized.

The initial search is text only; the results set may be 10 or 100 possible clips. You can then view thumbnails to help identify the required clip. Once a likely file has been located, then you can view a low-resolution stream, maybe 30 kbit/s. Once that is established as the correct file, you could then view a high-resolution stream, perhaps at 500 kbit/s. The alternative would be to order a dub of the master tape.

So streaming media is used as the core technology for the location of the relevant content and then for subsequent viewing of the media library.

media	stream rate	file size (15 min clip)
search result set		1 kBytes
thumb nails		20 kBytes
low-res proxy	30 kbit/s	3 MBytes
hi-res streaming media	500 kbit/s	56 MBytes
videotape	25 Mbit/s	2.8 GBytes

Figure 16.7 The hierarchy of media proxies.

Finding the material

It has often been said that if you cannot find a tape, what is the point in keeping it? The storage costs for videotape are not small. The vault requires climate control to maintain a long life. So to leverage the asset value of a library you need to make it easy to find the required material for potential reuse or re-purposing.

The usual way to locate the material is to use some form of search engine. These are usually text based, so you could search for keywords in the clip description or in a transcript of the soundtrack. With video material there are many possibilities beyond a straight text search. You could search for picture qualities, like color and texture, or for a person's face.

The first step in setting up the catalog is to generate an index that can be used by the search engine.

Indexing

The index uses data about the content data, called metadata. The capture of metadata has always been a problem because it usually relies upon physical typing of records into a database. Most tapes will come with basic information. Some examples of metadata are:

Title	Bit rate
Artist	Copyright
Author	Duration
Format	

Metadata can include keywords about the clip. To aid the searching, keywords should not be just physical attributes of the scene, emotional characteristics can be added – 'happy, sad, sexy' – and clearly these have to be entered manually.

There are automated ways of collecting information. Material shot for television often has closed captions; these can also be used for keyword generation and also for scene change detection (closed captions carry a marker). Another source of metadata is a transcript of the soundtrack derived by a speech-to-text software application. Keyword extraction can then be applied to the transcript.

Speech-to-text needs a clear soundtrack to get an accurate transcription. The early products were based on systems developed for automated call centers by telecommunications companies. Although these can produce good results with dictated speech, they are not so accurate with the average soundtrack from a video clip. Some of the more successful products that are used for indexing

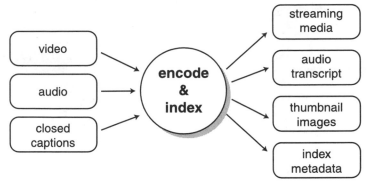

Figure 16.8 Encoding and indexing.

utilize the Hidden Markov model for analysis of the phones (a phone is the basic unit of speech). Some systems can also learn to recognize the voice of a number of different speakers. So a transcript of the dialog between two speakers can be annotated with the names of each speaker.

Once derived, the index metadata is exported to a database where it can be interrogated by the search engine.

Previewing material

There are two ways to preview material: as stills and as video. The results set for a text search can return a single still image (like a QuickTime movie poster) to represent the clip. More detail can be seen from a storyboard of thumbnail images. These are extracted as part of the indexing process. A video analysis engine detects the cuts, fades and dissolves that indicate a scene change and then grabs a reference still frame. This is converted to a JPEG image so that it can be dropped into HTML. The associated time code is listed with the thumbnails as a navigation aid.

Although digital asset management systems can be used with any media repository, tape or file on disk, they do offer an attractive solution for the management of streaming media content. Editorial personnel can use the search facilities during the production processes. The production of rich media brings together a number of publishing disciplines – text authoring, graphic design, web development and video production. The asset management system makes it much easier for the different skills to cooperate in the production of the final product. From a public media portal the consumer can also use a general search engine to identify wanted content.

The Dremedia user interface shows many of the features (see Figure 16.10). At the top left of the screen the user enters the search criteria. Underneath the results set shows relevant clips. Selecting a clip show the storyboard for the clip,

scene
change

web page of thumbnails

grabbed thumbnail
[jpeg]

Figure 16.9 Video indexing.

along with the audio transcript (on another tab). The audio and video can then
be played from any thumbnail location. The alternative is to navigate from the
transcript, so you can play from any point in the text.

Indexing workstation

In many ways the indexing workstation is similar to, or can even be based upon,
a regular encoding workstation. Many products have combined the two to give
a simple solution for the capture of library material. Consider a television news
station. The live newscasts can be captured and indexed using the closed
caption feed or generating an audio transcript. The station can then build up a
back catalog of newscasts, so the traveler can pick up their local news wherever
they are in the world. The index gives random access to wanted features without
the need to view the entire program. The main use will be for editorial staff to
look up old stories.

Figure 16.10 Dremedia t-m Production Suite showing thumbnails. © Dremedia.

Proprietary indexing tools

There are three established indexing products, Virage, Convera and MediaSite, and one newcomer, Dremedia. All have similar features, generating a storyboard of video scenes and a text transcript, but differ in the details. If you are evaluating products to use for indexing, some of the points to look for are the accuracy of the speech transcription and the ease and cost of integrating into the rest of your asset management framework. The relevance of the result set from the search engine depends strongly upon the quality of the original

Figure 16.11 Digital asset management indexing.

metadata used to generate the index. Very little information can be gleaned from the video alone; the best results are from the audio transcript. For high productivity, the automated collection of metadata is essential, so a good speech-to-text engine is a prerequisite for an efficient operation. It is also a complex task. It is one thing recognizing a small vocabulary for a telephone answering system. Understanding normal speech, with a wide vocabulary and in a variety of languages and regional accents, is a complex process. The recent development of sophisticated speech decoding algorithms means that a good transcript can now be generated on a modest workstation (twin Pentium CPU), making its wide application a reality.

Virage

Virage pioneered video indexing with the VideoLogger. The basic product indexes the video into a visual storyboard. Audio plug-ins provide speech-to-text conversion using the IBM ViaVoice. Speaker identification can be added to the speech transcript. The VideoLogger can also analyze the video media to recognize faces, and use optical character recognition to decode on-screen text (captions and graphics) for use in the index.

Virage has partnered with BBN Technologies to provide advanced audio analysis. This has been optimized for the transcription of broadcast news. The television news organizations have been early adopters of digital asset management as an essential tool to aid journalists in their research of the archives. The BBN analyzer can also identify and log proper nouns: peoples' names, company names and place names, often a problem for basic speech engines.

Another Virage product, MediaSync, is a plug-in to the VideoLogger. This lets you synchronize PowerPoint slides to an audio and video stream for swift preparation of rich media presentations.

A number of encoding stations can be linked together with a VideoLogger to make a comprehensive multiple-format streaming capture and encode system called SmartEncode. The encoding is not limited to streaming formats, but can also be standard resolution MPEG-2 for regular television broadcast. This allows streaming preview copies to be made alongside the broadcast material.

Convera

Convera started out as Excalibur. Their main product is the RetrivalWare catalog and search engine that is used for large text asset libraries. The Screening Room is a modular product for video content management that can make video assets searchable in the same way as text.

Once other modules are captured and indexed, Screening Room can be used to edit the content. It may just be trimming metadata and annotating, or it may be the re-purposing of material, by dragging and dropping scenes from the storyboard to assemble clips into a new program. The rough-cut sequence can then be exported as an Edit Decision List (EDL) to an external non-linear editor for 'sweetening'.

Sonic Foundry Media Systems (MediaSite)

Sonic Foundry purchased MediaSite in 2001. The MediaSite product is a spin-off from research at the Carnegie-Mellon University, comprising index and search modules. Sonic Foundry is supplying a range of integrated modules for publishing rich media, live and on-demand.

Dremedia t-m Production Suite

Dremedia take an alternative view to indexing. No manual collection or entry of metadata is required. The search index uses an automatically generated transcript of the soundtrack. The product combines high-performance speech analysis and a powerful search engine.

It is more than just an indexing system. The transcript is synchronized to video frames. This means that a rough cut of a program can be made on the transcript, without the need to use a video editor. The same principle can, of course, be equally applied to radio programming. Video or audio material becomes navigable from the transcript, using the search engine to find wanted text strings or words, offering the possibility of real productivity gains in production and in re-purposing.

The power of the t-m Production Suite stems from two technologies: one is the high-performance speech analyzer for recognizing continuous speech (SoftSound) and the other is Autonomy's Dynamic Reasoning Engine (DRE) to produce accurate searches.

No doubt you have often cursed a simple text or Boolean search and the attendant poor results sets. In contrast, the DRE uses powerful probabilistic modeling techniques to produce concept-based searches with high relevance ratings.

Real-time webcast analysis – iTVNow

The Dremedia speech analyzer can capture the soundtrack of a webcast and generate a transcript in real-time. The asset manager engine can use the transcript to automatically search for files that are conceptually linked to the webcast while the stream is being transmitted. A synchronized result set of

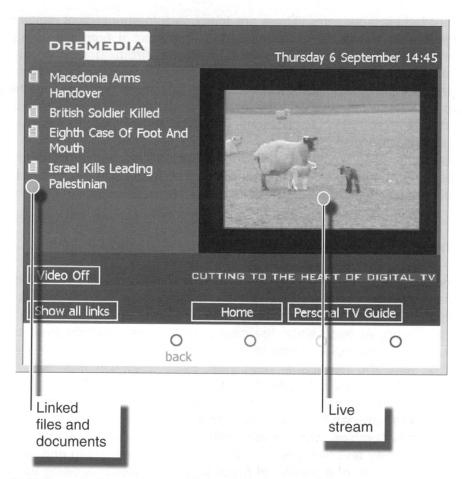

Figure 16.12 Dremedia iTVNow. Live asset linking. © Dremedia Limited.

relevant files can then be displayed after a short delay. These files could be audio and video, but could also be any document, PDF reports, word processor files or HTML links. Such a product has many potential applications; as an example, the financial community monitoring incoming agency feeds could associate live news with other information related to a particular stock. This is a very good example of the real productivity gains that can be achieved by combining streaming media with asset management.

Asset management frameworks

The indexing and search engines in themselves do not make a complete asset management system. A framework is required to link the index and catalog with the other business systems. There are four principle suppliers of digital asset management systems that can be used to construct a complete integrated solution: Ascential (Media360), Artesia, Bulldog (from Documentum) and eMotion. When selecting a system, apart from the obvious price/performance comparisons, it is most important to see how the system integrates with the rest of your business. It is quite possible that the professional services to drop the product into your other applications will cost more than the core asset management product.

These systems can manage very large media archives and promise potential savings in manpower – essential for the low-cost production demanded by the ever-increasing media output channels.

Summary

The last 100 years have seen a steady evolution of new media channels. The first mass communication media, print, was joined by radio. Alongside the development of radio the telephone opened up personal communication. Then came television. At each stage the new medium was originally treated as a variant of its predecessor. Some of the first radio news broadcasts used the anchor to read the newspaper headlines. Early television was like a radio broadcast with pictures. Gradually the creators of content learnt how to exploit the new medium in a way that broke from the stereotypes of its forerunners.

The barriers between the electronic media are becoming blurred. Interactive television can combine web content with off-air television. Telephones and radios can display text and graphics. Web browsers have audio and video.

The old paradigm of a handful of major television networks being the prime source of video programming has long gone. Cable and satellite can deliver several hundred channels to the home, but television is still mass media – 200 channels for a population of millions is hardly bespoke programming. Streaming adds a new and high-capacity delivery vehicle for video content that can be personalized for each viewer. It may be special content or targeted ads.

The quality delivered to the viewer has increased steadily since the mid-1990s, with improvements in codecs and broadband access for the last mile, and in 2002 could rival VHS, with many quality improvements in the offing.

QuickTime dominated multimedia production. RealNetworks pioneered the introduction of streaming to the Internet community. Now Windows Media have joined the fray with the integration into the operating system. MPEG-4 promises to open up streaming beyond the environment of the PC. Breaking away from the bounds of the rectangular video picture offers new possibilities for immersive and interactive experiences. The player could be a cellular phone, a PDA, a games console or a high-definition television receiver.

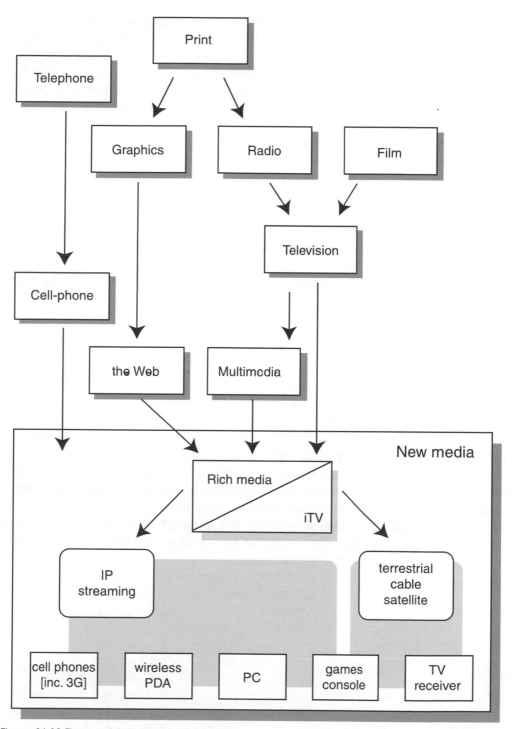

Figure 16.13 The road from print to rich media.

There is no doubt that the first streaming pictures were less than satisfying, but AM radio in the 1920s and television in the monochrome days both provided a great source of entertainment. The advances in delivery technologies, including broadband and CDNs, are offering both the consumer and the corporate user a whole new way to communicate. It is a very flexible medium, offering everything from live webcasts, distance learning and the whole gamut of corporate communications.

It is important that suitable content is selected for the medium. Take the movie industry. The realistic limit for the last mile is going to be 1 Mbit/s for the next decade. Will an on-demand movie streamed at that rate compete with the consumers' expectations of DVD quality? This quality gap will stretch further when the high-definition DVD becomes available. The DVD supports a higher data transfer rate than the last mile and the players are low cost, so perhaps streamed movies are not a good application for webcasting.

Many corporate applications of streaming replace the face-to-face presentation, saving on traveling costs and time. Other applications offer entertainment and information to the public.

And finally

There are many enigmas about webcasting. Many wild claims have been made about streaming – some have come to fruition, but some defy the laws of physics. The monetization of webcasting has proved more difficult than many people thought. There are many reasons for this, but the facts must be faced – much content has been of poor technical quality with indifferent production values. Consumers are happy to pay for good quality – look at the sales of CDs, DVDs and games. Once the issues of distribution are solved there are many indications that content will be sold very successfully.

The killer apps will have to exploit the strengths of the medium: the immediacy, the interactivity, the ability to personalize content, the rich media and, through the Internet, the global reach.

Glossary

Agnostic A system that can handle different streaming architectures.

Asynchronous Two devices, typically a transmitter and receiver of data, that are not synchronized. The receiver uses a buffer to store incoming data and processes at its own rate. Usually feedback to the transmitter will indicate buffer overflow.

Broadband There is no rigorous definition, but usually taken to mean connections that can carry data at rates higher than 100 kbit/s.

Browser A client-side application used to view HTML files, usually from the Web, but can be served over a LAN from a local server. Typical examples are Microsoft Explorer and Netscape Navigator. The streaming player is usually used as a plug-in to the browser.

Caching The temporary storage of often-used content in a proxy or edge server.

Capture The conversion of content from regular audio and video to a computer format.

CIF The common intermediate format of the H.261 video-conferencing standard: 352 × 288 pixels for luminance and 176 × 144 pixels for chrominance.

4CIF Picture source format with 704 × 576 pixels for luminance and 352 × 288 pixels for chrominance.

16CIF Picture source format with 1,408 × 1,152 pixels for luminance and 704 × 576 pixels for chrominance.

Codec A compression and decompression algorithm. The encoder will use the codec to compress the media file, which is decompressed by the media player.

DCT Discrete Cosine Transform. The basis of the spatial compression used by the MPEG standards.

DSL Digital Subscriber Line. A broadband connection that can carry voice or data traffic. The Asymmetric DSL (ADSL) uses a legacy copper pair to provide high-speed downloads to the client alongside the analog telephone service.

Encoding The compression and packetization of video and audio to a streaming format.

Frame 1. A single television picture, the result of a scanned raster. An interlaced frame comprises two fields.

2. A packet of data used in telecoms circuits.

H.261 ITU video-conferencing standard.

H.263 Development of H.261 for low bit rate applications like video phones.

Huffman coding A variable-length coding scheme where the most-used characters have a shorter code than the lesser-used characters.

Indexing The generation of a content catalog index by the extraction of metadata from the content.

Interlace scan The odd then even lines of a television frame are scanned alternately.

Intranet A private network for sharing similar content formats to that available over the public Internet, but for corporate use only.

JPEG Joint Picture Expert Group. A compression standard for continuous-tone still images.

JPEG2000 A compression standard for continuous-tone still images using wavelet compression.

MDCT Modified Discrete Cosine Transform. A perfect reconstruction cosine modulated filter bank. It has the property of time-domain aliasing cancellation.

Metadata Attributes of data or 'data about data'.

MP3 MPEG-1, layer 3, audio codec.

MPEG Moving Pictures Expert Group.

MPEG-1 Audio and video compression for CD-ROMs.

MPEG-2 Television compression standard.

MPEG-4 Rich media object coding standard.

MPEG-7 Metadata framework for multimedia.

MPEG-21 Framework for integrating multimedia resources and to facilitate value exchange.

Multicast A means of live webcasting to a large audience that requires a single stream to be transmitted by the server, rather than one per client. Each viewer connects to the multicast, so the network routers send copies of each datagram of the stream to all the clients participating in the multicast. Can potentially save network resources, but is not well supported on the WWW.

Narrowband A dial-up connection to the Internet typically using a 28 k or 56 k analog modem over a regular telephone line.

NTSC The US analog color television standard. The National Television Standards Committee devised a system that was backwards compatible with the RS-170 monochrome system. It has a field rate of 60 Hz and 525 lines. It has since been supplanted by the ATSC standards for high-definition digital television.

PAL Phase Alternating Line, the color television standard used in most of Europe (France used SECAM). It has a field rate of 50 Hz and 625 lines.

Plug-in A small software application that plugs into a web browser and renders file formats that are not supported by the browser. These include Flash vector graphics and streaming audio and video decompressors.

Progressive scan A frame is scanned top-to-bottom on one pass.

QCIF Quarter size CIF image format, 176×144 pixels for luminance and 88×72 pixels for chrominance.

Rich media A combination of audio, video, graphics and text, in a synchronized and possibly interactive presentation.

SIF The standard image format of MPEG-1 encoding: 352×240 pixels, 30 fps for NTSC; 352×288 pixels, 25 fps for PAL.

Telecine A device used to transfer movie film to a television format, where it can be stored on videotape. To match the film rate of 24 frames per second to television at 30 frames per second every fourth field is repeated, called the 3:2 sequence.

Unicast A one-to-one stream from a media server to a client player.

Abbreviations

AAC	Advanced Audio Coding
AAL	ATM Adaptation Layer
ACE	Advanced Coding Efficiency (Profile)
ADSL	Asymmetric Digital Subscriber Line
API	Application Programming Interface
ASF	Advanced Streaming Format
ATM	Asynchronous Transfer Mode
AVI	Audio-Video Interleaved
BIFS	Binary Format for Scenes
CDN	Content Delivery Network
CELP	Code Excited Linear Prediction
CIF	Common Intermediate Format
DAI	DMIF-Application Interface
DCT	Discrete Cosine Transform
DMIF	Delivery Multimedia Integration Framework
DRM	Digital Rights Management
DS	DMIF Signaling
DSL	Digital Subscriber Line
DVMRP	Distance Vector Multicast Routing Protocol (used by MBone)
FTTC	Fiber To The Curb
HFC	Hybrid Fiber Coax
HTTP	HyperText Transfer Protocol
HVXC	Harmonic Vector Excitation Coding
IETF	Internet Engineering Task Force
IP	Internet Protocol
ISDN	Integrated Service Digital Network
LPC	Linear Predictive Coding
MBone	Multicast Backbone
MDCT	Modified Discrete Cosine Transform
MMS	Microsoft Media Server

MOSPF	Multicast Open Shortest Path First protocol
MP3	MPEG-1, layer 3, audio codec
MPEG	Moving Pictures Experts Group
MSBD	Media Streaming Broadcast Distribution
OD	Object Descriptor
PNA	Progressive Networks Audio
QCIF	Quarter Common Intermediate Format
QoS	Quality of Service
RTCP	Real-Time Control Protocol
RTP	Real-Time Transport Protocol
RTSP	Real-Time Streaming Protocol
SDP	Session Description Protocol
SMIL	Synchronized Multimedia Integration Language
SVG	Scalable Vector Graphics
TCP	Transmission Control Protocol
UDP	User Datagram Protocol
UID	Unique Identifier
VOP	Video Object Plane
VPN	Virtual Private Network
VRML	Virtual Reality Modeling Language

Index